Praise for *The Actor's Book of Improvisation*

"Now I will be able to refer my students and the directors and actors who consult with me to this book, which will give them an idea of how to do improvisations properly."

> —Nina Foch,
> Actor, Professor, and Creative Consultant to Directors and Actors

"One of the most important books which should be a part of any serious actor's arsenal."

> —Michael Shurtleff,
> Author of *Audition*

"Finally, a book which corrects the misuse of improvisations and teaches actors, directors, and teachers how to use this very valuable tool."

> —Delia Salvi,
> School of Theater, Film, and Television, U.C.L.A.

"Finally, a clear explanation of how to utilize the technique of improvisation, directly connecting it to a character and situation. I strongly recommend it to anyone seeking growth as a performer or wishing to enrich teaching with truly useful improvisational techniques."

> —John Cauble,
> Department of Theater, U.C.L.A.

PENGUIN BOOKS

THE ACTOR'S BOOK
OF IMPROVISATION

SANDRA CARUSO has been teaching drama and directing plays for twenty years in public and private high schools, professional acting schools, and universities, and now teaches privately in Los Angeles. For several years she has conducted a class at UCLA with her husband, Dee Caruso, in which actors and writers collaborate. Ms. Caruso has trained with many distinguished acting teachers, including Sanford Meisner, Lee Strasberg, and Uta Hagen, and has directed a number of plays for theater and television. She is currently producing and directing a weekly cable television show.

PAUL CLEMENS has been a professional actor for more than fifteen years and has performed extensively in theater, film, and television. As a writer, he is the co-creator of a one-man play based on the life and works of Edgar Allan Poe, in which he also has performed. He makes his home in Los Angeles and enjoys drawing and sculpting.

THE
ACTOR'S BOOK
OF
IMPROVISATION

SANDRA CARUSO

AND

PAUL CLEMENS

PENGUIN BOOKS

PENGUIN BOOKS
Published by the Penguin Group
  Penguin Books USA Inc.,
  375 Hudson Street, New York, New York 10014, U.S.A.
Penguin Books Ltd, 27 Wrights Lane,
  London W8 5TZ, England
Penguin Books Australia Ltd, Ringwood,
  Victoria, Australia
Penguin Books Canada Ltd, 10 Alcorn Avenue,
  Toronto, Ontario, Canada M4V 3B2
Penguin Books (N.Z.) Ltd, 182–190 Wairau Road,
  Auckland 10, New Zealand

Penguin Books Ltd, Registered Offices:
  Harmondsworth, Middlesex, England

First published in Penguin Books 1992

10 9 8 7 6 5 4 3
Copyright © Sandra Caruso and Paul Clemens, 1992
Foreword copyright © Lowell Swortzell, 1992
All rights reserved

LIBRARY OF CONGRESS CATALOGING-IN-PUBLICATION DATA
Caruso, Sandra.
  The actor's book of improvisation / Sandra Caruso and Paul
Clemens.
    p. cm.
  Includes index.
  ISBN 0 14 01.5440 X
  1. Improvisation (Acting) I. Clemens, Paul. II. Title.
PN2071.I5C27 1992
792′.028—dc20   91-13979

Printed in the United States of America

Set in 11 on 13 Caledonia with Caledonia Bold and Futura Condensed for display
Designed by Robert Bull Design

11.95 / 7.17
May 1996

FOREWORD

When the authors sent me the manuscript of *The Actor's Book of Improvisation* with an invitation to write a Foreword, my immediate reaction was to decline politely because on first glance it appeared to be one of those recipe books I deplore in the teaching of the performing arts. The field is inundated with paperback collections of scenes that afford lazy actors easy access to plays they have never read and therefore have no right to perform. Responsible students select scenes they know, those most appropriate to the assignment and to their own artistic needs. Instead of allowing an editor to perform their work, they do it themselves, and so expand their knowledge of dramatic literature as well as their repertories of roles. These students recognize that even in this age of "instant" information no shortcuts exist in good acting. Genuine performances cannot be jerry-built, suggested, or expedited, but only *fully experienced*, first by the performers and then, through them, by their audiences.

So upon closer examination of this manuscript I was relieved and pleased to discover that Sandra Caruso and Paul Clemens have not written a recipe book or created a formula for quick success. Instead they provide a series of challenges to actors to play characters in genuine dramatic situations derived from a variety of stimulating sources. Readers must take these situations and make of them what they will by improvising out of their own imagination and creativity. So, despite the many lists of situations that appear throughout the book, this is not a collection of scenes to be quickly memorized and, once performed, just as quickly forgotten. The situations offered here are springboards from which to leap into the lives of characters who have been created by dramatists or novelists or drawn from actual real-life situations. *But* (and this *but* makes all the difference in the world when this book is compared with those standard collections of scenes I hate so much) the characters and situations are *unfinished* and must be completed as each performer chooses. Herein lies the real difference which compels me to endorse this book, for it is in the depth and dimension of the actor's exploration of these situations that lasting learning and development will take place.

Exploration is the operative word in *The Actor's Book of Improvisation*, as it is in all acting. It also explains why I believe this text can be useful not only to performers but also to playwrights and directors. They also need the experience of working through dramatic situations by weighing possibilities and making final decisions that stimulate and expand their creativity. Each decision must be justified, first by the individual character making it, then by the other characters involved in the situation at hand. And, of course, once this process has taken place, the performers will have justified themselves as artists.

The rich array of dramatic situations to be found in these pages offers actors myriad possibilities to explore characters and a multitude of decisions to make—and then to remake because each can be repeated from many vantage points, the more the better to foster greater dramatic understanding. George Bernard Shaw once reminded us that there are two tragedies in life: "One is not to get your heart's desire; the other is to get it." For me, the most valuable situations to explore here are the most paradoxical, those that can be traversed backward and forward with no simple solutions, no right or wrong decisions except those which we as searchers come to believe as truths.

In pursuing these possibilities we find that the conclusion of all our investigations will be to end up where we began and see it with new eyes. Each time we perform these situations we may discover that we know ourselves for the first time, both as increasingly alert artists and as ever more aware human beings.

Lowell Swortzell
Professor of Educational Theatre
in New York University
April 28, 1991

ACKNOWLEDGMENTS

I wish to extend my sincere gratitude to the following: My many acting students, who tested most of the situations in this book; without them, this book never would have been written. My acting teachers, for their energy and talent; Sanford Meisner, my first acting teacher, who taught me "to act before you think"; Stanley Burnshaw, who encouraged me to write this book; and Gary Mackay, who helped me through my hysterics while learning to use a computer. Paul Clemens and I wish to extend our sincere gratitude to Vicky Bijur, our literary agent, and all the people at Viking Penguin who worked on the book with us: Lori Lipsky and Nicole Guisto in editorial, and Teddy Rosenbaum and Sam Flores in production editorial—all of whom were benign taskmasters.

Sandra Caruso

CONTENTS

INTRODUCTION

Improvisation has long been acknowledged as one of the most valuable resources actors have at their disposal. Yet, surprisingly, there has never been a single, handy, comprehensive book of material on which to base improvisations.

Until now.

You are holding in your hands a virtual cornucopia of source material for improvisations. It is hoped that this book will finally answer the long-standing needs of both acting, teachers and students, whether on the professional or academic level. Uta Hagen, in her book *Respect for Acting*, says that "Improvisation techniques could fill a separate book." This is that book.

The Actor's Book of Improvisation consists of dramatic situations culled from a wide variety of sources, such as plays, films, novels, news items, etc. This material has been broken down into nine separate chapters. Most of these specialized chapters isolate a specific aspect of acting—i.e., subtext, discovery, etc.—and then provide situations pertaining to it. These situations, when tackled by actors, will force the actors to become aware of these particular areas of focus and, with time, will help them improve their handling of them. Each chapter uses improvisations in different ways, as techniques for attacking specific acting problems. The particular structuring of the situations, with their further division into specific areas of concentration, is a unique approach to improvisation.

Acting has been described as the ability to be truthful in imaginary circumstances. Although this does not purport to be a book on acting technique, it will nevertheless aid the actor in learning to be truthful within a very wide variety of imaginary circumstances.

Unlike theater games and other forms of commonly known improvisation, the situations in this book are more structured. Though the dialogue will be spontaneous, the actual performed improvisations resulting from these situations will be built around a "skeleton" of background information and character details. This will lend an added dimension not seen in most off-the-cuff improvisations. The situations in this book are *not* set up in the following manner: "Two people are sitting on a park bench.—Now improvise." Also, unlike work done by professional comedic improvisation groups, the situations in this book are geared specifically toward the actor's development rather than the audience's entertainment. They are presented in such a way that the actors will approach them much as they would an actual scene. In certain instances, the situations will require preparation and sometimes even research.

This book, then, provides a sort of "missing link" between the more common forms of improvisation and an actual working text. When actors have done structured improvisations such as those in this book, they can then approach a written scene or a full script with greater sensitivity and awareness.

It should be noted that when actors are left to invent their own situations for improvisation, repetitions of the same themes tend to occur; this allows for little growth. The experience of any human being is, of course, limited by the breadth of his or her personal knowledge. But by working with this book, actors are bound to find themselves in situations outside the scope of their individual experiences and thus can expand their horizons and stimulate their imaginations. The actors will learn that they can become *any* character in *any* situation.

The variety of situations presented in this book will call upon the use of the actor's full dramatic resources. Just as a workout helps an athlete prepare for an upcoming event, this workbook provides situations that encourage actors to stretch themselves to better prepare them for any work that lies ahead.

Of special note is the fact that most of the improvisations in this book have been tested in an acting laboratory in order to pinpoint likely problems and pitfalls inherent in the material. The information gathered in this experimentation process has been distilled and implemented in the form of "Comments," which accompany each situation. These are intended only as general guidelines, however; the actors should feel free to use what Stanislavsky termed their "independent creativity" in determining the outcome of a given scene, which may run contrary to the source material.

A NOTE TO THE ACTOR: *Don't tell the story!* Background information given for each improvisation is intended only to facilitate your understanding of the character—history, motivations, etc. It is *not* the actor's job to fill the audience in with exposition. If you get involved in too much explanatory dialogue, any real tension or excitement you feel will be dissipated, and as a result the improvisation will become artificial and lifeless. Also, this allows actors to hide behind words rather than relate to each other. Student actors, in particular, often feel they must supply as much background material as possible. An example of this common mistake might go something like this: An actress playing a mother says to her daughter, "Your father and I have been divorced for twelve years and are planning a reunion." Logically, the daughter would know how long her parents have been divorced. The mother would not have to supply her daughter with this information. So don't do it in these improvisations! Also, don't get bogged down in unnecessary verbiage. Remember—to quote Sanford Meisner, "An ounce of behavior is worth a pound of words."

To use this book successfully, treat each situation with respect. In other words, internalize and personalize the information given, trust that it has been assimilated, and then let the improvisation happen. In this way, the character's needs can emerge organically. You should not become "directors" guiding the course of events in your mind. If you allow yourself to be truly spontaneous, the improvisation can flow freely into interesting and sometimes unexpected areas.

If a situation is based on a film or play you may have seen, *do not* try to reproduce the writer's dialogue or the specific performances of the actors. This often happens unintentionally, so it is a good thing to be on the lookout for. Where you merely mimic what has already been done, you miss the real opportunity for growth.

Last of all, always remember the cardinal rule of acting: You must have a clear objective, knowing what you want from the other character(s), whether they be real or imaginary. Sometimes these objectives are given in the situation; other times, you must find them for yourself. This rule applies to every situation in this book.

If you approach these situations honestly, bringing to them your own imagination and understanding, the road to growth and discovery should be wide open to you.

A NOTE TO THE TEACHER: It is unlikely that a teacher would have at his or her fingertips the variety of material presented here. This book, then, can become a portable library of dramatic source material. Also, it may inspire the actors to investigate further the dramatic literature on which many of these situations are based. The teacher may wish to assign the actual source material as a follow-up to an improvisation.

A few tips: Because the source for a given situation is either serious or comedic does not mean that the resulting improvisation must fall into that category. For example, a scene from *Dracula* could be approached just as successfully from a humorous perspective as from the standpoint of straight melodrama. By the same token, the time period of a given situation can be altered in some cases, either for humorous effect or to add a new dimension to the scene. Sexes of characters can sometimes be changed as well. For example, a scene between two men might work just as well between two women. Whether or not this can or should be done will, naturally, depend on the nature of the situation. In the world of improvisation, the possibilities are limitless.

Finally, if you feel that certain background information is crucial to the class's understanding of a specific scene, then give the information to the class at the start of the improvisation. In this way, the actors' temptation to "tell the story" will be reduced.

A word of caution: Since some of the situations in this

book are of a mature nature, discretion is advised—particularly with regard to the use of this material in schools below college level.

More than anything, *The Actor's Book of Improvisation* should be viewed as a user-friendly guide to that challenging and often unpredictable realm called improvisation. Ultimately, it is the goal of this book not only to fill a great need but also to take both actors and teachers on new and exciting journeys.

A USER'S GUIDE

Source: Here will be listed the original source from which the particular situation has been taken. When a source says "Film by," this means the film was directed and written by the same person.

Characters: Here will be listed the number and sexes of the characters, followed by the characters' names, their relationship to one another, and miscellaneous identifying information. (In some instances, where a character's name is not considered intrinsic to the exercise, it will not be given.)

Place: Here will be listed the specific locale in which the situation occurs.

Background: Here will be given story information necessary for the actors' understanding of their characters and the situation. This leads to the point at which the improvisation is to begin.

Situation: This is where it all comes together. Here will be given the details of the specific situation on which the improvisation will be based.

Comments: Here will be listed notes and tips to the actors and teachers—helpful hints as well as warnings of possible pitfalls inherent in the material. This section often contains supplemental background information that may further enhance the actors' understanding of story and character.

•

Note: The situations within each chapter have been organized according to sex and number in the following manner:
   One male, one female
   Two females
   Two males
   Ensemble—any situation with more than two characters

The titles of each situation are in alphabetical order within each grouping.

There are a number of improvisations which are taken from the same source. In these cases, the reader is referred to the corresponding pages for further background. There are several improvisations from the same source where no reference is indicated. This is because there is no connection between the incidents and the situations are, therefore, not dependent on one another.

PART I

HOLDING
THE MIRROR
UP TO NATURE

1

RELATIONSHIP

Almost every scene in dramatic literature deals, to some extent, with aspects of relationship. Whenever more than one character is present in a scene (with the exception of certain more avant-garde works), the characters interact or respond to one another in some way. Even in a solo scene, a character may deal with his/her relationship to the surroundings.

To avoid overgeneralization, the following material focuses on situations in which the relationship between characters forms the central element, or "spine," of the scene: a fulcrum or catalyst for the thoughts, emotions, and actions of the characters.

Many good examples of this can be found in *Who's Afraid of Virginia Woolf?* and *Long Day's Journey into Night*, where the relationships among characters form almost the entire substance of the given work.

The characters in these improvisations must be familiar with intimate details of the others, such as their habits, lovemaking, family background, fears, humor, vulnerable spots, and so on. Everything they do or say is based on their knowledge of one another. The performing actors may not be familiar with the source material, but they are most likely cognizant of the problems of universal relationships, such as long-term marriages.

The basic background elements will be given from which the actors must then draw on their personal knowledge of similar relationships. Whether the relationship is between husband and wife, mother and daughter, father and son, friends, lovers, etc., the actors must examine themselves and recall their own relationships in order to truthfully explore these improvisations.

RELATIONSHIP

List of Situations

One male and one female

Two females

Two males

Ensemble

———— **1** ————

Source: *Anne of the Thousand Days*, a play by Maxwell Anderson (Situation #1)

Characters: One male and one female: Henry VIII, King of England, and Anne Boleyn

Place: A room in Henry's castle

Background: Henry VIII is married to the Spanish queen, Katharine of Aragon, whom he does not love. He wants to have a son as heir to the throne, but she has been unable to give him one. Anne is a lady of the court on whom he has set his sights. Being king, he is used to getting any woman he desires. Anne, however, is in love with another man, Percy, Earl of Northumberland. Anne's sister, Mary, has already been Henry's mistress, but he has tired of her. He now wants to divorce Katharine and marry Anne.

Situation: Henry has his first meeting with Anne and propositions her. She tells him of her love for Percy (whom Henry later has put to death, as Anne feared he would). The irony is that Anne is the first woman Henry ever really loved, and she doesn't love him. She is very frank with him, even admitting that she has been in the next bed while he was making love to her sister and doesn't think much of him as a lover. She realizes that he has the power to make her his or to kill her if she disobeys.

Comments: The actors should not be intimidated by the fact that this play takes place in the 1500s and that the people involved are kings and queens. They must not think they have to be formal and talk differently. Henry wasn't particularly formal anyway; he was quite down-to-earth.

See *Anne of the Thousand Days*, #2, page 46.

2

Source: *At Mother's Request*, a film for television by Michael Tuchner, teleplay by Richard DeLong Adams, based on an actual murder case

Characters: One male and one female: Frances, a mother, and her teenage son

Place: Their home

Background: Frances hates her millionaire father because he is a miser who plans to disinherit both her and her mother. The two of them plot to kill him through the son. Frances and her son have an unnaturally close relationship upon which Frances capitalizes. She knows her son loves his sister a great deal.

Situation: Frances tells her son that his sister is ill but that, with enough money, she could be saved. The grandfather has the resources but refuses to help. Frances gives her son a gun and persuades him to kill his grandfather. If he doesn't do what he's told, she threatens to withdraw her love.

Comments: In the actual situation, Frances convinced her son to do this deed for her. The actors can leave the

decision open-ended. The main element in the relationship is the strong attachment the boy has for his mother.
He is terrified of losing her.

———— 3 ————

Source: *The Bedroom Window*, a film by Curtis Hanson,
based on the novel *The Witnesses*, by Anne Holden

Characters: One male and one female: Terry and his lover,
Sylvia

Place: Terry's bedroom at two A.M.

Background: Terry is having an affair with Sylvia, who is
married to his boss, an influential man. They have left
an office party and come to his apartment. They are
making love when Sylvia hears a scream. She rushes to
the window and sees a man raping a woman. Since he
is right under a streetlight, she gets a good look at him.
Terry, still in bed, does not see him at first, and the man
has rushed off by the time Terry gets to the window.

Situation: Terry tells Sylvia that they must go to the police
and identify this man. Sylvia refuses because she does
not want their affair to be exposed. She is married to a
very important man, and this exposure would destroy
them both. Terry is in conflict because he wants to protect Sylvia, but he also knows that it will haunt him the
rest of his life if he lets this rapist get away.

Comments: The actress playing Sylvia must realize that
Sylvia has everything to lose and is desperate to save
herself. She is not in love with Terry; he is someone
with whom she is having a casual affair. Terry is infat-
uated with Sylvia and does not want to lose her, but he
is an ethical person and it goes against his grain not to
help someone in trouble. Not only should this rape be

reported, but, by doing so, other rapes could be prevented. This girl might have been killed had Sylvia not come to the window, thus scaring off the rapist. If the next girl is killed, *they* will be responsible.

4

Source: *Broadway Bound*, a play by Neil Simon

Characters: One male and one female: Jack and Kate Jerome, a middle-aged couple

Place: The Jerome house, Brighton Beach, Brooklyn

Background: Jack and Kate have been married for more than thirty years; they have two sons, one seventeen and the other in his twenties, Eugene and Stanley. A year ago, Kate heard from a friend that her husband was involved with another woman. She chose to ignore it. Lately, she heard that he had been seen with this woman again. He has been coming home late, and this night Kate is especially upset because she had fixed a great dinner but nobody was there to eat it. Her two sons had gone to their room to write something rather than eat.

Kate has spent her life cleaning the house, sewing, setting the table, and fixing dinner for her family. She never travels anywhere or does anything exciting. This has disturbed Jack. He has found in this other woman a zest for life that he feels his wife lacks.

Situation: Jack comes home late, long after dinner has been put back in the refrigerator. For the first time, Kate asks him if there is another woman, never letting on that she knows there is. Jack denies it at first, then admits that a year ago he had become involved with someone. But he reassures his wife that the affair is over and that he has not seen her for a year. Kate finally reveals to him that she knows he saw this same woman recently in a restaurant. He is forced to admit this is true. Kate keeps asking him questions about her; she wants to know what this woman has that she can't give him. He begs her not to ask him, but she persists, and he tells her what she doesn't want to hear.

Comments: This improvisation is about a relationship, but it is also an exercise in confrontation and subtext. Until all is revealed, there is great subtext going on for both characters. The actors must be very clear about this relationship and what these two people want from each other.

5

Source: *The Godfather, Part II*, a film by Francis Ford Coppola, screenplay by Coppola and Mario Puzo, based on the novel *The Godfather* by Mario Puzo

Characters: One male and one female: husband and wife, Michael and Kay

Place: Their living room

Background: When Kay married Michael, he was a lawyer planning to lead a "normal" life. However, Michael's father was the head of a Mafia family who, upon his death, made Michael the new Godfather. Since he became Godfather, Michael has changed. He has become hardened owing to his involvement in many killings. Obviously, Kay had not expected this kind of life and she cannot bear it. Previously they had two children, but Kay has recently had an abortion, not wanting to expose another child to the evil of this family. She told Michael it was a miscarriage. He was away at the time, and this is the first time he has seen her since she lost the baby.

Situation: Michael wants to tell Kay how badly he feels about the miscarriage and that he wasn't there for her when it happened. She confesses the truth, targeting the hate she has for what he has become. He takes revenge, forbidding her to ever see her other children again.

Comments: The actor must keep in mind the tremendous ego of this man. He is head of a Mafia family, and *nobody* crosses him. His own wife is no exception. His pride cannot let this go unchecked, but he is also deeply hurt. He loves Kay, and the true substance of his life is his wife and two children. Family is very important to the Mafia. Kay loved the man she married, not the one he has become. There is blood on his hands.

———— 6 ————

Source: *In the Boom Boom Room*, a play by David Rabe (Situation #1)

Characters: One male and one female: a father and his daughter, Chrissy

Place: The living room of their house

Background: The father is a bigoted slob who has been in and out of prison for theft. He used to enter his daughter in vodka-drinking contests. Recently he has been in the hospital for treatment of his genitals due to venereal disease. He felt emasculated by the nurses' putting medications on him. Chrissy, his daughter, is a go-go dancer in a bar called the Boom Boom Room. Her mother tried to have her aborted. She has prepared a homecoming dinner for her father, whom she has missed greatly and whose comfort she needs.

Situation: The father comes directly home from the hospital. They are both very happy to see each other. Eventually, however, he attempts to seduce Chrissy, trying to regain the feeling of manhood he lost at the hospital.

Comments: The actress may deal with this any way she likes. However, this situation has never occurred before with her father, and it comes as a tremendous shock. The actor playing the father must come to terms with the state of mind he is in when released from the hospital, a state of mind which eventually drives him to seduce his own daughter. Both of these people are emotionally deprived and very much in need of each other, although in different ways.

See *In the Boom Boom Room*, #2, page 28.

_____ 7 _____

Source: *I Oughta Be in Pictures*, a play by Neil Simon

Characters: One male and one female: Herb, the father, a Hollywood screenwriter, and his teenage daughter, Libby.

Place: Herb's living room in Los Angeles, early morning

Background: Libby, a girl in her late teens, has been living in New York with her mother. Her parents have been divorced fifteen years, and she has not seen her father since she was a small child. The father, an unsuccessful screenwriter, is presently living in Los Angeles. Unbeknownst to her father, his daughter has decided to move to Los Angeles to live with him. She wants to be an actress.

Situation: Libby arrives early in the morning while her father is still asleep and a little hung over. She reveals her relationship to him and the reason she is there.

Comments: The actors should decide what these people

know about each other and what their preconceived ideas have been all these years. The outcome should be resolved during the improvisation. They should also be clear about their attitudes toward the mother. Also, the actor must be aware that Herb has lived alone for many years. The decision to take in a teenage girl at this point in his life cannot be made easily.

_____ 8 _____

Source: *Les Liaisons Dangereuses*, a play by Christopher Hampton, based on the novel by Pierre Choderlos de Laclos

Characters: One male and one female: the Vicomte de Valmont, a good-looking, sophisticated man in his mid- to late thirties. He is amoral and manipulative. Madame de Tourvel, a woman in her late twenties/early thirties. She is a young lady renowned for her religious devotion and the happiness of her marriage

Place: The sitting room of Madame de Tourvel

Background: Valmont, on a bet with his friend the Marquise de Merteuil, a woman as amoral and manipulative as he (and a former lover to boot), has successfully seduced the virtuous young Madame de Tourvel into having an affair with him. Her husband has long been out of town. What started as a game between Valmont and Merteuil has become more than he bargained for because Valmont has violated his own cardinal rule and fallen in love with his intended victim, Madame de Tourvel. Valmont and the Marquise, having been born pre-revolutionary aristocrats, have had nothing better to do with their time than play games of deceit and sexual manipulation, a sort of living chess game with real human beings as the pawns.

Situation: So that he does not become a laughingstock in the eyes of his friend the Marquise, Valmont must bring to a speedy end his messy emotional entanglement with Madame de Tourvel. Under the ambiguous pretext of it being "beyond his control," he tells her (lying through his teeth) that he has become bored with the relationship and wishes to end it. She is understandably shocked by this news, for she has risked everything in allowing herself to love this man. His announcement devastates her. Valmont, however, is no less devastated himself; but, unlike her, he cannot openly show his true feelings. He has, with this single act, given up his one real chance at happiness for the sake of personal vanity and social acceptance by the Marquise (herself a desperately unhappy woman).

Comments: It must be understood that the Marquise holds Valmont in an almost hypnotic spell, which has its roots in their past relationship and divests him of control over his own life. In one sense, then, what Valmont so callously does to Madame de Tourvel, truly *is* "beyond his control."

---------- **9** ----------

Source: *Long Day's Journey into Night,* a play by Eugene O'Neill

Characters: One male and one female: James and Mary Tyrone, husband and wife. Mary is in her mid-fifties, and James in his mid-sixties

Place: The living room of their Connecticut home

Background: When their child, Edmund, was born, Mary

experienced a lot of pain. A cheap hotel doctor prescribed morphine for the pain, thus transforming Mary into an addict. She and James now have two children, Jamie, who is an alcoholic, and Edmund, who is ill with consumption (tuberculosis). The husband and two sons have watched Mary retreating into the haze of her addiction during the course of many years. She is not in this state all the time; she has her lucid moments, but as the day wears on, she drifts away from the family. She goes on talking about the past, rarely relating to her present life. She ignores whatever disturbs or troubles her, pretending the disturbance doesn't exist. She blames her husband, James, for her situation. She blames many of their problems on his miserliness. If James had called in a real doctor instead of relying on a cheap hotel "quack," she might never have become addicted to morphine. He left her night after night in a hotel room while he was performing in a theater. He was a popular matinee idol, and Mary sometimes feels she gave up too much for him, including a career as a concert pianist. There are many factors that have caused Mary to become what she is today—"a ghost haunting the past."

Situation: On this day Mary has resumed her use of drugs. James begs Mary to stop taking the morphine because it prevents her from relating to the family. It has become unbearable to watch her. He pleads with her to stay in reality and be part of the family. She is longing to get to the drugstore for more morphine rather than face this painful conversation. James is at his wit's end at this point and desperately wants his wife back.

Comments: Mary is steeped in self-delusion. She blames her husband or her children for her troubles. Mary and James love each other deeply but have hurt each other too much. This is an unusually complex play with complex characters. The actors cannot do all the preparation necessary when given this situation for the first time in class. However, there is much they could bring to it from their own life in addition to the facts given here. The situation of a painful marriage in which one person is trying to escape from reality is a recognizable theme. After working through this improvisation, the actors should be encouraged to explore the actual text, since this would help further their understanding of the play. They will find that after having improvised the material, they can play these characters with greater depth and honesty. In fact, José Quintero, the director of the play's American première, used improvisation extensively during rehearsals as a means of exploring the characters and situations in a more immediate way.

_____ **10** _____

Source: *The Man with the Satin Hat,* a documentary film about Max Linder, who was a director/performer in France during the silent screen era; directed and narrated by his daughter, Maud Linder

Characters: One male and one female: husband in his forties and wife, seventeen

Place: Their bedroom, the year 1925

Background: Max Linder was a famous actor, director, and producer in France. He was also extremely successful internationally and the precursor of all the great comedians, such as Charlie Chaplin and the Marx Brothers, who took many of their routines directly from him. While in his forties, he married a seventeen-year-old girl. They were very happy together and the union produced a baby daughter. Max Linder had been a lady's man until this point in his life. This was his first real love. Then, at the height of his career, with a wife he loved and an infant he adored, he committed suicide. His young wife slit her wrists as well. Nobody ever knew why they did this. Their daughter was raised by friends and later collected her father's films, which she incorporated into a documentary.

Situation: The actor and his young wife make the decision to commit suicide together. Since nobody knows the real reason behind this seemingly happy couple's action, the actors will have to create their own reasons. Let the decision be part of the improvisation. The reasons might be discussed beforehand; or one of the partners might present the idea to the other for the first time in the improvisation.

Comments: Remember that the couple did this at a time when they were both sitting on top of the world, at least in the eyes of others. This improvisation does not necessarily have to be morbid. Since the situation is not peculiar to this particular couple, the actors need not feel hemmed in by the specific biographical background and may supply their own. This successful man could be in any profession.

11

Source: *Mourning Becomes Electra*, a trilogy by Eugene O'Neill (Situation #2, from *Homecoming*, the first play of the trilogy)

Characters: One male and one female: husband, Ezra Mannon, and his wife, Christine

Place: The bedroom of their home

Background: Mannon has just returned from a long period
of fighting in the war. (The play takes place in 1865 and
it is the Civil War, but it could be any war.) He has had
a difficult time, and the only thing that held him together
was knowing that he would be coming home to his wife,
Christine. Unbeknownst to Mannon, Christine stopped
loving him on their honeymoon. While he was at war,
she took a young lover, Adam Brant, whom Mannon
knows. However, Mannon does not know of the affair.
Christine and Mannon have just made love and Mannon
has told Christine he missed her.

Situation: It is about three A.M. and they both awaken.
Mannon senses something is wrong and confronts Christine. She doesn't want to discuss it, nor does she want
the lamp lighted, but he insists. He tells her he feels as
though she went through the motions of lovemaking like
a slave, not really desiring him although he desired her
deeply. She admits that she is disgusted by lovemaking
with him and confesses that she has a lover. She owns
up to the fact that she has hated him throughout their
marriage.

Comments: The actress playing Christine must justify her
hatred and cruelty toward her husband. The actor playing Mannon must prepare his part in terms of his exhaustion from years of battle and his great need for his
wife's love.

See *Mourning Becomes Electra*, #1, page 29.

12

Source: *Pennies from Heaven*, a British television miniseries by Dennis Potter

Characters: One male and one female: Arthur, a sheet music salesman, and Eileen, a small-town schoolteacher

Place: A forest in a small town at night in the 1940s

Background: Arthur is a traveling sheet music salesman, who escapes from his unhappy life and unsatisfying marriage through the music and lyrics of the romantic songs he sells. Eileen is a schoolteacher in her thirties. She is single and lives with her father and brothers. She has had an argument with her family and has left in tears to be alone in the woods. Arthur had seen her recently with her schoolchildren and then again in a local music shop. He has fallen in love with her on sight and believes she is the ideal woman of his dreams.

Situation: Arthur has followed Eileen into the woods. There he approaches her for the first time and expresses his feelings for her. To her, he is a complete stranger; someone who has been watching her and is now professing his undying love.

Comments: The girl would certainly be cautious at first, but even when the sense of danger has passed, she is still faced with a very unusual situation.

13

Source: *Promises in the Dark*, a film by Jerome Hellman, screenplay by Loring Mandel

Characters: One male and one female: Gerry and his girl friend, Buffy—both high-school students

Place: Buffy's bedroom

Background: Buffy has been receiving chemotherapy treatments for cancer, and as a result of the cancer, she has had to have one of her legs amputated.

Situation: This is the first time since that operation that she and her boyfriend have been alone together. Now he must deal with this situation, trying to make her understand that he loves her no matter what, that she is still attractive to him despite the surgery. The situation reaches its critical point when she asks him to lift up the hem of her nightgown and look at the stump of her leg.

Comments: Gerry attempts to be as delicate and gentle with her as possible, knowing that her self-confidence is at an all-time low. The girl tries very hard not to show her terror at the possibility of rejection. The scene was handled with great sensitivity in the film. However, the actors may choose a very different or even opposite approach, i.e., the boyfriend not being able to respond sympathetically at all. Also, the actress playing Buffy might not feel terror; she might find humor in the situation. As a matter of fact, the actors must find *some* humor in this situation or they won't survive it. They must be warned against self-pity; whatever their choices are, they should fight to be brave. The actors should discuss and understand what their relationship had been before the operation—a very close one.

_____ **14** _____

Source: *The Seahorse,* a play by Edward J. Moore

Characters: One male and one female: a young sailor, Harry, and Gertrude, an unattractive, overweight woman, who owns and operates a bar for sailors

Place: Gertrude's bar

Background: A man once ran out on Gertrude, leaving her

devastated. Her father was killed in a brawl at the same bar that she is now in charge of. She makes a good living from sailors because the bar is located near the docks. She has let herself go because she feels she could never hold a man again. A young, good-looking sailor, Harry, comes to the bar often and has spent many nights with Gertrude.

Situation: Harry brings Gertrude a gift of a wedding gown. He truly loves her and wants to marry her. She is furious with him because she thinks he's making fun of her. She will not believe he loves her.

Comments: This part can also be played by a woman much older than the sailor. The actress must keep in mind that it isn't so much what she looks like but how she feels about herself. The actor must try his best to communicate the depth of his character's feelings for Gertrude.

15

Source: *The Sound of the Mountain,* a film by Mikio Naruse, based on a novel by Yasunari Kawabata (Situation #1)

Characters: One male and one female: husband and wife

Place: The kitchen of their apartment

Background: A son and his young wife live with the son's parents. The son is a philanderer and comes home late at night, leaving his wife alone most of the time. His mother feels that his father is spending too much time with the daughter-in-law and has become too close to her. She feels as though she is losing her husband.

Situation: In a meeting with her husband, she requests that the son and his spouse move out because she is not comfortable having them living there. The husband pleads for them to stay because he wants to rescue his son's marriage. It is also because he has found happiness with his daughter-in-law.

Comments: The plea to save his son's marriage is absolutely sincere. There has been no involvement between the father and his daughter-in-law. Neither of them is really aware of their feelings for each other at this point: it's all subliminal. The father, however, discovers something about himself in this discussion with his wife.

16

Source: *The Sound of the Mountain*, a film by Mikio Naruse, based on a novel by Yasunari Kawabata (Situation #2)

Characters: One male and one female: a father-in-law and his daughter-in-law

Place: A park

Background: The daughter-in-law is living with her husband's parents. Her husband is a callous, philandering man who comes home late and drunk most evenings. She becomes pregnant but has an abortion because she doesn't love her husband anymore. The father-in-law has supported her through her loneliness. In the meantime she has fallen in love with him because he is kind and gentle to her. He has fallen in love with her also; however, neither of them acknowledges this. The father has tried very hard to patch up the marriage by talking to his son. His own relationship with his wife is not a good one. She has "let herself go," and he is no longer attracted to her. One day his daughter-in-law calls him at the office and asks him to meet her at a park.

Situation: They meet in the park and for the first time admit their feelings for each other. This is a relationship that cannot be consummated owing to circumstance.

Comments: This is not a sordid love affair. The daughter-in-law simply feels she cannot live with this secret anymore. These are two very decent, proper people who would not purposefully hurt anybody. The father-in-law is quite old-fashioned and would fight to save the family unit.

———— 17 ————

Source: *Tell Me That You Love Me, Junie Moon,* a film by Otto Preminger, screenplay by Marjorie Kellogg, adapted from her novel

Characters: One male and one female: Arthur, a man who has a severe case of epilepsy, and Junie Moon, whose face is acid-scarred

Place: A kitchen in the house where they live

Background: These people live together in a rented house. They met in a nearby hospital and found themselves drawn together because they are both misfits. Junie Moon's face is disfigured on one side by acid, and she always wears a large-brimmed hat to cover the scar. She never expects any man to love her again. Arthur has a very severe case of epilepsy and has been fired from many jobs because of his seizures. He is very good-looking.

Situation: Arthur comes home one night very happy because he finally got a new job. He decides to tell Junie he has fallen in love with her. She does not accept this because she does not believe a good-looking man like this could possibly love her. Arthur also never believed anyone could love him because of his seizures.

Comments: Arthur must find a way to make Junie Moon believe he really loves her. Both characters have physical problems that have affected their lives profoundly. The actors must pay attention to this.

───────── **18** ─────────

Source: *Torch Song Trilogy*, a play by Harvey Fierstein

Characters: One male and one female: mother and son, Arnold

Place: Son's apartment

Background: The mother has come to visit her son, Arnold. Her husband, to whom she was married for fifty years and whom she loved deeply, has recently passed away. Arnold has just lost a male lover who was killed in a street fight. The two men had lived together for only a matter of months and Arnold is still grieving over the loss. His mother does not yet know that her son is homosexual. She also does not know that he and his lover adopted a young boy who now lives in the apartment.

Situation: Arnold needs to tell his mother about the loss of his lover; he must share the grief with somebody. At some point the mother realizes that the lover to whom her son is referring is a man. This comes as a shock. He also tells his mother about the young boy he has adopted. Arnold compares the loss of his lover to the mother's loss of her husband, a comparison she very much resents. She attempts to talk her son out of his life-style.

Comments: It is important for the actress playing the mother to understand this woman's background and why Arnold's behavior would be unacceptable to her.

————— **19** —————

Source: *Autumn Sonata*, a film by Ingmar Bergman

Characters: Two females: Charlotte, a concert pianist in her early sixties, and her daughter, Eva, a woman in her thirties

Background: Charlotte, who has been away for seven years on world concert tours, comes to live with her daughter. Charlotte's lover, a musician with whom she had been touring, has recently died and she is without companionship. She abandoned her family and her husband for this lover but is now alone and needs her daughter. She has another daughter, Helena, who has an incapacitating disease similar to muscular dystrophy. Charlotte had Helena institutionalized. Eva and her husband Viktor, unbeknownst to Charlotte, have brought Helena to their house to live with them.

Situation: Eva confronts her mother with what she feels was her mother's desertion of the family. She also reveals that Helena is now living with her. Charlotte has much to answer for and must defend her actions as best she can. She needs the security of her daughter's home and her love.

Comments: Charlotte's profession meant everything to her, and the actress playing her must realize that. She was a strong, independent woman willing to make any sacrifice necessary to become the world-class pianist she now is. This is the first time in her adult life that she has needed anyone. The actress playing Eva must realize how deep Eva's feeling of abandonment is and that forgiveness, if even possible at this point, cannot be easy for her.

———— 20 ————

Source: *Cloud Nine*, a play by Caryl Churchill

Characters: Two females: late twenties or early thirties

Place: A park

Background: Neither of these women is very happy with her life. One is married but bored with her husband; the other is divorced and a lesbian.

Situation: Both women are sitting in the park, watching their children playing nearby. The lesbian woman, after a conversation in which she determines that the other woman is unhappily married, suggests that they become lovers.

Comments: In the actual play, the woman approached agrees to try this new kind of relationship. The actresses should not, however, decide beforehand what the outcome will be. Remember, this life-style is completely foreign to the woman approached. The actresses must also remember the presence of the children.

———— 21 ————

Source: *The Glass Menagerie*, a play by Tennessee Williams

Characters: Two females: Amanda, the mother, in her sixties, and Laura, the daughter, in her twenties

Place: The living room of their home

Background: Laura had a childhood illness that left her partially crippled. She had to wear a brace on her leg, and she now has a noticeable limp, about which she is very self-conscious. She is frightened of the world and painfully shy. Her mother, Amanda, sends Laura to typing school to acquire some skills and independence because she believes Laura may never marry. Amanda has paid a year's tuition in advance to this school; money not easy for her to come by. Amanda had once been a Southern belle. She had many suitors and a life of luxury, but now she is poor. Her husband deserted the family years ago. Amanda also has a son, Tom, who lives with them. He comes home late at night and is on the verge of leaving the family. Whenever Laura is upset, she retreats to playing with her collection of glass animals or listens to old records her father left behind. Amanda has just come home from the typing school, having inquired about Laura's progress. Much to her dismay, Amanda was informed by the headmistress that Laura attended school only the first day. She had become sick in class, left, and never returned. Laura, who has been pretending to attend school every day, has been going to the park instead. She can't handle the pressure of taking typing tests.

Situation: Amanda confronts Laura with her knowledge of Laura's deception. Laura eventually confesses how she has been spending her days and the reason why. Amanda sees Laura's actions as the end of hope for her daughter's independence. She wonders what they will do with the rest of their lives.

Comments: The actress playing Laura must decide what it is that terrifies her about the outside world. She must also decide which leg is lame and practice walking on it. Amanda is a desperate woman who sees her life going down the drain. Having been very popular herself, Amanda cannot understand why Laura is socially as well as literally crippled. It never occurs to Amanda that Laura's problems may have something to do with the pressure she puts on her.

_____ **22** _____

Source: *In the Boom Boom Room,* a play by David Rabe (Situation #2)

Characters: Two females: two strippers—Chrissy and Susan, Chrissy's friend

Place: A dressing room in a nightclub

Background: Chrissy has been betrayed by everyone since the day she was born, including her own parents. Her mother tried to abort her and has hated her ever since (for being born). Her father sexually abused her. She has been taken advantage of sexually and emotionally by every man she's ever dated and she's now at the end of her rope. Her boyfriend, out of jealousy, has beaten her badly. Her only friend is Susan, the girl with whom she shares her dressing room. She desperately needs friendship at this moment.

Situation: Chrissy is devastated and comes to Susan for help. Susan eventually reveals that she is interested in Chrissy sexually and wants to make love to her. Chrissy realizes Susan only wants her body, just like everyone else in her life.

Comments: Chrissy has never experienced a lesbian relationship. The last thing she needed right now was for her only friend to make a pass at her. She now knows there is nobody she can trust. The actress must be aware of how devastating this encounter is for Chrissy at this moment in her life.

See *In the Boom Boom Room,* #1, page 11.

--------- **23** ---------

Source: *Lovers and Other Strangers*, a play by Renee Taylor and Joseph Bologna

Characters: Two females, mother and daughter

Place: The living room or kitchen of the parents' home

Background: The parents are old-world Italians who do not believe in divorce for any reason. Their children, however, are contemporary and do not believe in staying in an unhappy situation.

Situation: The daughter informs her mother that she is going to get a divorce. The mother tries everything possible to talk her out of this decision.

Comments: Each person is fighting for her own happiness and beliefs. The daughter must be clear in her mind what her reasons for divorce are. The mother must be clear about why she cannot allow a divorce to come about.

--------- **24** ---------

Source: *Mourning Becomes Electra*, a trilogy by Eugene O'Neill (Situation #1, from *Homecoming*, the first play of the trilogy)

Characters: Two females: the mother, Christine, in her forties and the daughter, Lavinia, in her twenties

Place: The father's study

Background: Lavinia suspects that her mother is having an affair with Lavinia's lover. She follows her mother to a hotel in New York, where she observes her meeting their mutual lover. Then she eavesdrops outside the hotel room door. When Christine and Lavinia have returned home, Lavinia requests that her mother meet her in the father's study.

Situation: Lavinia confronts her mother. She threatens her, saying that she will tell her father unless her mother promises never to see their mutual lover again.

Comments: In order for this improvisation to work, it is essential that the mother greatly fear the father's finding out about her affair. Both women must want this lover strongly. The two women must also find the love they have for each other; although it may be hidden, this should not be left out. It is significant that Lavinia asks to see her mother in the father's study, where his personal belongings surround them.

See *Mourning Becomes Electra*, #2, page 17.

————————— **25** —————————

Source: *'night, Mother*, a play by Marsha Norman

Characters: Two females: a mother, Thelma, in her sixties and her daughter, Jessie, in her thirties

Place: Their living room at night

Background: Jessie's husband left her a few years before, and she has not found someone new. Her son is a thief and drug user. She is epileptic and lives with her mother in the country. She has been severely depressed for a year, and believes she has no reason to go on living.

Situation: Jessie announces to her mother that she intends to commit suicide that night. Jessie has hidden a loaded gun and has made elaborate plans. She must reveal her plans to her mother because Jessie has been managing the household and wants her mother to take over the responsibilities. Her mother tries desperately, using every means at her disposal, to change Jessie's mind.

Comments: The actress playing Jessie must justify her decision both to herself and to the mother. Both actresses must decide what the relationship between the characters has been. The actual play is rich in background detail.

——— 26 ———

Source: *All My Sons*, a play by Arthur Miller

Characters: Two males: the father, Joe Keller, and his son, Chris Keller

Place: The front yard of the Kellers' home, right after World War II

Background: During the war Joe Keller manufactured airplane cylinders that were faulty and caused the death of many boys. His son, Chris, lost a whole battalion of men in this manner. But until now, Chris never realized that his own father was manufacturing the faulty equipment. Joe did it for profit. He would have lost the whole business if he had recalled the planes. In Joe's mind, he was doing it so Chris would inherit a profitable business. Meanwhile, Joe's other son, Larry, has been reported missing in action. In actuality, he committed suicide because he knew about his father's actions. Larry was going to marry Annie, the daughter of Joe's old partner. Chris now wants to marry her. She has just found out from her father that not only had Joe knowingly sent out faulty parts but he also let Annie's father take the rap for it. Annie has revealed what she knows to Chris.

Situation: Chris has just received this information from Annie and confronts his father with it.

Comments: The actors must be aware of the deep love between father and son. Chris thought of his father as a great man, and this new information is traumatic for him.

The actor playing Chris must think about the men he lost and how much he cared for them. (He was responsible for them as well.) The actor playing Joe must justify in his mind why he did what he did.

———— 27 ————

Source: *I Never Sang for My Father*, a play by Robert Anderson

Characters: Two males: the father, Tom Garrison, in his seventies; the son, Gene Garrison, in his forties

Place: The bedroom of the father's house in New England

Background: Tom's wife died a few weeks before, and he's having trouble coping. He is also having memory lapses. Gene has come home with his fiancée, Peggy, to persuade his father to move to California with them. Gene has to stay in California because his two children from a previous marriage live there, and Peggy, who is a doctor, has her practice there. Tom is growing older now and is becoming less and less able to care for himself. He was the local mayor for many years and is used to being in a position of authority. He fights desperately against relinquishing control.

Situation: Tom tries to persuade Gene and Peggy to move into his house because he does not want to move to California. At this point in his life, he feels unable to make the change. He wants to stay in his own territory, where he feels safe. Gene does not want to leave him alone because he realizes his father is no longer able to care for himself.

Comments: Gene and his father, who have never been very close, understand that this is their last opportunity to break through the emotional barriers that have devel-

oped through the years. The actors should not decide
beforehand whether this closeness can be achieved or
not. Either it happens or it doesn't. The actors should
decide what incidents have occurred in the characters'
history to cause these emotional barriers.

———— **28** ————

Source: *Manhunter*, a film by Michael Mann, based on the
novel *Red Dragon* by Thomas Harris

Characters: Two males: Will Graham, a detective in his
late thirties/early forties and his son, a boy about eleven
or twelve

Place: A supermarket

Background: Will Graham was responsible for tracing and
uncovering the identity of a serial killer named Dr. Han-
nibal Lecter. Lecter was a psychiatrist responsible for
the brutal killings of nine people, some of them his pa-
tients. To help track Lecter, Graham put himself into
the disordered mind-set of the killer, forcing himself to
see and experience things the way the killer might. Finally, having discovered Lecter's identity, Graham
phoned the police. However, Lecter surprised Graham
during his phone call, attacking him with a knife and
putting him into the hospital. After Graham recovered
from his physical wounds, he spent some time in a psychiatric ward recovering from the damaging emotional
and psychological effects of merging his mind so thoroughly with the mind of a psychopath. Graham's son
knows very little about the details behind his father's
hospitalization, but he knows something is wrong. He
loves his father very much and wants to understand and
help him if he can.

Situation: The son confronts his father with his knowledge of a tabloid article he has seen that deals with Graham's treatment owing to his experiences with Lecter. Graham has never talked openly with his son about this experience. Now, when confronted by him, Graham explains to his son—as gently and sensitively as possible—the terrible realities of his profession and the emotional/psychological costs involved. Sensing how difficult this is for his father, the son must try to give him a way out. Eventually he brings the conversation around to some superficial topic, such as what brand of coffee to buy.

Comments: The deep love and affection that exists between father and son must be present at all times—influencing both their words and their actions. Graham, while wanting to tell his son the truth, must decide how far to go in relating unpleasant details to him, such as how Dr. Lecter killed his victims. Graham doesn't want to lie to his son, but he doesn't want to give him nightmares or cause psychological scars. This scene must be approached with great sensitivity and awareness because it is a major turning point in the relationship between these characters. The actors must also be aware of the public environment in which the scene takes place.

----------- **29** -----------

Source: *QB VII*, a novel by Leon Uris

Characters: Two males and one female: Sir Adam Kelno (Polish); his wife, Angela (French); their son, Stephen, in his twenties. Adam and Angela have been married since World War II, approximately thirty years. They met at a Polish section hospital, where she was a nurse and he was a doctor trying to save the lives of Polish prisoners.

Place: The couple's home in London

Background: Sir Adam Kelno was knighted by the Queen for his work in medicine. He had been a Polish political prisoner at the Jadwiga concentration camp. He was able to survive because of his medical expertise. Although he was a prisoner, his life was spared. In later years he brought suit against a writer, Abraham Cady, who slandered him in print. As the trial came to its conclusion, evidence was introduced by the defendant's attorney that conclusively proved that the basis for the defendant's allegations was in fact real and substantial. Namely, that the plaintiff, Dr. Kelno, by then a prominent physician, had at one point collaborated with the Nazis, engaging in cruel medical experiments and operations on Jewish prisoners at Jadwiga. He was more humane with non-Jewish prisoners.

Situation: The wife and son have been in the courtroom for many days listening to various evidence. This is the first proof they have heard about Sir Adam's crimes. They confront him at home after the trial.

Comments: The actor playing the husband must find a way of justifying his actions to himself as well as to his family. He must be specific in his mind regarding his actions at the prison. He loves his family very much and does not want to lose them. The actors playing the wife and son must place firmly in their minds, at the start of the scene, what they have just heard at the trial and must still be feeling the impact of the horrors described in graphic detail therein—horrors committed by a man they love and thought they knew.

———— **30** ————

Source: *White Nights (Le Notti Bianche)*, a film by Luchino Visconti, based on a Dostoyevsky short story

Characters: Two males and one female: Mario, a shy young man; Natalia, a pretty young girl; and Natalia's previous lover

Place: A canal bridge in Livorno, Italy

Background: Mario met Natalia one night while she was sobbing on a canal bridge. His heart went out to her and he befriended her. She told him she was in love with someone who left a year before because of some trouble he was in. He was not able to marry her at the time, but he promised to return in a year and to meet her on this bridge. He did not show up, and she is heartbroken. She becomes friends with Mario but not lovers because she still believes that the man she loves will come for her. She knows he is back because someone has seen him. She writes him a letter, which she asks Mario to deliver. Mario tears it up; he has fallen in love with Natalia.

Situation: They have been out dancing this evening and have had a wonderful time. It is the first time Natalia has been able to forget her grief. Mario admits to Natalia that he never delivered the letter. He has, by this time, convinced her that her former lover has no intention of coming back. She accepts this tonight for the first time and realizes she has been living a lie. She allows herself to have a good time with Mario and begins to fall in love with him. They are standing near the canal bridge, and they see a figure standing there. She realizes it is "him." Though she has fallen in love with Mario, she realizes she still loves the other man as well.

Comments: Natalia is torn as to what she should do. Her

decision cannot be an easy one. The actor playing the man who returns must be clear in his mind as to why he left for a year, why he has delayed in contacting her on the time agreed upon, and why he cannot reveal the reason for his absence. Although the film on which this improvisation is based was set in Italy, the locale could be anywhere, in any country.

RELATIONSHIP

Cross-References

*Other improvisations in this book that involve
Relationship can be found in the following categories:*

CONFRONTATION/CONFLICT

One male and one female

Two males

Ensemble

CLIMACTIC MOMENT/DISCOVERY

One male and one female

Two females

Two males

Ensemble

SUBTEXT

One male and one female

Two females

Ensemble

UNUSUAL CIRCUMSTANCES

One male and one female

2

CONFRONTATION/ CONFLICT

Webster's dictionary defines *confrontation* as "facing, especially in challenge: to oppose." *Conflict* is defined as "a clash between hostile or opposing elements or ideas."

Obviously, a fine line exists between confrontation and conflict, yet they do differ. One may have confrontation without conflict. For example: a man is confronted by his employer and accused of embezzlement. Instead of protesting the accusation, the employee readily admits his guilt. One may also have conflict without confrontation. For example: two roommates who have widely differing views on a variety of subjects decide, for the sake of equilibrium, never to discuss their differences. Although their ideas are in conflict, they don't confront each other directly. However, usually you don't find one without the other. For that reason, confrontation and conflict have been combined in this chapter.

Acting involves making choices, and the avoidance of confrontation or conflict, while at times dramatically valid, is usually not the most interesting choice. Of course, the avoidance of confrontation or conflict may be the key to a particular character. In such an instance, the actor should respect that trait. Nevertheless, the choice to explore confrontation and/or conflict within a given situation can be tremendously exciting, both for an actor and an audience.

Therefore, the following improvisations have been designed to center specifically on situations in which con-

43

frontation and/or conflict are not only inherent but inevitable. They are constructed in such a way that there is no easy escape. The cards are on the table, and the game can't proceed until a confrontation takes place. Acting is about confronting.

Often, actors, particularly in film and television work, are not allowed the luxury of building to these moments. They are frequently called upon to enter into a confrontation suddenly, out of sequence or context. Some of the following improvisations will facilitate these moments of sudden confrontation and/or conflict, allowing the actor to deal with this problem in a focused manner.

Confrontation within a scene may occur between lifelong friends or complete strangers. Characters may clash after twenty-five years of marriage or because someone took their place in line. The improvisations in this chapter will allow the actors to explore confrontation and/or conflict within a wide range of relationships and situations.

CONFRONTATION/CONFLICT

List of Situations

45

Ensemble

———— **1** ————

Source: *Anne of the Thousand Days*, a play by Maxwell Anderson (Situation #2)

Characters: One male and one female: Henry VIII, King of England, middle-aged, and Anne, Queen of England, in her twenties

Place: The Tower of London, where Anne is imprisoned and awaiting execution

Background: Anne has not been able to give Henry a son as heir to the throne. He does not want their daughter, Elizabeth, to be the heir because of her sex. Henry asks Anne to give him a divorce. He wants to marry Jane Seymour in the hope that she will give him a male heir. (Anne gave birth to two sons, but they were stillborn.) Anne will not sign the papers granting Henry a divorce because if she is no longer queen, her daughter, Elizabeth, will not be entitled to the throne. Anne is therefore falsely accused of adultery and treason, offenses punishable by death.

Situation: Henry has come to the tower to see Anne. He

pleads with her one last time to sign the paper granting him a divorce, in return for which he offers her her life.

Comments: It is important for the actors to remember that Anne is the only one of Henry's wives whom he truly loved. Henry is tormented by the thought that she might have committed adultery while they were intimate. As a way of getting even with him, Anne taunts Henry with the fact that he'll never know for sure. Another reason she won't sign the paper is that she suspects Henry's offer is empty. He will probably have her killed anyway. However, it is not an easy decision for her to make, nor would it be easy for Henry to have her executed.

See *Anne of the Thousand Days*, #1, page 6.

_____ **2** _____

Source: *The Crucible*, a play by Arthur Miller (Situation #1)

Characters: One male and one female: John Proctor and his wife, Elizabeth

Place: The living room in the home of John and Elizabeth Proctor, Salem, Massachusetts, 1692

Background: This scene takes place at the time of the Salem witch trials. Elizabeth found her husband, John, having an affair with Abigail and forbade him to see her anymore. He agreed to this. It has now been seven months and John has kept his promise, but Elizabeth has still not let him near her bed. Abigail, to get revenge on Elizabeth for keeping John from her, has accused her of being a witch.

Situation: Elizabeth asks John to go to Abigail and tell her she is a whore and that he no longer cares for her. John is reluctant to do this. To Elizabeth this is a sign that he still has feelings for Abigail. This angers him because he has been faithful for seven months with no gratification from his wife. If Abigail believes John doesn't care for her anymore, she'll let Elizabeth go. But as long as she thinks it is Elizabeth who is keeping her from John, she'll see to it that Elizabeth is labeled a witch.

Comments: The actors must be aware of the effect of sexual repression on both of the characters. They must also be aware that the witch hunts were very real. A person who did not confess to being a witch was usually hanged.

———— 3 ————

Source: *The Crucible*, a play by Arthur Miller (Situation #2)

Characters: One male and one female: a married man, John Proctor, and his ex-lover, Abigail Williams

Place: A shack in the woods at night in Salem, Massachusetts, 1692

Background: This scene takes place at the time of the witch trials in Salem. Abigail has accused John Proctor's wife, Elizabeth, of being a witch so that she will be hanged and John will be free to be her lover. Abigail brought a doll with a needle stuck in it to the court, saying that Elizabeth Proctor had done this. Abigail claimed to have been pricked all over as if from a needle. The people in Salem at that time believed in this kind of witchcraft.

Situation: Tomorrow is Elizabeth Proctor's trial. John has asked Abigail to meet him in the woods. She believes he called her there as his lover. Abigail is very happy to see John, telling him she knew he would come to her. He is still attracted to her, but he tells her his true mission there is to save his wife's life. He asks her to testify in court that she made up the story about the doll. John threatens to expose her as a liar if she doesn't volunteer to help him. She reminds him of their torrid affair and retaliates by announcing that she will make it public.

Comments: There is great conflict for John in this scene. He is still very attracted to Abigail, and his wife has refused to have sexual relations with him for the last seven months as a punishment for his affair. He does, however, love his wife and is desperate to save her. Abigail knows how to work on John's desires. The actress can decide whether or not Abigail believes that Elizabeth is pricking her body or whether she's just saying it to make John believe it. Arthur Miller insinuates in the last scene that Abigail is, at this point, a little crazy.

————— **4** —————

Source: *David*, an autobiographical novel by Marie Rothenberg

Characters: One male and one female: Marie Rothenberg, a young single working mother, recently divorced, and Charles Rothenberg, her ex-husband

Place: Two locales: the New York office where Marie works as a secretary, and a motel in California near Disneyland

Background: Neither Charles nor Marie has remarried; however, Marie is planning to marry, in the near future, the man she is presently seeing. Charles fears that after Marie's marriage he will not be able to see much of their son, David. He persuades Marie to let him take David on a week-long vacation to the Catskills. In reality,

Charles kidnaps his son and takes him across the continent to California.

Situation: Charles has telephoned Marie. She reacts with anger and panic, demanding to know where he has taken their son. Her outburst sets off a rage in Charles, causing him to threaten her with never seeing David again. Terrified, she believes her initial reaction to be a blunder and tries desperately to remedy the situation.

Comments: The actors should explore this relationship. They must investigate the reasons for the divorce and the causes of such deep resentment. *David* is based on a true story, in which the father ultimately did great harm to his son. The wife may not know to what extent he will go, but she senses grave danger for her son.

5

Source: *A Day in the Death of Joe Egg*, a play by Peter Nichols

Characters: One male and one female: husband, Bri, and his wife, Sheila

Place: Their home

Background: Bri and Sheila have a ten-year-old daughter named Joe, who is practically a vegetable and has been so since birth. Sheila feels guilty because she believes she caused the child to be this way by holding back while giving birth. Joe has to be bathed, exercised, and fed. The only sound she makes is "Aah." Sheila and Bri never go out together because no one else could care for Joe. They both love their daughter, but the marriage is beginning to suffer owing to the confining nature of their lives.

Situation: Bri confronts Sheila with the fact that they must send Joe to an institution if they are going to save their marriage. This is not the first time he has brought this up, but today he gives Sheila an ultimatum. Because of the guilt she feels, she cannot let her daughter go.

Comments: One of the elements that made this play a success is that it was not played like a soap opera. These two people have lived with this tragedy for many years and have used humor as a means of coping with it. The issue here is to save the marriage. The actors must understand the strain this tragedy has put on their relationship. The husband really is at his wit's end.

6

Source: *Harold and Maude,* a film by Hal Ashby, screenplay by Colin Higgins

Characters: One male and one female: Harold, an off-beat young man in his early twenties, and his mother, in her fifties

Place: The sitting room of the mansion in which Harold and his mother live

Background: Harold is a strange young man, who is obsessed by death. A favorite pastime has been to commit elaborate "suicides"—meticulously prepared staged simulations. By now his mother has become quite used to these displays and regards them with a weary, slightly annoyed resignation.

Recently Harold met and fell in love with Maude, a woman in her seventy-ninth year, who is a feisty, free-spirited eccentric. Maude's love of life has proved infectious, rubbing off on Harold, who has begun to emerge from his world of darkness. Harold now sees the beauty of life and nature and the positive potential within himself. As a result of this personal awakening, he has come to feel deep love for Maude and wishes to marry her. To him and to Maude, the difference in their ages is irrelevant.

Situation: Harold tells his mother about Maude and his intention to marry her. At first she is delighted because she has tried desperately for some time to get Harold interested in women. Then Harold shows his mother a recent photo of Maude, and her mood changes drastically.

Comments: It is of utmost importance to the mother to see Harold married—it is her dream. Therefore, it is quite a letdown when she finds out who the bride-to-be is. Harold, seeing absolutely nothing wrong with his choice, is disappointed with his mother's reaction.

An interesting sidelight is that, although Maude never directly discusses it in the film, she is a concentration-camp survivor.

--------- 7 ---------

Source: *The Heiress*, a play by Ruth and Augustus Goetz, based on the novel *Washington Square* by Henry James (Situation #2)

Characters: One male and one female: Morris, Catherine's suitor; Catherine, a woman in her late thirties, an heiress

Place: The living room of Catherine Sloper's town house on Washington Square in the mid-1800s.

Background: Catherine's father, Dr. Austin Sloper, often told her that she was a plain, dull girl and that men would be interested only in her money. Morris Townsend, a handsome young man, proposed to Catherine a decade earlier, when Catherine was still in her twenties.

Catherine's father forbade the marriage, knowing Morris to be a fortune hunter. Despite this, Catherine made arrangements to elope with Morris; he was to pick her up at midnight. But earlier that day she told him that her father had disinherited her. She believed that this wouldn't make any difference. However, Morris never showed up that night, and she was devastated.

It is now ten years later, and Morris has been traveling aimlessly, living by his wits and on a small inheritance. Dr. Sloper has since died, and Morris wants Catherine to take him back. Catherine is stronger now and hardened.

Situation: Morris, now lonely and desperate, is outside the door begging Catherine to let him in. He wants to marry her in earnest this time. Catherine can no longer be disinherited because her father is dead, and she is now very rich. In her heart, she believes that Morris is still only after her money. Catherine listens to his cries outside the door.

Comments: In the play, Catherine never responds to Morris vocally. She eventually turns out the lights and goes upstairs to bed. Even though Catherine has become embittered, the actress must remember that this character still loves Morris and finds it painful to lock him out. The actress might make the decision to let him in to see what the exchange might be.

The actor playing Morris must remember that his character is at his wit's end, and he needs Catherine to take care of him. The actor must make the decision as to whether or not Morris really loves her.

See *The Heiress*, #1, page 106.

——— 8 ———

Source: *Macbeth,* a play by William Shakespeare (Situation #1)

Characters: One male and one female: husband, Macbeth, leader of the Scottish army, and his wife, Lady Macbeth

Place: A room in Macbeth's castle outside the banquet hall

Background: Lady Macbeth has convinced her husband to murder Duncan, the reigning king of Scotland. Macbeth will then become king, and she will become queen. Duncan has been invited to a banquet at their castle this evening. They plan to murder him in his sleep and then make it look as if his bodyguards committed the crime, by placing bloody daggers in the hands of the sleeping guards whose wine they will drug.

Situation: The banquet is under way, and Macbeth has vacated the dining room suddenly because he cannot face Duncan, whom he's going to murder in a few hours. He is having second thoughts. Lady Macbeth is searching for her husband and finds him outside the dining hall. She tells him it is not wise to disappear, since he is the host; it might appear suspicious. Macbeth tells her he would like to abandon their plan. She confronts him, questioning his manhood and his breach of promise to her.

Comments: The actors might not be able to relate to becoming king or queen, but they should be able to relate to the thirst for power. Macbeth could not become king any other way. Lady Macbeth is the stronger personality of the two. She has power over her husband—sexual as well as emotional.

See *Macbeth,* #2, page 167.

_____ 9 _____

Source: *Night Must Fall,* a play by Emlyn Williams (Situation #1)

Characters: One male, one female: Dan, a young man hired to care for Mrs. Bramson, who is an invalid; Olivia, a young woman in her twenties or thirties, the niece of Mrs. Bramson

Place: The home of Mrs. Bramson

Background: Olivia lives with her aunt, Mrs. Bramson, an invalid confined to a wheelchair. Olivia is engaged to be married. However, she finds both her fiancé and her aunt unexciting. There is a murderer at large who decapitates women. The police have found one of the heads buried on the Bramson property, and, understandably, this has unnerved Mrs. Bramson. She has hired Dan to protect her. He is charming, and she adores and trusts him completely. Olivia, however, who has by now fallen in love with Dan, suspects he is the murderer. (In fact, he is.) When his luggage was being carried upstairs, she noticed a hat box that was unusually heavy. She guessed what was probably in it.

Situation: Olivia is probing Dan to find out more about him because she knows relatively little. This is really the first time either Dan or Olivia has felt anything for another person. Dan is comfortable with Olivia and begins to open up to her. She eventually confronts him about the hat box.

Comments: The actress playing Olivia must deal with the conflict of loving this man and yet realizing that he is probably a murderer. The actor also has a conflict in that he loves her, but she is the only one who suspects his guilt. The actors should note the contrasting character-

istics of Dan and Olivia: Olivia is an educated, sophisticated woman of some wealth. Dan is lower-class,
uneducated, has no money, and is very resentful of the
people for whom he works. He is used to fabricating
stories about his past to make people feel sorry for him.
He is very charming and has been able to gain the confidence of all the women he's killed. The actress playing
Olivia should be aware that the lack of excitement in
Olivia's life will color her reaction to Dan. This is a
woman desperate to escape from boredom.

See *Night Must Fall*, #2, page 144.

____ 10 ____

Source: *The Obscene Phone Caller*, a real-life news item

Characters: One male, one female: the president of a university and his wife.

Place: Holding room of a police station

Background: The president of a university is charged with
placing obscene phone calls from his campus office to a
woman he didn't know. He apparently made ten calls to
her home. The police have tapes of the conversations,
which lasted from twenty minutes to one hour. The calls
contained explicit language in which he talked about
having sex with his young son and daughter. In actuality,
he has no son, and his daughters are adults. He also
discussed having group sex with what turned out to be
a fictitious family. He has just been arrested.

Situation: His wife has just been brought to the police
station. The husband must face his wife and tell her about
his crime.

Comments: The challenge here for the actors is that these are two cultivated, well-educated, successful people who have to face this difficult moment in their relationship. The actors should have no preconceived notions about their reactions to this. The husband has never done this before, and he is as bewildered by it as is his wife. In the actual news story, he confessed to having been a victim of child abuse, but the actor may wish to find his own motivations for what has driven him to these acts.

11

Source: *The Owl and the Pussycat*, a play by Bill Manhoff

Characters: One male, one female: Felix, a male writer, and Doris, a hooker who lives upstairs

Place: Felix's apartment at two A.M.

Background: Felix complained about the noise being made by Doris, a hooker living in the same apartment building. The complaint resulted in her eviction. She conducted her "business" in her apartment. Now that she has been evicted, she has no place to live and of course no source of income. Felix is desperate to meet a writing deadline.

Situation: Doris knocks at Felix's door, posing as a lost little girl. He falls for this and opens the door. She then bursts in demanding that he put her up in his apartment, since it was his fault that she no longer has a place to live. No matter what he does, she will not leave. He has no money to get rid of her. He has a very important meeting in the morning involving one of his writing projects, and he sorely needs his sleep. She is wide awake and talkative because this is the time when she usually works.

Comments: These two are strange bedfellows. Both of their professions are very important to them. Felix is a work-aholic and has no time for pleasure. Although he is rather appalled by Doris's profession, she is quite lively and appealing. The two gradually experience a growing attraction for each other.

_____ 12 _____

Source: *Running on Empty*, a film by Sidney Lumet, screenplay by Naomi Foner

Characters: One male, one female: a man in his early sixties and his daughter, in her late thirties/early forties

Place: A restaurant

Background: The daughter and her husband have been on the run from the FBI for many years because of their activities as political activists in the 1960s. This constant running has been very hard on their children. The daughter has been estranged from her parents for many years, also as a result of her one-time activism. She has recently contacted her father and requested that he meet her at a certain restaurant. He has agreed to this.

Situation: The father and daughter meet for the first time in many years. Eventually, she brings herself to ask her father to take custody of her eldest child, a boy in his mid-teens. Also, she apologizes for the pain she caused her parents. The resolution of this situation will be left up to the actors.

Comments: Whatever the outcome, this is a difficult and sensitive situation for both characters. The actor playing the father must bear in mind that although this is his own daughter, whom he loves, he has been hurt by her emotionally in the past and has disapproved strongly of her political stance and her activism. This has caused much grief to both him and his wife. What she is now asking of him must not be an easy decision. His whole life will be disrupted by taking in a teenage boy. The actress playing the daughter must understand how difficult it is for her to confront her father in her totally vulnerable, emotionally naked state. She must bear in mind both the guilt she feels and the desperate need she has to find stability and a normal home environment for her son.

———— 13 ————

Source: *The Shining*, a film by Stanley Kubrick, screenplay by Kubrick and Diane Johnson, based on the novel by Stephen King

Characters: One female, one male: Wendy Torrance and her husband, Jack Torrance

Place: The Overlook, a resort hotel high in the Colorado Rockies, closed for the winter months

Background: Jack Torrance, a former schoolteacher, was fired for having physically beaten a student. His wife, Wendy, knows her husband is capable of violence. There had even been an incident at home in which Jack, who had been drinking, dislocated his son's shoulder. Recently, Jack has been made winter caretaker of the Overlook Hotel. He considers his position all-important—his last chance at having a position of responsibility. He is obsessed with maintaining this position at all costs—if need be, even the lives of his wife and son.

Situation: For some time Jack has been at work on a novel. As yet, Wendy has seen none of it. At the beginning of this improvisation, she comes upon the box containing the manuscript of this "novel." As she begins to examine the pages, she quickly discovers that all the writing consists of endless typographical variations on the single sentence: "All work and no play makes Jack a dull boy." With each page she views, a horrible realization begins to dawn on her—she and her young son, Danny, are trapped in a snow-bound hotel with a madman who was once her loving husband. At this point, Jack surprises her, coming up behind her and asking her opinion of his "novel." The confrontational phase of the scene proceeds from here as Jack, possessed by the dark forces inhabiting the hotel, confronts Wendy with his suspicion that she wants to take their son away, abandoning him. The beginning of this improvisation is a solo moment for Wendy.

———— 14 ————

Source: *The Shoe Store*, a real-life news item

Characters: One female, one male: a shoe-store owner and his female employee

Place: A shoe store

Background: The woman has been employed at this shoe store for the past twenty years. Her employer has discovered that she has been taking home a pair of shoes every week.

Situation: The owner confronts his employee with the above.

Comments: The actors must accept that this is true. The woman should decide what her motivation is for stealing so many shoes.

_____ **15** _____

Source: *The Prime of Miss Jean Brodie*, a play by Jay Presson Allen, adapted from the novel by Muriel Spark

Characters: Two females: Jean Brodie, an English teacher in her prime, and a headmistress, Miss MacKay

Place: The headmistress's office in a girls' private school

Background: Jean Brodie is a flamboyant, stimulating teacher, who has great influence over her "girls." Miss MacKay is a rigid, frustrated headmistress, who does not approve of Miss Brodie's teaching methods, which are of a personal, emotional nature. Miss Brodie shares her experiences about men with her students but always in the context of teaching an important lesson. One of the students has written a highly sexual letter about Miss Brodie and her so-called flings with two male teachers in the school: one with a wife and six children and the other a confirmed bachelor. These are, of course, the fantasies of a sexually aroused adolescent girl.

Situation: Miss MacKay calls Jean Brodie into her office to read her this letter, found by the school's gardener. Jean Brodie, of course, finds it rather amusing and makes some spelling corrections on it. Miss MacKay does not quite see it the same way and believes that Miss Brodie must have done something to stimulate these fantasies. She asks for Miss Brodie's resignation. Miss Brodie refuses to resign because she believes she is a great teacher. She has devoted her life to this profession and to this school in particular.

Comments: Miss Brodie's relationship with Mr. Lowther, the music teacher (a bachelor), is purely platonic; she goes to his house on Sundays with the girls. Her relationship with the art teacher, Mr. Lloyd, is of a romantic nature but has probably never been consummated. However, the actress can determine for herself the extent of her involvement with these two men. She must keep in mind that Miss Brodie is a passionate woman and a complete contrast to Miss MacKay, who is well past her prime, if indeed she ever had one. The actors can compose their own letter beforehand and read it aloud in the improvisation or it can be read silently. The play takes place in Scotland, but the situation could easily be transposed to any country.

———— 16 ————

Source: *Child's Play*, a play by Robert Marasco (Situation #2)

Characters: Two males: Father Mozian, headmaster of a Catholic boys' school, and Jerome Malley, a teacher at the school. This scene could also be done with two females in a Catholic girls' school

Place: The headmaster's office

Background: It has been brought to Father Mozian's attention by a teacher that Malley has been receiving pornographic magazines at school through the mail. Malley is a teacher of long tenure, but the headmaster feels he must be dismissed. Malley never ordered these magazines and does not understand why they are being sent. Also, Malley's mother, to whom he is very close, is quite ill. Malley is nearing his emotional breaking point. The teacher who leveled the false charges against Malley wants to get Malley fired so that he can take over the senior class.

Situation: The meeting between the headmaster and Malley. Malley tries to defend himself, but the headmaster's response is unsympathetic. Malley's increasingly harried emotional state does not strengthen his positon.

Comments: The actor playing Malley must understand that his long-standing teaching position at this school means nearly everything to him. The actor playing Father Mozian must understand that, from his character's point of view, he is fully justified in wanting Malley dismissed.

The actor playing the priest should be cautioned not to play the character as a "holy man." The priest is someone doing his job. This does not mean he lacks compassion, however. The actor playing Malley cannot resort to anything like the threat of a lawsuit. He must confront the headmaster right then and there.

17

Source: *An Enemy of the People,* a play by Henrik Ibsen, adapted by Arthur Miller

Characters: Two males: Dr. Stockman and his brother, Peter Stockman, mayor of Clear Water Springs

Place: The home of Dr. Stockman in the town of Clear Water Springs

Background: Dr. Stockman has discovered that the water in the town is poisoned. This is a tourist town, which makes a fortune from the springs. People come from all over to use the springs as health baths; they are the main attraction of the town.

Situation: Dr. Stockman calls his brother, Peter Stockman, to his home to tell him of his discovery, assuming that Peter will do the right thing—namely, inform the townspeople and the visitors that the water is contaminated. However, Peter is more politically minded and financially oriented than his brother. He attempts to persuade the doctor to keep his findings quiet because it would be a financial disaster for the town if word of this leaked out. When Dr. Stockman refuses to agree to this, Peter threatens to ruin his reputation as a doctor and run him out of town.

Comments: Both actors must strongly justify their own point of view in this matter. They must also deal with their relationship as brothers. The actors have to accept the fact that the doctor's findings are accurate. The water is poisoned because the springs are too close to a toxic dump.

———— 18 ————

Source: *The Family Man*, a film for television by Glenn Jordan, teleplay by William Hanley, based on *The Monogamist*, a novel by Thomas Gallagher

Characters: Two males: Eddie Madden, about fifty, and his son, Denny, late teens

Place: A New York street at night

Background: Eddie Madden owns a New York City garage at which his son, Denny, works. Eddie is a devout Catholic and a dedicated family man. He has been happily married and has two children, Denny and a daughter, Oona. Recently, Eddie met an attractive young single woman named Mercedes, who asked to rent the room above his garage. They soon found themselves drawn to each other and began an affair. Eddie's wife began to notice little differences in her husband's behavior and started to become suspicious. One night, as Denny was leaving work late, he saw his father and Mercedes getting into a car together. He then knew the truth about his father's infidelity but found himself torn about what to do. He decided not to tell his mother or sister and, instead, made up his mind to confront his father directly.

Situation: It is closing time at Madden's garage, and the father and son take a walk together. As they walk, they discuss various things, but underlying everything is Denny's knowledge about his father. His father suspects that his son may know but says nothing about it. At some point, Denny openly confronts his father about the affair.

Comments: The actor playing Denny must take into account the boy's concern for his mother and for the future of his family. It's been a great burden on him to carry around this knowledge. The actor playing the father must have a clear picture of his relationship with his wife and Mercedes, and, of course, his son.

_____ **19** _____

Source: _Lone Star_, a play by James McClure

Characters: Two males: an older and a younger brother

Place: A local bar

Background: The younger brother has smashed up his older brother's car. That car was the most important thing in his brother's life. He had his first sexual experience in the car and many more after that. He nurtured the car with many coats of paint through the years. It was his prize possession. The older brother is a Vietnam vet.

Situation: In a roundabout manner, the younger brother breaks the news to his older brother that he slept with his brother's wife while he was in Vietnam. He does this to soften the blow about having demolished the car.

Comments: The characters are drinking, but this does not mean the actors should play the scene as if drunk. Rather, the alcohol breaks down their inhibitions. The older brother tends to be volatile anyway, which is why the younger brother is terrified of telling him about the car. The older brother is totally ignorant of his younger brother's involvement with his wife.

20

Source: *Lost in America,* a film by Albert Brooks, screenplay by Brooks and Monica Johnson

Characters: Two males: the owner of a hotel/casino and a customer

Place: The office of the casino owner in Las Vegas

Background: A man and his wife have liquidated their savings and have decided to travel across America as free spirits. He was a big advertising man in Los Angeles. They are presently staying in a Las Vegas hotel/casino. In the middle of the night, the wife went downstairs and gambled away all their money.

Situation: The husband goes to the casino owner and requests that their money be returned. He is desperate. Utilizing the techniques of his trade, he tries every means at his disposal to persuade the owner. For example, he proposes the refund be used as an advertising gimmick to promote the hotel's humanity and goodwill. The owner is not impressed. The husband, however, is not a man who gives up easily.

Comments: The advertising man must not give up, no matter how stubborn the casino owner becomes in his refusal to refund the money.

This situation was basically humorous in the film. It has, however, a tragic undertone. Therefore, it may turn out to be a serious improvisation. It is best for the coach not to introduce it as humorous or serious. Let the actors take it wherever it goes.

_____ **21** _____

Source: *Mass Appeal*, a play by Bill C. Davis

Characters: Two males: an older priest and a seminary student

Place: The priest's office in a large city church

Background: The seminary student has been dismissed from the parish because he was felt to be too revolutionary in his views. He rocked the boat by not sticking to traditional doctrine in his sermons.

Situation: The student asks the priest to stand up for him before the congregation. The priest feels that this is too much to ask, since his own position would be put in jeopardy. If he speaks up for the young man, there is a good chance he will be removed from his pulpit and sent to some small-town church. He needs the support of this congregation; this is his whole life. The student feels that the priest should be stronger. He knows that the priest agrees with the contents of his sermons but lacks the courage of his own convictions.

Comments: The actors should decide on the specific content of the student's sermons and why they are so threatening to the congregation. Both must know whom they are dealing with in the higher echelon of the church. The actor playing the priest must also deal with his fears. The actors should be cautioned not to portray these characters as "holy men."

————— **22** —————

Source: *The Meeting Between Pope John Paul II and His Would-be Assassin in 1981,* a real-life news item

Characters: Two males: Pope John Paul II and his would-be assassin

Place: The assassin's jail cell

Background: During a public appearance, a young man shot at the pope, hitting him in the shoulder. The pope was not seriously injured.

Situation: The pope has come to the prison to meet his would-be assassin face-to-face. It is now several months after the attempted assassination.

Comments: The assassin is not Catholic. This was to have been a political assassination. The actor playing the part must have a strong sense of why he was driven to do this. The actor playing the pope must not play this part as a cliché but should have some awareness of papal protocol. He must deal with his own human feelings about someone's attempt to kill him. The actor playing the pope must also be cognizant of this man's enormously prominent role in world religion. The pope knows his actions will be looked upon as an example to the world. The actors should not be concerned with nationality.

————— **23** —————

Source: *The Winslow Boy,* a play by Terence Rattigan

Characters: Two males: Ronnie Winslow, a twelve-year-old cadet, and his father, Arthur Winslow

Place: The living room of their home

Background: Ronnie goes to a military boarding school. He was kicked out for suspected stealing of a five-cent postal money order. He came home from school with a letter of dismissal and hid outside the house, afraid to face his father. He let himself be seen by his sister and mother, who then hid him upstairs. The father found out and asked to see him.

Situation: The father and son meet. Ronnie claims he is innocent of the charges. Mr. Winslow must find out if he is lying, because if Ronnie is telling the truth, Mr. Winslow intends to take the false accusation of his son to the highest court in the land.

Comments: There are a number of elements to deal with here: Ronnie's fear of his father; the humiliation of being kicked out of a prestigious military school—something that could affect the rest of Ronnie's life; the injustice of being falsely accused; convincing the father of this injustice; the father's hurt feeling because his son hid from him. It must be of vital importance to the father to get the truth from Ronnie. This play is based on an actual case.

24

Source: *Billy Budd, Foretopman*, a novella by Herman Melville

Characters: Three males: Billy Budd, an innocent sailor; his superior, the master-at-arms, Claggart; the captain of the ship, Captain Vere

Place: The office of Captain Vere on board ship

Background: Billy Budd is an honest, hard-working, very handsome sailor, who is loved by his shipmates. He befriends Claggart, who, for some unknown reason, falsely accuses him of stealing food and instigating mutiny among the crew.

Situation: Captain Vere calls Billy into his office regarding this matter of mutiny. Billy is completely bewildered by the accusation. Captain Vere cannot take the chance of simply believing Billy because mutiny is serious. He must be certain. Billy has a speech impediment that manifests itself when he is under great pressure. He becomes so frustrated at being unable to defend himself verbally against Claggart's false charges that he strikes out at Claggart, accidentally killing him.

Comments: The actor playing Claggart must find his own motivation for destroying Billy Budd. Captain Vere, deep in his heart, knows Billy to be innocent but chooses to make an example of him because of his fear of mutiny. This novella was based on an actual case, which took place in 1797, a time when sea captains greatly feared mutiny. Mutiny had become so widespread a problem that Vere reacts strongly to even the mere suggestion of it. The actors must be forewarned not to play this any differently because it is set in 1797. It is about injustice which can occur in any century.

_____ **25** _____

Source: *Born on the Fourth of July,* a film by Oliver Stone, screenplay by Stone and Ron Kovic, based on Kovic's autobiography.

Characters: Two males and one female: Ron Kovic, a handicapped Vietnam veteran in his late twenties; a husband and wife in their late fifties

Place: The husband and wife's home in the country

Background: During the Vietnam war, Ron Kovic, a young enlisted man, accidentally killed a young fellow soldier. This incident has haunted him for many years. Paralyzed from the waist down owing to a bullet wound, Kovic gets around in a wheelchair.

Situation: Ron Kovic arrives at the husband and wife's home and confronts them, confessing that he was responsible for their son's death. He tells them he shot their son accidentally, mistaking him for the enemy.

Comments: The main issue here is Kovic's feeling compelled to confess and the parents' response to what he tells them. The actor playing Kovic must be clear about what has brought him to this point, and the actors playing the parents, aside from dealing with the feelings of the moment, must be clear about their relationship to their dead son and understand how his death has affected their lives. Since Kovic's handicap is not intrinsic to this situation, the part can be played without the handicap and wheelchair, although the handicap may create more interest.

_____ 26 _____

Source: *Golden Boy*, a play by Clifford Odets (Situation #3)

Characters: Four males: Joe Bonaparte, a young fighter, and the father and two brothers of a fighter who was just killed by Joe in the ring

Place: The dressing room of the dead fighter

Background: Joe was an accomplished violinist who gave up music to fight and earn a lot of money. He rose to the top and became a champion. He knocked out his opponent in this evening's bout, killing him accidentally. At heart, Joe is not a fighter; it goes against his nature, but he does it because he wants to be successful.

Situation: Joe goes to the dressing room of the fighter he has just killed and faces the man's father and two brothers.

Comments: The actors should have no preconceived notions about how they will deal with this situation.

See *Golden Boy*, #1, page 162, and #2, page 164.

_____ **27** _____

Source: *Lemon Sky*, a play by Lanford Wilson

Characters: One male and two females: husband and wife, and their sixteen-year-old foster daughter

Place: The home of the foster parents

Background: The foster daughter tells the wife that she was molested by the husband in their basement.

Situation: This improvisation is divided into three scenes. In the first scene, the girl tells her foster mother that she was molested by the father. In the second scene, the wife confronts her husband with this accusation, and he denies it. In the third scene, all three characters are involved. The husband calls the girl in and accuses her of lying.

Comments: Only the husband and the girl know what really happened, and the actors must each decide this beforehand. If the girl is lying, she has to have good reason. The actress playing the mother should make some decisions about her husband's history. This will have an effect on how she receives the accusation.

_____ **28** _____

Source: *A Meeting Between Rapists and Rape Victims*, a television documentary

Characters: Males and females—number indeterminate: a group of men—convicted rapists; women who have been raped; and a counselor

Place: A room in a maximum-security prison set up for an encounter group

Background: The women in this group have been psychologically damaged by their rape experiences. The men in the group are not the ones who raped these particular women.

Situation: In a therapy session, the women confront the rapists under the guidance of a counselor.

Comments: Both rapist and victim must be very specific in their own minds about what they did and what happened to them. The men must grapple with what events and feelings have driven them to their crimes. Each of the women must be clear on the trauma she has experienced and how it has affected her life.

_____ **29** _____

Source: *Piano*, a play by Anna Deveare Smith

Characters: Two males and one female: husband, Eduardo, and wife, Alicia; Eduardo's brother, Antonio

Place: The living room of Alicia and Eduardo's elegant home in Cuba, 1898

Background: During this period in history, there was a revolution going on in Cuba. The Cuban rebels, with the help of the United States, were waging guerrilla warfare against the Spanish. In retaliation, Spanish officials herded thousands of Cubans into camps and kept them prisoners under ghastly conditions. Alicia, Eduardo, and Antonio are from Spain. Alicia and Eduardo have opened their home to everyone; they have no enemies. However, Antonio, who is a Spanish general, is the one responsible for the camps. Carlitos, the son of Alicia and Eduardo, has been kidnapped by the Cuban

people. In exchange for his return, the rebels have requested that two thousand prisoners be released. The
decision lies in the hands of Antonio.

Situation: Alicia and Eduardo beg Antonio to agree to the
exchange and return their son to them. Part of their
argument is that the people he was asked to release are
not criminals. They are innocent; their only crime is that
they are Cuban. Alicia and Eduardo are appalled by the
camps. The important issue at the moment, however, is
that Antonio is Eduardo's brother, and if he loves his
brother, he will do whatever he can to get Carlitos back.
If he does not do this, their son will be killed.

Comments: The actors should not get too tangled up in the
history. This is a confrontation between people. It is
about two desperate parents, whose son has been kidnapped. The uncle is the only one who can save him.
The actor playing Antonio must find his own reasons for
his actions. He must believe that the people imprisoned
in the camps are bad. Also, Antonio is attracted to Alicia,
which might be of use to the actor.

————— **30** —————

Source: *Sandburg's Lincoln*, a television mini-series, based
on the biography by Carl Sandburg

Characters: One male and two females: Lincoln and Mary
Todd, his wife; Mrs. Ord (General Ord's wife)

Place: An outdoor ceremony during the Civil War, in which
Lincoln has just addressed the troops.

Background: Mary Todd got a late start and missed out on
riding with her husband to see the troops. The president
asked Mrs. Ord to ride with him in place of Mrs. Lincoln.

Situation: Arriving late, Mary sees her husband walking

back from the ceremony with Mrs. Ord. She has a jealous fit and, in front of everybody, accuses Mrs. Ord of trying to steal her husband, like some "little harlot." Mrs. Ord tries to defend herself but doesn't want to say that it was the president who asked her. Lincoln himself explains this to his wife. Mrs. Ord is naturally taken aback but must remain tactful because she is talking to the First Lady. The president then takes his wife aside to talk to her privately.

The second half of this improvisation is between Lincoln and Mary. Although he makes his anger plain, Lincoln convinces his wife of his devotion. What is truly behind her anguish is the recent loss of their young son Willie. She is still grieving. She fears losing her husband now, too. Lincoln is concerned about her mental and emotional state. Her anguish is painful for him to see.

Comments: This scene requires two mature actors, who are able to understand the dynamics of the relationship involved. These two people love each other. Mary has become unbalanced by the pressures of being First Lady. Lincoln must deal with his conflicting feelings of anger and love. He is a compassionate man, but he, also, is under great pressure. The actors must remember that this is a couple with marital problems and that being the president and First Lady doesn't make them behave in any special manner when they are alone.

_____ **31** _____

Source: *Scattered Clouds*, a film by Mikio Naruse

Characters: One male and two females: a widow and her sister, and a man who killed the widow's husband in an automobile accident

Place: A restaurant in Tokyo

Background: A husband and wife formed a happily married couple. The wife was expecting a baby. He was a bright young man with a great career. They were preparing to leave for Washington, D.C., on business when, one day, the husband was crossing the street and a car skidded in the rain, killing him. In that split second the wife's life changed drastically. She found herself with no financial resources and was forced to abort her child. The driver of the car was found to be innocent. This was based on Japanese law, which limits the rights of women. The driver requests a meeting with the widow because he would like to make amends. The widow's sister insists that she go.

Situation: The three meet in a restaurant. The man offers the widow a large sum of money to be paid on a monthly basis. He feels badly that the court did not demand restitution. She refuses the money because she doesn't want money from the man who killed her husband. Her sister implores her to take it.

Comments: The man responsible for the accident is as much a victim as the widow. He cannot be happy knowing the pain he has caused her. If she would let him assist her financially, it would help him to survive this tragedy.

———— **32** ————

Source: *Triangle*, an original situation

Characters: Two males and one female: husband, wife, and wife's lover

Place: The lover's home

Background: The wife has been having an affair for quite some time without her husband's knowledge. The husband and the lover know each other but are not close friends. Up until now, the husband has had no suspicions. But he has just learned of his wife's affair by listening in on a telephone conversation between his wife and her lover. At the wife's suggestion, she and her husband drive to the lover's home.

Situation: The wife and her husband meet with the lover and discuss their situation.

Comments: The actors must be very clear on the nature of their past involvement with one another. The husband and wife need to explore the problems in their marriage beforehand. The wife cares a great deal about both men, though in different ways.

CONFRONTATION/CONFLICT

Cross-References

Other improvisations in this book that involve Confrontation or Conflict can be found in the following categories:

RELATIONSHIP

One male and one female

Two females

Two males

Ensemble

CLIMACTIC MOMENT/DISCOVERY

SUBTEXT

UNUSUAL CIRCUMSTANCES

FANTASY

THEATER OF THE ABSURD

SPECIAL PROBLEMS

One male and one female

Two females

Ensemble

3

CLIMACTIC MOMENT/ DISCOVERY

Actors are at times called upon to enter into a situation at its climactic moment. It can be extremely difficult, however, to enter into a situation without the luxury of preparation. Yet, occasionally, in our own lives a sudden occurrence or accident will thrust us unprepared into a climactic moment. A lover can unexpectedly reject us. We can be fired without warning. There are many moments such as these, which instantly transform our lives. An example of a play with a sudden climactic moment is Tad Mosel's *All the Way Home*, in which a family hears that the father has been killed in an auto accident.

Other types of climactic moments are the result of a gradual emotional buildup. An example of this would be the moment in which Othello kills Desdemona. The climactic moments found in this chapter are not necessarily the climax of the respective dramas. A play, for example, may have a number of climactic moments that lead up to the primary, or central, climax. Though the hotel room scene between father and son in Arthur Miller's *Death of a Salesman* is certainly a climactic moment, it is not the climax of the play.

As with CONFRONTATION/CONFLICT, these improvisations are particularly valuable for film and television actors, since films and TV shows are usually shot out of sequence. The actor will frequently find himself in the uncomfortable position of having to plunge headlong into a climactic moment without first getting his feet wet. This can also apply to the audition process, in which the actor is given little or no time for preparation of scenes, scenes that are often climactic.

Many climactic moments are discoveries as well and can therefore be deeply challenging. Characters in an improvisation are constantly making discoveries, just as they do in a play or a film. However, there are moments when characters discover something about themselves or other characters that causes major change. For example, in Reginald Wilton's *I, Spud*, a person awakens to discover that a loved one has turned into a large potato. Another classic example would be Oedipus's discovery that he has married his mother. Characters in situations such as these experience profound transitions in their perspective on themselves and their world.

The improvisations in this section can also be used to particular advantage by the working actor "trapped" within the confines of a long stage-run. During an extended run the problems of anticipation and lack of spontaneity can crop up with a vengeance. The use of improvisational situations similar in context to those in this chapter—but based on moments or scenes from the actual play in which the actor is currently marooned—can help create a new and revitalized perspective from which to work.

Most, though not all, climactic moments involve discovery. For example, the execution of a condemned man would qualify as a climactic moment but not necessarily as a discovery, since the climax would be the anticipated one. By the same token, discovery may not always constitute a climactic moment. For example, a person may discover that he has a few gray hairs he hadn't noticed before.

In many cases, climactic moments are interwoven with

discovery (and vice versa). Therefore, these two elements have been combined under the single umbrella of this chapter. Through this combination actors can learn to experience emotional buildup and release, and/or to receive new information that changes them instantly in some way. These situations are constructed specifically to exercise such objectives.

CLIMACTIC MOMENT/DISCOVERY

List of Situations

Ensemble

———— **1** ————

Source: *Adam,* a film for television by Michael Tuchner, teleplay by Allan Leicht, based on a true story (Situation #2)

Characters: One male and one female: John and Reve Walsh, husband and wife, the parents of Adam

Place: A hotel room

Background: A couple's young son, Adam, has been missing for several weeks. The police have been searching for him, and they have found a body.

Situation: John and Reve are in a hotel room waiting for a phone call from the police regarding the identity of the body. The call comes, and they are notified that it is the body of their son. The body was found decapitated.

Comments: It is essential that the husband and wife establish their relationship to each other and to Adam. The telephone ring will have to be worked out ahead of time. It is crucial to the situation.

This is based on a true case, which led to major reforms in the tracing and locating of missing children. John Walsh, Adam's father, spearheaded these reforms. He went on to establish the Adam Walsh Foundation for Missing Children. Eventually, Walsh became the host of a syndicated television program—*America's Most Wanted*—which has been responsible for the capture of many dangerous criminals. Although the above information is not intended to be used in the improvisation itself, it may give the actor some key as to the nature of this man's character.

See *Adam*, #1, page 179.

2

Source: *The Ballad of the Sad Café*, a play by Edward Albee, based on the novel by Carson McCullers

Characters: One male and one female: husband and wife

Place: The bedroom of newlyweds in a small Southern town

Background: The wife is afraid of sex because her mother died giving birth to her. Therefore, she equates sex with death. It took her husband eight years to get up the courage to propose to her because of her intimidating temper. She dominates the entire county because everyone is afraid of her.

Situation: This is their wedding night, and the husband discovers for the first time that his wife is terrified of sex. She keeps him away at gunpoint.

Comments: The actors must accept the fact that the characters have not slept together before marriage. This is not unusual for the provincial community in which the characters live.

————— 3 —————

Source: *Cause Célèbre*, a play by Terence Rattigan

Characters: One male and one female: Alma Rattenburg, a married woman in her thirties, and George Wood, her eighteen-year-old servant and lover

Place: Alma's bedroom

Background: George has been hired in the household as a repairman, chauffeur, etc. Alma is married to a much older man whom she calls Rats—her nickname for him. She is very fond of her husband, but they have not had sexual relations for a long time. He is not in good health and knows he cannot give his wife what she wants. When George comes to live with them, he finds a very lonely and unhappy lady of the house. Alma breaks down in front of him one day, and this brings them together. George becomes her lover. The husband is aware of what is going on, but he says nothing. However, he starts getting nasty and strikes his wife in a drunken stupor. George can't stand the fact that Alma's husband is keeping them from happiness. One night he takes a mallet and strikes the husband, killing him. Alma is upstairs in bed and knows nothing of the incident.

Situation: George comes up to Alma's bed, where he sleeps every night. She starts getting affectionate with him, but he can't return it. Finally, he tells her what he has done. She can't understand it or believe it at first. Then she finally comprehends the truth of what he is telling her.

Comments: The actors should be aware that this was not premeditated murder; it happened on impulse. These two people are not just having a casual affair; they love each other, and each wants to protect the other from criminal charges. The play was based on an actual case. It culminated in the first double trial in English legal history in which the defendants tried to exonerate each other and take all the blame on themselves.

—————— 4 ——————

Source: *Day After the Fair*, a play by Frank Harvey, based on *On the Western Circuit* by Thomas Hardy (Situation #2)

Characters: One male and one female, newlyweds: Anna, a simple servant girl, and Charles Braddock, a young lawyer of high social class

Place: The couple's new home during the Victorian era

Background: Anna had spent two nights with Charles before he entered the military service. When she found out that she was pregnant, she decided to correspond with Charles. However, Anna, being illiterate, persuaded her mistress, Edith, to write the letters for her. Edith became intrigued with this correspondence, and she and Charles became entrenched in a very intimate love affair by mail. Charles thought all the time that he was writing to Anna. Anna, being inarticulate, gave Edith free rein in the writing of these letters. Eventually, Anna told Edith that she was pregnant by Charles and wanted him notified. Reluctantly, Edith obliged her by writing a beautiful letter in which she told him that she loved carrying his child and demanded nothing of him. Charles wrote back that he wanted to marry Anna. Edith and her husband arranged an elaborate wedding for them. In this scene, they have been married for a short time, and Charles finds it hard to communicate with Anna. Her letters were intelligent and passionate, but her behavior does not reflect this.

Situation: Charles wants Anna to write a thank-you letter to Edith for the wedding. Anna is forced to confess to Charles that she cannot read or write and that Edith composed and wrote all the letters. Charles now realizes that, in one sense, it is Edith with whom he fell in love, not Anna.

Comments: Charles knows he is trapped in his marriage. The actors must accept the social conventions of the Victorian era. Charles is a lawyer by profession, and Anna is a servant. During this period, that meant that there was a huge gap in educational levels. Charles is married to Anna for life, and Edith is married to her husband for life. Divorce is not a possibility. Anna is relieved to have a legitimate father for her child. The actress can decide how she feels about Charles.

See *Day After the Fair*, #1, page 140.

_____ **5** _____

Source: *Fatal Attraction*, a film by Adrian Lyne, screenplay by James Dearden (Situation #1)

Characters: One male and one female: Dan, a married man, and Alex, a woman with whom he had a short-lived affair

Place: The lobby of an airport

Background: One weekend when his wife was out of town, Dan had an affair with Alex, a woman he met at a business meeting. To him, this was just a casual fling. To her, it was a great deal more than that. To put it mildly, she is not willing to let go of the relationship.

It is now many weeks later, and Alex is very upset because Dan has refused to take her phone calls. She has recently been to a doctor and has found out that she is pregnant.

Situation: Alex corners Dan at an airline terminal as he is about to board a plane. She announces to him that she is pregnant and intends to keep the baby. She feels that this will ensure a close relationship with him forever. This is definitely not what he had in mind. He loves his wife and wants to keep his family together.

Comments: The actor must accept that this is his child. His major fear is putting his family in jeopardy. Alex is not going to let go; she is obsessed with this relationship.

See *Fatal Attraction*, #2, page 160.

--------- **6** ---------

Source: *Fatal Attraction,* a film by Adrian Lyne, screenplay by James Dearden (Situation #3)

Characters: One male and one female: husband and wife

Place: The kitchen of their country home

Background: See background in previous situation #1. Dan has continued to ignore Alex. She now decides to take her revenge. The husband and wife have gone to their country home to get some peace. They have bought their daughter a pet rabbit, which she adores.

Situation: Dan's wife, Beth, comes home and finds the rabbit boiling in a pot on the kitchen stove. Hearing her screams, Dan rushes into the kitchen. He quickly realizes who is responsible for this wicked deed. Now aware that Alex will stop at nothing, he decides to tell his wife about the affair.

Comments: The husband's discovery is that he has become involved with a dangerous maniac. The wife discovers both the murdered rabbit and her husband's betrayal. The actors should have no preconceived ideas as to the outcome. They must also have a very clear image of the boiling rabbit or the immediacy of this situation will not come across believably. It is a very short leap in their minds from a murdered pet to a murdered child.

See *Fatal Attraction*, #1, page 90, and #2, page 160.

———— 7 ————

Source: *Fences*, a play by August Wilson (Situation #2)

Characters: One male and one female: the husband, Troy Maxon, and his wife, Rose

Place: The backyard of the Maxon home in a poor urban area

Background: Troy and Rose have been married for eighteen years. They have one son, Corey, who is now in high school. Troy has an older son from a previous marriage. Drowning in the bills and hardships of life, Troy has felt unsuccessful as a man. He was seeing another woman for many years without Rose's knowledge. When this other woman became pregnant, Troy was forced to tell his wife about the relationship. Needless to say, Rose was deeply hurt. She had been faithful to Troy throughout the marriage and had never suspected his affair. The baby has now been born, the mother having died in childbirth.

Situation: Troy has just come from the hospital and is carrying the baby. He presents it to Rose, telling her that the baby has no mother and that he wants her to bring it up.

Comments: The actress may make her own decision about her reaction. In the play, the wife decides to take the baby, at the same time spurning her husband. But every woman would react differently, and it is preferable for the actress to make no preliminary decision regarding her response. Troy's response will, of course, depend on the actions of the wife. Note: Actors will need to use a doll for the baby.

See *Fences*, #1, page 117.

8

Source: *Hay Fever*, a play by Noël Coward

Characters: One male and one female: Judith, a famous semiretired actress, and Richard, her daughter's boyfriend

Place: Judith's summer house in the country. A room in this house with much of her memorabilia in it

Background: Judith has invited several guests for the weekend, and her daughter, Sorel, has invited her boyfriend, Richard. Judith's husband, David, is somewhere in the house. Sorel is off flirting, thus leaving Judith alone with Richard. Richard is in awe of Judith because she is a famous actress/singer whom he has always admired.

Situation: Richard asks Judith to sing for him, which she does. They have martinis together while she shows him pictures of her career in her photo album. They become flirtatious with each other, and he kisses her on the neck, but as a *fan* not a lover. She totally misunderstands this and takes the kiss to mean that he is in love with her.

She is delighted and announces that she is going to tell her husband, David, right away. She dramatizes how hard he might take it, but she is convinced she has found the love of her life. Richard has gotten himself in much deeper than he ever expected, and he tries to get out of it gracefully without offending Judith.

Comments: The actress playing Judith can take great license with the fact that she (Judith) takes herself very seriously as an actress. She dramatizes everything to its fullest. She sees this as the love affair of the century and indulges in the pain of having to break the news to her husband and daughter.

9

Source: *The Heartbreak Kid,* a film by Elaine May, screenplay by Neil Simon, based on a short story by Bruce Jay Friedman

Characters: One male and one female: young newlyweds

Place: An elegant restaurant in Miami, Florida

Background: The couple have been on their honeymoon for a week. The husband has come to despise his wife and wants out of the marriage. On the first day of their arrival at their hotel, the wife contracted a terrible sunburn, which made it necessary for her to stay in the hotel room for a few days. During this time, the husband has been going to the beach by himself and has met a girl with whom he has fallen in love. He soon decides to break the news to his wife that he wants out of the marriage.

Situation: The husband and wife are sitting in an elegant restaurant eating lobster. This is when he chooses to tell her he wants the marriage annulled. He keeps trying to cheer her up with the prospect that this restaurant has great lobster and "yummy yum" pecan pie (her favorite).

Comments: In the film, he never mentions the other girl, and this creates great subtext for the actor. For the actress, this is an exercise in discovery.

_____ **10** _____

Source: *A Killing in a Small Town,* a film for television by Stephen Gyllenhaal, teleplay by Cynthia Cidre, based on a nonfiction book by John Bloom and Jim Atkinson

Characters: One male and one female: husband and wife

Place: The couple's living room

Background: A long time ago the wife had an affair with her best friend's husband. Her friend has only just found out about it and confronts the wife. Although the wife repeatedly assures her the affair is finished, she will not be consoled. She proceeds to threaten the wife with an axe. Turning the tables on her, the wife grabs the axe and strikes her friend. She not only kills her but strikes her forty-three times after she is dead. Following the murder, she calmly goes into the shower, cleans up, and returns home. That evening she and her husband receive a call from her friend's husband, telling them that his wife has been murdered.

A few weeks have passed, and the woman has recently been questioned by the police because she was the last person to have seen her friend alive.

Situation: The wife confesses to her husband that she murdered her friend. Initially, it was in self-defense. But continuing to strike her friend forty-three times, long after she was dead, is something she herself doesn't understand. At this point, she also tells her husband about the affair.

Comments: When the wife finally confesses her heinous crime, it is as much a discovery for her as it is for her husband. Up until now, she has not been in touch with what she has done. The actress must find personal reasons that drove her to such a violent act. The husband has to deal with the discovery of his wife's affair and her shocking crime.

11

Source: *Love Letters*, a film by Amy Jones

Characters: One male and one female: Anna, the daughter of a woman now deceased, and her mother's long-lost lover

Place: The mother's grave in a cemetery

Background: Anna's mother died very recently. While sorting through her mother's possessions, Anna found some old love letters. Apparently, the mother had been corresponding for fifteen years with a man whom she loved. On her deathbed, the mother gave Anna a ring. After reading the letters, Anna realized it was this same man who gave her mother the ring. Anna is recovering from a traumatic love affair with a married man, which has left her in an emotional state.

Situation: When Anna goes to put flowers on her mother's grave, she notices that someone has left gardenias there. She looks up and sees a man walking away. She approaches him, and he immediately recognizes her because she looks so much like a younger version of her mother. He also notices that Anna is wearing her mother's ring.

Comments: This is not an improvisation with much inherent conflict. It involves the discovery of two people who have cared deeply about the same person for many years and who are finally meeting. Anna is suffering from both the breakup of her relationship and the loss of her mother. The man has just lost the only woman he ever loved. Because of the circumstances of their lives, they were unable to be together for the last fifteen years. Their correspondence was all they had. In order for this improvisation to work, it is important that both actors have a clear picture of the mother and their relationship with her.

─────────── **12** ───────────

Source: *Not Without My Daughter,* a nonfiction book by Betty Mahmoody with William Hoffer

Characters: One male and one female: the mother, Betty, an American woman, and her husband, Moody, an Iranian man

Place: An apartment in Iran, which belongs to Moody's relatives. It is a filthy environment—rarely cleaned, meals eaten off the floor, and infants laid on the carpet, where they urinate

Background: In August of 1984 a housewife from Michigan, Betty Mahmoody, accompanied her husband, Moody, to his native Iran for a two-week vacation. They had been happily married in the States, where he was a successful doctor. They met when Betty was his patient. Toward the end of their stay in the United States, Moody lost his position at the hospital. He became depressed. The political situation in Iran began to change, and so did Moody. He told his wife he wanted her and their four-year-old daughter, Mahtob, to meet his family in Iran and promised that they would return in two weeks. When they arrived in Iran, Moody's relatives behaved in an antagonistic manner toward Betty and her daughter because they were Americans and women. Betty was forced to stay restrictively covered at all times. The food was prepared in a most unsanitary fashion. The rice actually had bugs in it, but Moody's family ate it anyway. Betty found most of the food inedible. Betty and her daughter were extremely unhappy and could hardly wait to go home.

Situation: After two weeks, Moody announces to his wife that they will not be going home. In Iran, he, as the man, has total power over his wife and child, and they must do as he says. They cannot leave the country without his permission, which he says he will never grant. Betty reminds him that her father is dying of cancer and she wishes to get back to Michigan to see him. Moody tells her that she cannot see her father again and is not to telephone or write her family. He says he will see to it that she and Mahtob are watched at all times, and he warns her not to disobey him.

Comments: The actress and actor must accept the laws of Iran. There truly is no way for Betty to disobey her husband. It ultimately takes two years for Betty and Mahtob to escape from Iran. They are complete slaves to Moody and, at the point of this improvisation, have no other friends to turn to. Moody's behavior comes as a complete surprise to Betty. The moment they arrived in Iran his personality changed drastically. He became violent and beat Betty if she did not completely submit to him. Being an independent American woman, submission is difficult for her.

13

Source: *The Phantom of the Opera,* a novel by Gaston Leroux

Characters: One male and one female: the Phantom—a middle-aged composer/teacher/mentor, and Christine, a young singer in the Paris Opera

Place: The Phantom's subterranean lair beneath the Paris Opera House—a grotto in which everything is lit by candlelight

Background: The Phantom is the infamous "ghost" that has been haunting the Paris Opera. Christine is an up-and-coming ingénue in the company. The Phantom loves her and thinks of her as his "angel of music." He turns out to be not a ghost but a real man. His face is disfigured, and so he wears a mask. The Phantom kidnaps Christine, bringing her down to his lair. He wants her to sing an opera that he has written for her. Christine, being strangely attracted to him, lets him become her mentor and performs his music.

Situation: Christine has an overwhelming desire to see the Phantom's face. Eventually, she tears off his mask and sees his badly disfigured face. No one has ever clearly seen the Phantom before (certainly without his mask) because he has stayed hidden. This is a moment of shocking revelation for Christine, and for the Phantom as well, although for different reasons.

Comments: The actors will have to use their imagination regarding the appearance of the Phantom's face. It is important for the actress playing Christine to be aware of her character's conflicting emotions toward the Phantom. If her initial horror at seeing his face is not mixed with some feeling of tenderness for him, there can be no real place for this improvisation to go. The actor playing the Phantom must be acutely aware of his character's fear of exposure to Christine. To him, she is an idealized being, and he has a deep need for her to see him in this same idealized light.

As presented here, this is not a "horror film" situation but more the *Beauty and the Beast* love story made famous by the Andrew Lloyd Webber musical. This does not mean, however, that the actors should not feel free to take a different approach to the material. As mentioned in the introduction to this book, such divergence can often lead to interesting and exciting results.

───────── 14 ─────────

Source: *The Picture of Dorian Gray*, a novel by Oscar Wilde (Situation #1)

Characters: One male and one female: Dorian Gray, a good-looking man in his twenties, and Sibyl Vane, a pretty young actress. The two are lovers

Place: The dressing room of the theater where Sibyl has just performed Juliet

Background: Dorian loves Sibyl for the characters she plays. He invited his friends to the theater this evening to see Sibyl perform. He has raved about her, and she has humiliated him by giving a dreadful performance. His friends have all left the theater very disappointed.

Situation: Dorian tells Sibyl he does not want to see her again because her performance was so disgraceful. She tells him she performed badly because she no longer needs to transform herself into different characters now that they are in love. *He* is now her whole life, not the theater.

Comments: Sibyl makes the discovery that Dorian does not really love her for herself but only for the characters she plays. Dorian discovers that she is not really like these characters whom he "loved." In Wilde's story, Sibyl commits suicide after he leaves the dressing room. This will give the actress some idea of the intensity of Sibyl's feelings for Dorian.

See *The Picture of Dorian Gray*, #2, page 190.

_____ **15** _____

Source: *Reds*, a film by Warren Beatty, screenplay by Beatty and Trevor Griffiths

Characters: One male and one female: John Reed and Louise Bryant, husband and wife, both journalists

Place: Their apartment

Background: Before they were married, Louise had an affair with the American playwright, Eugene O'Neill. At the time, O'Neill wrote her a passionate love letter proposing marriage. She stuck the letter into a book and forgot about it. Both John and Louise travel frequently on professional assignments and are thus separated for long periods.

Situation: John finds the letter and confronts Louise with it. She has *not* been involved with O'Neill since the time of her marriage. It comes out in the conversation that her husband *has* been unfaithful.

Comments: The actress may end this however she wants, but she must not take his infidelity lightly. It comes as a great surprise. The irony is that her husband is accusing her of infidelity, when *he* is actually the unfaithful one.

———— 16 ————

Source: *Resurrection,* a film by Daniel Petrie, screenplay by Lewis John Carlino (Situation #1)

Characters: One male and one female: Edna McCauley and her doctor

Place: A hospital room

Background: Edna and her husband were in an automobile accident. He was killed. She had just bought him a new car for his birthday and they had gone out for their first drive to celebrate. They loved each other very much.

Situation: She wakes up in the hospital room with the doctor present. He tells her about the accident and that her husband did not survive. She also finds out that her legs are paralyzed.

Comments: The actress need not feel compelled to become hysterical; there are a myriad of ways to react to this shocking news. Once again, the actress should have no preconceived idea of how she would respond. The actor playing the doctor should be cautioned not to become the "professional" but to relate to this woman on a human level.

See *Resurrection,* #2, page 199, and #3, page 319.

———— 17 ————

Source: *Sweeney Todd,* a musical play by Stephen Sondheim and Hugh Wheeler

Characters: One male and one female: Sweeney Todd, a barber in his fifties, and Mrs. Lovett, also in her fifties (Optional—dead body)

Place: A basement room in a seedy section of Victorian London, beneath a barber shop and meat pie shop

Background: A barber named Benjamin Barker was sent into exile on a trumped-up charge by a wicked, unscrupulous judge, who then publicly raped Benjamin's wife, Lucy, at a masked ball. As a result, Lucy lost her mind and the wicked judge wound up getting custody of Benjamin and Lucy's daughter, Johanna, and raised her as his ward. Fifteen years later, Benjamin Barker returns to his former London establishment but now under the alias Sweeney Todd. An old friend, Mrs. Lovett, tells him his wife committed suicide. Hell-bent on vengeance, he sets up practice once again as a barber, waiting for the time when the judge and his beadle will turn up as customers. But in the meantime, by way of preparation, he begins to cut the throats of innocent customers as well, disposing of the bodies by giving them to his cohort, Mrs. Lovett, who turns them into meat pies. By then, Sweeney is obviously quite mad and will stop at nothing to find fresh victims for his razor. Just prior to killing the judge, he finds a crazed, filthy beggar woman in his shop. "Don't I know you?" she asks, squinting at him. But not having time for this annoyance (the judge is now mounting the stairs to his shop), Sweeney cuts the woman's throat and sends her body down a chute into the basement below. Sweeney then slits the judge's throat while giving him a shave and sends *his* body down the chute as well. His final vengeance having been achieved, Sweeney then goes down to the basement to help Mrs. Lovett dispose of the bodies.

Situation: Sweeney helps Mrs. Lovett with the judge, then drags the body of the crazed beggar woman to the large bakery oven. But when Lovett opens the oven door, the firelight falls on the dead woman's face, and he suddenly recognizes her. It is his long-lost wife, Lucy. Mrs. Lovett then confesses she knew the woman's identity all along but wanted to spare him the knowledge of what his wife had become. She tells him she did it because she loved him and knew she would make a much better wife for him than Lucy.

Comments: The enormity of this realization presents numerous possibilities for the actor playing Sweeney. He should allow himself full latitude by not giving thought in advance to how his response will manifest itself. The actors must make a decision about how they want to deal with the body of Lucy, which is a focal point of the improvisation. It is suggested that they use an imaginary body. The important thing is that Sweeney must have a definite picture in his mind of the Lucy he loved, in contrast to her present appearance. If he doesn't really "see" her, the improvisation won't work. These circumstances are bizarre, but the despair over the loss of a loved one is universal.

_____ 18 _____

Source: _The Wild Duck_, a play by Henrik Ibsen

Characters: One male and one female (or two): Hjalmar Ekdal and his wife, Gina Ekdal (Optional—Hedvig, their daughter. See Comments)

Place: Their living room

Background: Hjalmar used to work for Mr. Werle, a wealthy factory owner. He met his wife, Gina, there. She was a servant for Mr. Werle. Hjalmar and Gina have been happily married for fourteen years and have a fourteen-year-old daughter, Hedvig. It is important to note that Hjalmar and his daughter adore each other. Mr. Werle and Hjalmar's father were partners years ago.

When funds were found missing from the company, Hjalmar's father was arrested. Hjalmar was left penniless. Mr. Werle went on to become rich. Gregor, Mr. Werle's son, hates his father for letting his partner take the blame. He left home, relinquishing his inheritance, and came to live with Hjalmar and Gina. He viewed Hjalmar as a saint and believed he would help the marriage by telling him the truth about Gina. He persuades Hjalmar to take a long walk with him to reveal this "truth." Hjalmar returns home a different man.

Situation: Hjalmar tells his wife that he has just been informed by Gregor that she had an affair with Mr. Werle just before she and Hjalmar were married. She admits to this, feeling that after so many years of a good marriage it shouldn't matter anymore. A letter then arrives in the mail from Mr. Werle notifying them that he is leaving a large sum of money to their daughter, Hedvig. This leads to further questioning by Hjalmar, in which he asks Gina, point-blank, whether Hedvig is his own child. She finally confesses that Mr. Werle is the father. Hjalmar then remembers that it was Mr. Werle who rushed them into marriage. This was to prevent any scandal because Werle had a wife of his own. Gina said she didn't tell Hjalmar at the time because she loved him and knew he wouldn't have married her if he had known the truth. Throughout the intervening years, she maintained her silence to spare Hjalmar the pain this knowledge would bring.

Comments: This improvisation will not work if Hjalmar is all-forgiving. This would not be characteristic behavior for him. He cannot bear the fact that he has been deceived all these years. Not only is he not Hedvig's biological father, but the actual father is Hjalmar's worst enemy. This play was written in the 1884, when it was considered a disgrace to be with child out of wedlock. But even today this situation would be a very volatile one. Not many men would be able to accept the fact that their child was fathered by another man, after having long believed it was their own.

This improvisation could be extended to the entrance of Hedvig. She worships her father, and it would be interesting to see the effect this revelation has on their relationship.

──────── **19** ────────

Source: *The Heiress*, a play by Ruth and Augustus Goetz, based on the novel *Washington Square* by Henry James (Situation #1)

Characters: Two females: Catherine, an heiress, and Lavinia, her aunt

Place: The living room of Dr. Sloper's town house on Washington Square, New York City, in the mid-1800s—the time is midnight

Background: Catherine is an heiress who will inherit a great deal of money from her father, Dr. Sloper. She is an only child whose mother died giving birth to her. Her father has never forgiven Catherine for that. He has always told her she is a plain and stupid girl, while her mother was beautiful and witty. Catherine has been courted by Morris, a handsome, worldly young man. Dr. Sloper told her that if she accepted Morris's hand in marriage, he would disinherit her. He believes Morris is only after Catherine's money, since he cannot imagine anyone loving her. She does not have much opportunity to meet men because, being painfully shy, she rarely goes out. Until now, she has believed what her father told her about herself.

Morris is to pick her up at midnight to elope. Catherine told Morris that her father would disinherit her if they married. She believes Morris loves her and that this will not frighten him away.

Situation: Catherine has all her bags packed and is waiting for the clock to strike midnight, at which point Morris will come to get her in his carriage. She has sneaked downstairs quietly so as not to awaken her father and her Aunt Lavinia, who also resides in the house. However, her aunt hears her and comes downstairs. By this time it is already past midnight. Catherine, who cannot persuade her aunt to go back to bed, tells her about the elopement. Her aunt is very happy for her because she never believed Catherine would find anyone. She is also fond of Morris. They eventually discuss the inheritance, and Catherine reveals that she has told Morris that she will be disinherited if they marry. Her aunt tells her that, knowing this, Morris may not come. Catherine does not believe this at first, but eventually she has to face reality.

Comments: The actresses must remember that, in the mid-1800s, life was different for women, and their happiness was very much wrapped up in their mate. Catherine will probably not have another opportunity, and she and her aunt both know that.

See *The Heiress*, #2, page 52.

———— **20** ————

Source: *Home for the Holidays,* a film for television by John Llewellyn Moxey, teleplay by Joseph Stefano

Characters: Two females: Chris and her older sister, Alex

Place: A bedroom in the family homestead

Background: Four sisters had gathered for the Christmas holidays at the home in which they grew up. During the course of their stay, someone has murdered two of the sisters. The murderer is Alex, the oldest of the four. She has felt a tremendous emotional burden all her life from being "the big sister," whom everyone else came running to for help. Her sanity has snapped and she has relieved the pressure by murdering her siblings, including (or so she thinks) Chris. Alex hit Chris across the forehead with a tire iron while they were out on a nearby country road. She saw Chris's body roll down a hill and into a ditch, apparently lifeless.

Situation: It is now some hours later. The police have found Chris's body and have placed it on a bed. Alex has been directed to this room by the police in order to view her sister's corpse. Unbeknownst to Alex, this is a trap designed to get her to reveal her guilt. When Alex sees her sister on the bed, she makes a believable show of grief for the benefit of the police. In the midst of this show, Chris, who is very much alive, opens her eyes and turns to stare at her big sister.

Comments: The two sisters must confront each other, one knowing that she attempted to murder the other, and the other knowing her sister's intentions. The actresses need to confer about the past relationship of these two sisters and what has brought them to this point. The reaction of the actress playing Alex should be governed, in part, by an awareness of the character's unbalanced mental and emotional state. It would be one thing to discover that someone you dearly loved and thought deceased was not dead after all. It would be quite another to discover that someone you had wanted out of the way and had murdered was, in reality, still alive.

21

Source: *Death of a Salesman*, a play by Arthur Miller (Situation #2)

Characters: Two males: Willy Loman, in his sixties, and Willy's boss, Howard, in his thirties

Place: Howard's office

Background: Willy had originally worked for Howard's father, who has been dead for over ten years. Willy was once one of the company's best salesmen, but he is no longer doing well. He has been traveling on the road all his life and has come to ask Howard to find him a job in the office. The truth is that he has not been making any money in the last few years. He has been going to his friend, Charley, to borrow money every week and telling his wife, Linda, that it was his salary. Needless to say, Willy is desperate. Unbeknownst to his wife, he has even attempted suicide. This job is his last hope of getting his life back on track.

Situation: Howard is playing an audiotape of his family. Willy must sit there listening to Howard brag about his family while hearing their voices. He finally gets Howard's attention long enough to ask for a job working in the office rather than on the road. Howard not only turns him down but ends up firing him. Willy finally begs, but Howard will not give in. Howard keeps reminding Willy that he has many people waiting to see him and that

Willy must pull himself together and get out of the office. Willy is on the verge of a nervous breakdown. The more upset Willy becomes, the more Howard wants him out.

Comments: The actor playing Howard must find a clear-cut motivation for his actions, e.g., he feels he is losing business with Willy and can't afford to keep him on. The part of Willy must be played by an actor of some maturity. He must take into account Willy's desperation and have an understanding of what would drive a man to this point.

See *Death of a Salesman*, #1, page 114.

—————— 22 ——————

Source: *Lie of the Mind,* a play by Sam Shepard (Situation #1)

Characters: Two males: Jake, in his twenties, and Frankie, in his twenties or thirties. They are brothers

Place: Two separate locales. Each brother is at his home speaking on the telepone.

Background: Jake and his wife, Beth, have terrible fights all the time, during which he beats her. This time he believes he has actually killed her.

Situation: Jake calls his brother, Frankie, on the telephone to tell him he thinks he has killed Beth. Frankie lives thousands of miles away and, therefore, cannot come right over. He must talk to Jake and get the facts.

Comments: In actuality, Jake has not killed Beth, though he has permanently damaged her brain. She is unconscious, and he is too frightened to think clearly. He beat her up in a jealous rage. The actor should personalize his reasons for beating up his wife. Despite his violence, he does love her and regrets his actions. But, although he is remorseful, he should still feel somehow justified in what he has done. Frankie feels responsible for Jake. He would not call the police because he wants to protect his brother.

See *Lie of the Mind*, #2, page 309.

23

Source: *Arsenic and Old Lace*, a play by Joseph Kesselring

Characters: One male and two females: Mortimer Brewster, a man in his late twenties/early thirties, and two elderly women, Abby and Martha Brewster, Mortimer's aunts

Place: Abby and Martha's living room

Background: Unbeknownst to Mortimer, his aunts are quite insane and have murdered close to a dozen lonely old bachelors by giving them poisoned elderberry wine. Abby and Martha did this in the belief that they were helping the old gentlemen to find peace. They have no concept of the immorality of their actions, or of the possible consequences. They believe, instead, that they have been doing beneficent and charitable work. Their nephew, Mortimer, a drama critic for a local newspaper, has no idea of his aunt's nefarious activities.

Situation: Mortimer is discussing with his aunts a play he will be reviewing that evening—a murder mystery entitled *Murder Will Out*. His attitude toward the probable nature of this play is disdain. He mockingly hypothesizes that a body will no doubt be discovered shortly after the curtain goes up, probably concealed in a window seat. At this point, Mortimer, by way of demonstration, opens the actual window seat in his aunts' home. He receives the shock of his life upon discovering a very real corpse concealed therein. The scene proceeds from this point with Mortimer trying to get some kind of sensible explanation from his aunts and them cheerfully providing information, making no attempt at concealment. They are completely unaware that what they have done is wrong. In the process of making his aunts see the light of reason, he discovers that this is not their only victim.

Comments: The actors must believe in the reality of the situation. The effect will be enhanced by sincerity. Also, the actresses playing the aunts must watch out for the trap of playing them all on one level—i.e., sweet. Mortimer must visualize the corpse.

_____ **24** _____

Source: *Blood Wedding*, a play by Federico García Lorca; and *The Graduate*, a film by Mike Nichols, screenplay by Buck Henry and Calder Willingham

Characters: Five males, three or more females, and ensemble: the bride, the groom, the bride's ex-lover, the best man, the maids of honor, a priest or minister, parents, relatives and friends.

Place: A church

Background: See comments.

Situation: A wedding ceremony is on. The bride is about to be married when suddenly her old lover comes in and interrupts the wedding. He tries to persuade her to leave with him.

Comments: Since this improvisation is based on *two* sources with differing background material but ending in precisely the same situation, it may be more interesting to let the actors invent their own background. They should, however, agree on the nature of their past relationships before performing the improvisation. The actress playing the bride must struggle to make this difficult decision, and it must be made during the improvisation, not beforehand.

_____ **25** _____

Source: *The Dead Zone*, a film by David Cronenberg, screenplay by Jeffrey Boam, based on the novel by Stephen King (Situation #1)

Characters: Three males, and one female: Johnny Smith, a schoolteacher in his late twenties/early thirties, Dr. Weizack, the director of a medical clinic, and Johnny Smith's parents

Place: Hospital room in the Weizack clinic

Background: Johnny Smith, a schoolteacher, had been engaged to another schoolteacher, Sarah. Shortly before their wedding, he had a terrible automobile accident and, as a result, remained comatose for five years.

Situation: Johnny Smith has just awakened from his coma. To him, the events of the accident seem like yesterday, even though five years have passed. At the beginning of the improvisation, only his doctor is with him. Johnny begins to suspect something unusual when he realizes there are no bandages on him and not a single scratch. Time, of course, has long since healed his physical wounds. The doctor discusses Johnny's situation with him, although to a very limited extent. Then the doctor decides to bring Johnny's parents into the room. From their reaction, Johnny suspects his situation is very unusual indeed, and he questions the doctor to get more information. At this point, he learns how long he has been in a coma. He then asks his parents about his fiancée and learns she is now married to another man.

Comments: How Johnny reacts to what he learns is, of course, up to the actor playing the part and should not be decided beforehand. There are many different ways that a man in Johnny's position might respond to the shattering news. There is no single "correct" way of reacting. The actor should establish what was happening in his character's life five years ago. He would probably note changes in his parents. The parents should have an idea of what the past five years have been like for them. Many things have changed since Johnny's accident.

See *The Dead Zone*, #2, page 142.

_____ **26** _____

Source: *Death of a Salesman*, a play by Arthur Miller (Situation #1)

Characters: Two males and one female: father, Willy Loman; son, Biff; and a female secretary

Place: A hotel room in Boston

Background: Biff has flunked math in school. He travels from Brooklyn to Boston to ask his father to convince his teacher to let him graduate. Willy Loman is a traveling salesman, who is no longer successful. He is playing big shot to a secretary who deals with some of his buyers. He intends to give her new stockings while his wife sits home mending old ones.

Situation: Biff knocks on the door of Willy's hotel room, and Willy, hearing who it is, tells the secretary to hide in the bathroom and be quiet. When he opens the door, he tries to get Biff to leave, saying he'll meet him downstairs. But Biff stays. Eventually, the woman appears and wants her stockings. She is getting tired of waiting. Willy gives her the stockings, gets rid of her, and attempts to explain her presence to Biff. He claims she is a buyer from one of the stores with whom he does business, but Biff does not believe this. Biff had worshiped his father and is devastated by this revelation. Seeing him give new stockings to this woman while his mother sits home night after night darning old ones is especially painful.

Comments: This scene demands great sensitivity on the part of the actors. This incident destroys a trusting, loving relationship forever. The mother must be clearly defined for the actors. Biff has a great attachment to his mother as well. Willy loves his wife deeply, but because he feels like a failure, he plays big shot to the secretary to make himself feel important. He attempts to explain this to Biff, but to no avail. The secretary is oblivious of the emotional turmoil Willy and Biff are experiencing. She is preoccupied with the stockings Willy promised her. The contrast between her insensitivity and the sensitivity of the son and father in this situation is an important element of the improvisation.

See *Death of a Salesman*, #2, page 109.

_____ **27** _____

Source: *Equus*, a play by Peter Shaffer
Characters: Two males and one female: Alan, a boy of seventeen; his middle-aged psychiatrist, Dr. Martin Dysart; and Jill Mason, a girl about Alan's age
Place: Dysart's office

Background: Once a month Alan would steal away at night to a local riding stable where he worked and take one of the horses—Nugget—for a midnight ride in a nearby field. This was a ritual, in which Alan, naked, would ride the horse bareback while reciting a kind of litany until achieving sexual climax. Alan had created a "religion," in which horses were symbols of both spirituality and sexuality. Alan met Jill, a girl who worked at the stable, and found himself attracted to her. One night Jill took Alan into the stable, which, to Alan, was the sacred temple of Equus, his supreme horse-God. (*Equus* is the Latin word for "horse.") There, the boy and girl disrobed and began tentatively to make love. Alan, however, felt suddenly guilty at making love to a girl under the watchful, accusing gaze of his gods and was unable to perform sexually. Jill, a compassionate and sensitive girl, attempted to reassure him. But Alan, in an explosion of humiliation, rage, and guilt, ordered her out of the stable. Then Alan was left alone to face his angry and accusing gods. At first, he attempted to placate them and beg their forgiveness. But finding this futile, he saw only one real and absolute escape from the accusing all-seeing stares. Picking up a metal spike used for cleaning horse's hooves, he leapt up in the air, blinding each of the horses in the stable. Following the blinding, Alan was sent to an institution for treatment.

Situation: It is night and his doctor has scheduled a special session with Alan to try to get him to relive what caused him to blind the horses. Dysart, at this point, already knows the full background of Alan's disturbance, with the exception of what exactly drove him to commit the crime itself. Dysart helps Alan to re-create the painful events in his mind, acting them out as he does so. As he relives the events, the actress playing Jill may then enter into the improvisation and interact—*but only with Alan* because this interaction takes place in Alan's memory alone.

Comments: Dysart's office, while always remaining an office to *him*, becomes, in Alan's mind, the stable. The actor playing Dysart should understand that Dysart has a sterile and unexciting marriage and secretly envies the boy his tremendous passion—a passion that, in order to cure the boy, Dysart must eradicate forever. There is, then, a tug-of-war going on inside Dysart, making the question of "curing" Alan a difficult one. In the play, there is a full psychological explanation for Alan's behavior, but it is rather complex. In this improvisation, the actor can create his own reasons why Alan was led to create his obsessive equine "religion."

Another valid way to approach this improvisation would be to have the actor playing Alan create his own reasons for blinding the horses.

--------- **28** ---------

Source: *Fences*, a play by August Wilson (Situation #1)

Characters: Two males and one female: husband, Troy Maxon; wife, Rose; and Gabe, Troy's brother, who is brain-damaged

Place: The backyard of the Maxon house in an urban neighborhood of a northern American industrial city

Background: Troy and Rose have been married for eighteen years. They have a son, Corey, who is now in high school. Troy has an older son in his thirties from a previous marriage. Troy and Rose love each other, but Troy has not felt very successful as a man and has been drowning in bills and other hardships of life. He has been seeing another woman for many years, his justification being that he needed this to go on living. This woman is now going to have his baby, and he is faced with telling Rose. She is totally unsuspecting and has been faithful to him all these years. Gabe, Troy's brother, is brain-damaged. He babbles constantly and has no real awareness of what's going on around him.

Situation: Troy tells his wife he is going to have a baby by another woman. Soon after he breaks this news to her, Gabe enters, talking away, oblivious of the tension between Troy and Rose. The two try to talk in between Gabe's babbling. Finally, Rose tells Gabe to go inside, guiding him to the door. Gabe goes inside, and the two continue talking.

Comments: This play was written for an all-black cast. However, the situation is universal. The only difference is that Troy wanted to be a baseball player but couldn't play in the major leagues—he was excluded from participating because of his race. (This was in the late fifties.) A white actor can find his own reasons for not feeling successful as a man. This improvisation can also be done just between the husband and wife, eliminating Gabe. However, the brother entering at this crucial moment creates interesting tension for the actors.

See *Fences*, #2, page 92.

_____ **29** _____

Source: *Fortunes of War*, a British television mini-series based on *The Levant Trilogy* by Olivia Manning

Characters: One male, one female, and ensemble: Guy and Harriet Pringle, husband and wife; a friend; and people at a party

Place: A wedding party in Cairo, Egypt, during World War II

Background: Because Guy was so busy and had so little time for her, Harriet decided to take an evacuation ship back to England, her home. News came to Guy that the ship was torpedoed and that there were no survivors. He has been grieving for his wife. However, Harriet never took the ship; instead, she went off with two friends, traveling for several weeks in a remote area where there were no newspapers. One day her friends heard the news about the ship and told her. Harriet realized her husband must assume that she is dead.

Situation: Harriet's friends bring her to the wedding party of a mutual friend, at which Guy is a guest. The husband and wife meet each other face to face.

Comments: It is important to note that these two people love each other deeply. He has grieved greatly over her presumed death. Once they reunite, the improvisation is pretty much concluded, since that is the climactic moment. However, it could continue—just to see what might develop. For example, obviously there were some problems in the marriage which originally provoked the wife to leave. These problems could be explored.

———— **30** ————

Source: *The Morning After,* a film for television by Richard T. Heffron, teleplay by Richard Matheson, based on the novel by Jack B. Weiner (Situation #1)

Characters: Two males and two females: two married couples—Charlie and Fran Lester and Frank Lester (Charlie's brother) and his wife, Carol

Place: A restaurant

Background: Charlie Lester is an alcoholic, though he does not admit it. His drinking has caused his wife, Fran, and their children much torment.

Situation: Charlie excuses himself to go to the bathroom. While he is away from the table, Fran breaks down in front of her in-laws. She tells them how sick her husband is and how she worries when he doesn't make it home at night, thinking that he's been killed in a car accident. Charlie comes back to the table and hears what she is saying. The situation progresses from there.

Comments: The actress playing Fran must realize that Fran has held in her feelings for some time and is now at the breaking point. She must be clear in her mind about the torment she has gone through. Charlie is in complete denial of his alcoholism. His wife's breakdown may or may not change him.

See *The Morning After,* #2, page 188.

———— **31** ————

Source: *The Sailor Who Fell from Grace with the Sea,* a film by Lewis John Carlino, based on a novel by Yukio Mishima

Characters: Two males and one female: Anne, a widowed

mother; Jonathan, her adolescent son; and Jim, a sailor, who has become her lover

Background: Anne has done her best to raise her son alone. Her husband was killed in the war (World War II), and she misses him deeply. Jonathan, now in his adolescence, has become quite a handful. The mother has recently met and become passionately attracted to Jim Cameron, a sailor. This is the first man she has felt a strong attraction to since her husband.

Situation: Jonathan, driven by curiosity and his own sexual awakening, has been spying on his mother and her lover through a peephole in the wall of his bedroom. The mother has just noticed a light coming from this peephole and rushes into the boy's room, followed by her lover, to confront him.

Comments: The actor playing Jonathan must be aware of the embarrassment his character would likely feel at getting caught. He must also be especially aware of the complex feelings he would have as a result of what he has witnessed. This role can, of course, be played by an older actor. The actor playing Anne should remember that this relationship represents the first sexual contact she has had since the death of her husband. This is a reawakening for her and, as such, is particularly intimate on an emotional as well as a physical level. She is very vulnerable. These factors should be considered in gauging her response to her son's spying. The actor playing Jim must take into account not only his character's response to finding the boy but his response to the mother's emotional state as well. Both older actors must be clear about exactly what the boy saw.

_____ **32** _____

Source: *Salvador*, a film by Oliver Stone, screenplay by
Stone and Richard Boyle

Characters: Two males and one female: Richard, a news
reporter; Maria, his fiancée; and an immigration officer

Place: Inside a bus at the Mexican/U.S. border

Background: Richard is American; his fiancée is from Salvador. They have been living in Salvador amidst constant
warfare and bloodshed. He has struggled hard for over
a year, making arrangements to bring Maria to the
United States. He wants to marry her there. As a reporter, he has caused trouble in Salvador, putting his
fiancée in jeopardy. He has promised her that once they
cross the border, she would be safe. She has lived in
great expectation of this safety. Eventually, they board
a bus bound for the Mexican/U.S. border.

Situation: Having finally reached the border, the bus is
pulled over. An immigration officer comes aboard and
asks to see the fiancée's green card, which she does not
have. She is instructed to leave the bus. This means she
will be sent back to Salvador. Richard pleads with the
officer because he knows she will be killed upon her
return.

Comments: Actors working with this material should have
some familiarity with the immigration problem. The
actor playing the immigration officer can make his own
decision regarding the outcome, knowing that he himself
would be in serious trouble if he allowed Maria to stay.
But if he forced her to return, he realizes he would have
her blood on his hands.

The actors must be aware of the physical boundaries
of the bus. They must be clear about the location of the

windows, aisle, seats, front door, etc. They must also deal with the movement of the bus and when it stops for the inspection.

_____ **33** _____

Source: *Sophie's Choice,* a novel by William Styron

Characters: Two males and two females: Sophie, a young Polish woman in her late twenties, her two young children (a boy and a girl), and a Nazi SS doctor

Place: Outside a Nazi concentration camp—at night

Background: Sophie is not Jewish; she is a Catholic Pole. Her father was a political activist in Poland, and she was taken to a concentration camp for this reason. She is standing in line with her two children as a Nazi doctor selects which people will go to the work-camp and which people to the gas chambers.

Situation: The Nazi doctor tells Sophie he wants to have sex with her. Then, upon discovering she's not a Jew but rather a Polish Catholic, he tells her that this gives her "a privilege—a choice." She herself must decide which child she will be allowed to keep and which will be sent off to the "showers" to be killed. She says she cannot choose. He then tells her he will take them both if she does not choose.

Comments: The actress will have to prepare in terms of her feelings concerning her two children. The actor playing the Nazi must find some inner justification for his actions or he will emerge as a one-dimensional "villain." Though his actions are monstrous, he still must seem real and believable. The children may be played by adult actors.

—————— **34** ——————

Source: *Tartuffe*, a play by Molière; English translation by Richard Wilbur

Characters: Two males and one female: Tartuffe, a holy man and friend of the family; Orgon, the husband; Elmire, his young attractive wife

Place: The living room of Orgon's house in Paris in the late 1600s

Background: Orgon has invited Tartuffe, a religious man, to come stay with him. He allows Tartuffe to manage all his money matters and leaves him alone with his wife and daughter for hours. He thoroughly loves and trusts Tartuffe. Various members of the household have been warning him that Tartuffe is seducing his wife and daughter and stealing his money. He refuses to believe this.

Situation: Orgon confronts his wife with this rumor. She admits it all to be true, but he still won't believe it. Elmire tells Orgon to hide under the table in the drawing room and listen to Tartuffe's advances. He agrees to do this, expecting to hear nothing but noble thoughts from his friend. When Tartuffe arrives, Elmire plays along with him while gallantly avoiding his overtures. The attempted seduction does not happen immediately. Tartuffe is clever about getting women under false pretenses. He finds the right moment to make his move while still disguised in his devoutness. Eventually, Orgon realizes the truth and comes out from under the table, much to Tartuffe's astonishment. A confrontation follows between Tartuffe and Orgon.

Comments: This improvisation is about Orgon's great shock in discovering Tartuffe's hypocrisy. He worships Tartuffe as if he were a saint. Even though this play is set in the seventeenth century, its themes of betrayal and hypocrisy are timeless. The actors should not let themselves be intimidated by the period aspects but, instead, should concentrate on the truth of the feelings involved and of the reality of their situation. If desired, the time period can be updated and Tartuffe could be a modern-day evangelist.

_____ **35** _____

Source: *White Heat*, a film by Raoul Walsh, screenplay by Ivan Goff and Ben Roberts

Characters: One male and the male ensemble: Cody Jarrett, a middle-aged man in prison for robbery, and a group of fellow prisoners

Place: A prison mess hall

Background: Cody Jarrett is a gangster, psychotic and without principles, save for a fanatical devotion to his mother. "Ma" Jarrett is the center of his emotional life, and she not only endorses her son's criminal activities but participates in them. She is the only person who can soothe his chronic headaches and calm him when he goes into a psychotic rage. Recently, Jarrett was caught by the police and sent to prison.

Situation: While the prisoners are eating in the prison mess hall, news begins to circulate in whispers that Cody Jarrett's mother has died. She was old and she died of natural causes. Eventually, this news reaches Jarrett, who is sitting at one of the tables finishing his meal. He had not expected his mother to die, and the news takes him completely by surprise.

Comments: News of this nature would, of course, come as a shock to almost anyone, but the actor playing Jarrett must take into account his character's specific psychological makeup. To say that Jarrett was a devoted son would be an understatement. Also, Jarrett's degree of dependency upon his mother must be considered in preparing for this improvisation. The actor must be very specific about Jarrett's relationship with her. As to *how* Jarrett's response manifests itself, this should, as always, be left up to the actor. And whatever his reaction, it should be spontaneous. Each of the actors playing the other prisoners should have his own individual relationship with and attitude toward Jarrett. The actor playing Jarrett should be clear on his relationship with each of them.

_____ 36 _____

Source: *Who's Afraid of Virginia Woolf?*, a play by Edward Albee

Characters: Two males and two females: two married couples—George and Martha (middle-aged) and Honey and Nick (mid- to late twenties)

Place: The living room of George and Martha's home—four A.M.

Background: George teaches history in a university where Martha's father is president. Nick teaches in the math department of the same university. George and Martha met Nick and his wife, Honey, earlier this evening at a faculty party. Following the party, Martha invited Nick and Honey back to her home.

George and Martha have long had a marriage based as strongly on mutual hatred as on love. This has manifested itself over the years in numerous "games" they play with each other and with other people. These games consist primarily of psychological/emotional abuse, manipulation, and intimidation, frequently couched in savage and sardonic wit. Nick and Honey are George and Martha's newest "victims." Martha attempts to sleep with Nick as vengeance against her husband, who has been insulting her in front of the guests. During much of the foregoing, Honey has been in and out of the bathroom throwing up, and by the end of the evening she is like a weakened, sick puppy, with no strength to fight about anything. Nick has cheerfully gone upstairs with Martha, not only to get back at George, whom he has grown to dislike, but also because he is physically attracted to Martha. He proves impotent, however, because of his advanced state of inebriation.

Also, for many years George and Martha have had an imaginary child—a son who has acted as an anchor for them, providing a kind of emotional glue that has held their marriage together. Neither has been biologically capable of having children, and rather than adopt a child, they conspired to create their imaginary son.

Situation: It is about four A.M. and George decides to take his ultimate revenge on Martha by symbolically "murdering" their child with both guests present as witnesses. He relates the contents of a telegram he supposedly received earlier that night, while Martha and Nick were upstairs together and Honey was curled up on the floor of the bathroom. This imaginary telegram contains the details of an automobile accident, which resulted in the "death" of their child. Martha, sensing what George is about to do, tries in vain not to listen, but George goes ahead anyway. This single act changes their lives dramatically.

Comments: Each character's response to this situation may be left up to the individual actors. However, given the very specific and complex psychological and life backgrounds of these characters, it is suggested that the actors have some familiarity with the source material. Reading Albee's play would be very helpful for this improvisation. But a familiarity with the play does not imply using the dialogue verbatim or attempting to duplicate the specifics of Albee's style. In fact, it is better not to. More important is the spirit of the work—the meaning behind the words.

CLIMACTIC MOMENT/DISCOVERY

Cross-References

Other improvisations in this book that involve Climactic Moments and Discovery can be found in the following categories:

CONFRONTATION/CONFLICT

One male and one female

SUBTEXT

One male and one female

SOLO MOMENT

One male

One female

UNUSUAL CIRCUMSTANCES

One male and one female

Two males

Ensemble

FANTASY

One male and one female

Two females

Ensemble

SPECIAL PROBLEMS

One male and one female

One male

Ensemble

4

SUBTEXT

Subtext is one of the most valuable and exciting tools an actor has. But although subtext is present in most dramatic material, it is central in some pieces and not in others. For example, in *The Odd Couple*, a play by Neil Simon, the characters openly state their feelings about each other; whereas, in a play such as *Betrayal* by Harold Pinter, a character will say one thing while layers of unspoken dialogue lurk beneath the character's façade.

There are times in our real lives when the only means of survival is to put on a "mask." Although actors do not usually wear these phychological masks when confronting each other, there are times when they must. Sometimes the character plays a role to disguise himself, but he must know what lies *beneath* the role. A device Eugene O'Neill uses in *Strange Interlude* is to have the characters pause during a scene to verbalize their inner thoughts. O'Neill's device may be applied to any of the improvisations in this chapter. Bear in mind, however, that this is to be used as an exercise and not to be done during the actual improvisation.

An example of a play built almost entirely around subtext is David Storey's *Home*. In *Home* two elderly men and two women sit in a garden and pass the time of day with apparently trivial conversation. In time it becomes evident that these people are actually inmates of an institution for the mentally ill.

Subtext in a scene involves two parallel streams of

thought: one spoken, one unspoken. Woody Allen's film, *Annie Hall*, made an amusing use of this in a scene between Allen and Diane Keaton. During a conversation between the two, subtitles begin to appear, expressing the characters' unspoken thoughts of the moment.

Throughout these improvisations it must be made clear (where applicable) that the actors are not to talk directly about what they really want from each other or about what is disturbing them. No direct references should be made regarding their needs and desires. During any of these improvisations, the instructor may wish to stop an actor and ask him to verbalize his thoughts. The actor is then forced to become immediately cognizant of the subtext.

There are numerous situations in life and on stage in which we are not able to expose our true feelings. In life, we are not always aware of our suppressed emotions and thoughts; in acting, we must be.

Every situation given in this chapter features subtext as the central element, intrinsic to all that is done or not done, said or left unsaid. These improvisations will focus the actors' attention on subtext in a direct way, increasing their awareness of this vitally important acting resource.

SUBTEXT

List of Situations

One male and one female

Two females

Two males

Ensemble

––––––––– 1 –––––––––

Source: *Above and Beyond,* a film by Melvin Frank and Norman Panama, screenplay by Melvin Frank, Norman Panama, and Beirne Lay, Jr.

Characters: One male and one female: Colonel Paul Tibitts and his wife, Lucey Tibitts

Place: Child's bedroom

Background: Colonel Tibitts has been selected by the Air Force to head the select group of men charged with dropping the atom bomb on Hiroshima. Because of the top-secret nature of the assignment, he is not allowed to discuss it with anyone outside the project, including his own wife. Naturally, the responsibilities of such an assignment have weighed heavily on him. He is acutely aware of the lives that will be lost—men, women, and children—as a result of his coming actions.

Situation: The Tibitts are standing over their baby in its crib. Lucey remarks that the baby looks so peaceful, he could almost be dead. The husband's reaction is way out of proportion to what she has said. He has on his conscience all the children who will die as a result of the bombing. Because of the pressure he's been under, there has been tension in their marriage, but he cannot share his feelings with his wife.

Comments: The colonel loves his wife and yet cannot let on why he is so upset about her remark. The subtext is very strong on his part. But the actor playing the husband must relate to his wife, and not concentrate only on the subtext. He's trying to forget what he has to do and focus on his family. His wife knows something is bothering him, but she has no idea what it is or what she's done wrong.

_____ 2 _____

Source: *The Anniversary Dinner*, an original situation

Characters: One male and one female: husband and wife

Place: A restaurant

Background: This couple has been married for three years. That morning the husband filed for divorce through the family lawyer, leased an apartment, made arrangements with a moving company to pick up his things in a week, and spent the afternoon with his mistress. Unsuspecting any of this, the wife spent her day house-hunting for a new home for both of them.

Situation: They are celebrating their anniversary dinner at an expensive and romantic restaurant, at which time they exchange gifts. The wife announces that since she has just turned forty, she would like to have a baby before it's too late. The husband never reveals how he spent his day.

Comments: The actor playing the husband must decide why he wants out of this marriage and why he decides not to tell his wife at this time. The wife's subtext is that she knows there are troubles in the marriage, but she won't face up to them.

———— **3** ————

Source: *Attempted Suicide*, a real-life situation, as reported in a magazine article

Characters: One male and one female: two adult strangers

Place: A street next to a hotel

Background: A man walking along the beach saw a woman standing on the roof of an ocean-view hotel staring out at the sea. Fearing that the woman was contemplating suicide, he went into the hotel lobby and informed the desk clerk of the woman's actions. The clerk then phoned the police, who came and brought the woman down. The woman, however, steadfastly maintained that she merely wanted to get a good view of the ocean, and so the police left her behind, having no concrete reason for detaining her.

Situation: The man who originally saw her standing on the roof has just seen the police leave and approaches her. He fears she may return to the roof and wants to be of help. The woman is cordial to the man and tells him she was on the roof merely to view the ocean. Underlying this, however, is the fact that she really *did* intend to commit suicide and fully intends to return to the roof in the near future. And the man, intuitively sensing this, tries somehow to reach her emotionally.

Comments: It is important that the woman know why she is attempting suicide. She must also remember that there is always the hope that someone will reverse her decision. The man, of course, doesn't want to live the rest of his life wishing he had prevented a tragedy. As a matter of fact, in reality, the woman did return the next day and completed her mission.

4

Source: *Betrayal*, a play by Harold Pinter (Situation #1)

Characters: One male and one female: husband, Robert Downs, and his wife, Emma Downs—both middle-aged

Place: Hotel room in Venice—summer, present

Background: Robert and Emma have been married for ten years. Robert went to the American Express office earlier that day to cash some traveler's checks. While he was there, the clerk told him that there was a letter addressed to someone with the last name of Downs. The clerk asked him if he was related and if he would like to take the letter. He noticed that the letter was addressed to his wife from his best friend, Jerry, who had been best man at their wedding. We do not know if Robert read the letter. He leaves it at the American Express office and goes back to the hotel room where his wife is lying on the bed reading a book.

Situation: Robert does not mention what is on his mind, but he raves about the inefficiency of the Italian mail service. He condemns the Italians for attempting to give a letter to a possible stranger just because he had the same last name as the person to whom the letter was addressed. Robert had no suspicion about an affair between his wife and Jerry until today. He brings up the

book Emma is reading, noting that it is about betrayal.
She says she hasn't finished it yet. Emma has guessed
what happened. After skirting the true issue at hand,
Emma offers the information that the letter is from Jerry,
which Robert already knows. Eventually, she tells him
that she and Jerry have been having an affair for five
years. She says she has taken a flat in London, where
they meet.

Comments: The important aspect of this improvisation is
that both the husband and wife know that he has found
out about her affair, and they don't talk about it directly
for some time. She eventually beats him at his own game,
telling *him* before he tells *her*.

_____ 5 _____

Source: *Betrayal,* a play by Harold Pinter (Situation #2)

Characters: One male and one female: Jerry and Emma,
two ex-lovers

Place: A restaurant

Background: It has been two years since Jerry and Emma
have met. They once had a lengthy affair, during which
they were both married to other people. They are still
married and now have children. During the affair they
had their own apartment, where they met. Emma's five-
year-old son was conceived by Jerry, not by her husband.
The affair simply came to an end; there were no bad
feelings.

Situation: They are sitting in a restuarant having drinks and
talking for the first time in two years.

Comments: Remember that this is based on a Pinter play,
and he is a master at subtext. The important element in
this improvisation is that the couple never talk directly

about their feelings for each other; they talk about their spouses and children. However, there is a strong undercurrent of yearning for the other person. They still love each other and want each other. They are not going to resume the affair, but the actors must ask themselves why they are meeting. The feelings for each other must be strong or this improvisation has no meaning.

_____ 6 _____

Source: _Birdbath_, a play by Leonard Melfi
Characters: One male and one female: Frankie and Velma
Place: Frankie's one-room apartment in a large city
Background: Frankie and Velma work together at a restaurant. This evening Velma told Frankie she could not go home. He offered to take her home with him. Velma is in a state of shock because she had a terrible fight with her mother at breakfast that morning. The fight occurred when the mother announced that she was going on a trip to meet some men. Velma was told not to go along because she was ugly and stupid and would frighten the men away. For Velma, this morning was the culmination of the years of abuse she had endured from her mother. For the first time, Velma fought back. She killed her mother with a knife used to cut the coffeecake. At the moment, she has no conscious memory of this.

Velma has never been sexually involved with a man.

Besides working in a restaurant, Frankie is a writer and basically a loner. He had a relationship with a girl, but she rejected him. His only companion since then has been his typewriter, at which he spends a great deal of time composing poetry.
Situation: Frankie and Velma arrive at his apartment. They

are two very lonely people. Frankie does not know about
Velma's crime, but as the evening goes on, Velma begins
to remember what happened and eventually reveals her
story to him.

Comments: The actress must explore the state of mind this
girl would be in following such a trauma. She blocks it
from her mind for a time: She knows she cannot go home
but is not sure why. Without deciding beforehand, the
actress must eventually allow something to trigger her
memory of the murder. She must also understand that
she desperately needs Frankie's protection. He is probably the only person who has ever been kind to her. The
actor playing Frankie should have no preconceived no-
tion about his reaction to Velma's revelation.

_____ 7 _____

Source: _Day After the Fair,_ a play by Frank Harvey, based
on _On the Western Circuit_ by Thomas Hardy (Situation
#1)

Characters: One male and one female: Charles Braddock,
a London lawyer, and Edith Harnham, who is unhappily
married to a brewery owner

Place: A restaurant during the Victorian era

Background: Edith Harnham has a servant girl, Anna, who
cannot read or write. Anna has a lover, Charles, who is
in the military service and with whom she wants to correspond. She asks her employer, Edith, to write the
letters for her. Because Anna cannot verbalize what she
wants to say, Edith composes the letters as well. Edith
begins to fall in love with Charles and Charles with Edith
as the correspondence progresses. Anna confesses to
Edith that she is carrying Charles's child and wants him

notified. Although painful for Edith, she writes this to Charles. Charles writes back that he will arrive on the following Wednesday. Edith does not announce this to Anna but decides to meet with Charles alone first, as Anna's guardian.

Situation: Charles and Edith meet in a restaurant. Charles has brought Anna's letters to show Edith, having no idea that Edith wrote them. Edith refuses to look at them, saying that they are private. Charles explains to her how he met this simple girl, Anna, spent only two evenings with her, and then forgot her. But when he received these beautiful letters he realized she was far more than a superficial date. As a result, he has fallen in love with Anna and has returned to marry her. Edith, now in love with Charles herself, attempts to reverse his decision, pointing out that Anna, being a servant girl, is not in his class and so the marriage would not work. However, he persists. Edith also realizes, as she speaks with Charles, that she and Charles would be suited for each other.

Comments: This is a very good exercise in subtext for the actress. She has much to conceal in terms of the contents of the letters, which he keeps attempting to disclose to her. She is in love with Charles and cannot reveal her feelings, which are intensified by his constant espousal of love for Anna. For the actor playing Charles, it is not so much a matter of subtext, though he would probably feel a strange attraction to Edith, which he doesn't understand. He wants Edith to consent to the marriage because he could not marry Anna without the consent of both Edith and her husband. An important point about this improvisation is that it takes place in the Victorian era. The actors must be cognizant of the mores of the time. It was a disgrace to have a child out of wedlock;

young girls could marry only with the consent of their guardians, and there was no divorce. There would therefore be no way for Edith and Charles to be together under these circumstances. This improvisation will not work if the actors aren't willing to play by these rules. Also, they must not fall into the trap of playing these characters in any stilted "period" manner. They would, however, address each other by their surnames.

See *Day After the Fair*, #2, page 89.

_____ 8 _____

Source: *The Dead Zone*, a film by David Cronenberg, screenplay by Jeffrey Boam, based on the novel by Stephen King (Situation #2)

Characters: One male and one female: Johnny Smith, a schoolteacher in his late twenties/early thirties, and Sarah, a woman of the same age

Place: A dayroom in the hospital, where Johnny is a patient

Background: Sarah and Johnny were engaged to be married five years ago. On the last night they saw each other, Sarah invited Johnny to spend the night, but, though tempted, he refused. They had not yet consummated the relationship because they wanted to wait for their wedding night. After saying good-bye to her that night, Johnny had a terrible automobile accident—a collision with a runaway oil-tanker. As a result of the accident, he remained in a coma for five years. He has now regained consciousness. Sarah, in the interim, married someone else and had a child. Johnny is still in a wheelchair but no longer has any visible injuries; they have long since healed.

Situation: Johnny and Sarah meet for the first time since the night of the accident five years ago. In Johnny's mind, the relationship is the same. Sarah has had five years of living, which have changed her.

Comments: These two people were very much in love and were meant for each other. But fate has dealt them a blow that, for various reasons, makes a continuation of their former relationship impossible. Much of this is not directly confronted in their conversation but is implied and understood.

See *The Dead Zone*, #1, page 113.

--------- **9** ---------

Source: *A Dill Pickle*, a short story by Katherine Mansfield

Characters: One male and one female: ex-lovers

Place: A restaurant

Background: You might say this relationship suffers from entropy. This couple separated several years ago. He was always very self-involved and talked mostly about himself, showing little interest in her. He is a petty person. For example: A waitress brings them food, which they don't touch, and he doesn't want to pay for it. They used to spend hours talking about the places they would visit together. He now brags about all the trips he has taken without her. In the meantime, she has gone nowhere because she couldn't afford to. She used to play the piano and really loved it, but she has since put the piano in storage because her apartment was too small for it. Neither of them has found another companion since their separation, and both of them need each other.

Situation: They have an accidental meeting at a restaurant.

There is still a sexual attraction. They talk about various
things from their past together, as well as what has happened in their lives since their last meeting. The unspoken dialogue that goes on throughout the scene is
that of each character trying to surmise any changes in
the other that will enable them to renew the relationship.
As much as they both need and desire each other, at
some point they both realize it's not going to work. When
they arrive at this conclusion, they should find a way to
part.

Comments: It is very important in this improvisation for
the actors to establish their previous relationship. The
actors should discuss some of the things they experienced
together, and each actor should be specific in his own
mind about the other's shortcomings. If the right preparation is done, they will be more sensitive to the present
dynamics between them. The actors must remember that
this is an exercise in subtext; the characters never directly
discuss their feelings.

──────── 10 ────────

Source: *Night Must Fall*, a play by Emlyn Williams (Situation #2)

Characters: One male and one female: Dan, a young man
hired to care for Mrs. Bramson, and Mrs. Bramson, an
older well-to-do woman confined to a wheelchair

Place: The living room of Mrs. Bramson's home

Background: There is a murderer at large who strangles
women and then decapitates them. Mrs. Bramson has
hired Dan for protection, not realizing that he is, in fact,
the murderer. Dan is planning to kill Mrs. Bramson this
evening. Because of the terror in the neighborhood, Mrs.

Bramson's servants have deserted her. She is terrified of being left alone even for a moment and panics every time Dan leaves the room. She adores him because he gives her so much attention and affection. Still, though she trusts him, there is doubt deep within her, which she is afraid to face.

Situation: Mrs. Bramson asks Dan to read to her from the Bible to soothe her nerves. He reads and then sings to her to further put her at ease. Eventually, he smothers her with a pillow.

Comments: It must be clear to the actor playing Dan that he has to gain Mrs. Bramson's complete confidence before he is psychologically ready to kill her. Once he gets her to put her head back and close her eyes, he can make his move. He must calm her down in whatever way he can—massaging her, singing to her, reading to her, giving her her medicine, and so on. He treats her like his mother, and she thinks of him as her son. The actor must deal with his motivation for killing Mrs. Bramson. He hates anyone he works for because they have power over him. The only way he can feel important is to gain the trust of women and then kill them. For some reason, it is only women he murders. The actor must decide what this reason is.

If a Bible is not available, the actor can use any reading material that would soothe Mrs. Bramson's nerves.

See *Night Must Fall*, #1, page 55.

——————— **11** ———————

Source: *The Plumber,* a film by Peter Weir

Characters: One male and one female: a man who claims to be the plumber, and the female occupant of the apartment

Place: The woman's apartment

Background: The woman is married, but her husband is at work. She has remained home to work on a book she is writing, and this time is valuable to her. The presumed plumber knows the couple's schedule.

Situation: A man knocks at the door. When she answers it, he explains that he is the plumber and wants to look at the pipes. She tells him she had not requested a plumber, whereupon he explains he was sent by the management of the building. At this point, she admits him into the apartment. As the scene continues from here, the man finds various ways of delaying his work and engaging the woman in conversation. During the scene, she comes to suspect, quite rightly, that he "ain't no plumber."

Comments: The actor who plays the "plumber" must decide why he is there, what he knows about this couple, and what he wants. However, while menace may be present, this improvisation should deal with subtleties and undercurrents. It should not be handled as some covert "horror" situation. The actors should be encouraged not to make the choice that he has come there to seduce her; it should be a much more complex reason. The actor playing the "plumber" must not feel obligated to reveal to the woman who he really is or why he is there. The scene will prove more interesting if these matters are dealt with obliquely, by implication rather than in a direct way. Also, the actress playing the woman must find

some justifying reason for not immediately taking overt
action when she realizes he's not a legitimate plumber.

_____ **12** _____

Source: *A Room with a View,* a novel by E. M. Forster
Characters: One male and one female: George Emerson
   and Lucy Honeychurch, both in their twenties or a little
   younger
Place: Lucy's home; the time is the early 1900s in England
Background: Lucy and George met while traveling in Flor-
   ence, Italy. During a street brawl Lucy fainted. George
   caught her and carried her to safety. Later, on a tour,
   they became momentarily separated in a field of flowers,
   and he grabbed her and kissed her passionately. It is
   now a few months later and Lucy is living at her home
   in England. She is engaged to be married to Cecil. Suddenly, George and his father show up to rent a cottage
   from Lucy's parents. Nobody knows about the two passionate meetings that took place between Lucy and
   George. One day, with Lucy and George present, Cecil
   reads a passage aloud from a book written by one of the
   women in the Italian tour. Without identifying them,
   this passage describes in detail the passionate kiss between Lucy and George. They didn't know they had been
   seen.
Situation: It is a few moments later, and the others have
   left the room. George grabs Lucy and kisses her. At that
   moment, she realizes she is in love with George and not
   Cecil. However, she must send George away because of
   her impending marriage. She does not reveal to him that
   she loves him but says she loves Cecil.
Comments: The actors must remember that this situation

takes place in Edwardian England, when it would have
been a great scandal for Lucy to break off her engagement
and run off with another man. Cecil is a decent person,
who loves her, and Lucy doesn't want to hurt him, but
she feels the difference when George kisses her. The
improvisation can begin with the reading of the passage.

————— 13 —————

Source: *The Sea Gull*, a play by Anton Chekhov

Characters: One male and one female: Nina, a young actress in failing health, and Konstantin, a young playwright in love with Nina

Place: A drawing room outside the dining room in a country
house owned by Konstantin's uncle—winter

Background: Two years ago Nina had been an actress in a
makeshift outdoor summer theater near this house. Madame Arkadina is Konstantin's mother and a successful
actress. Konstantin is a struggling writer, in love with
Nina, who wrote the play she had acted in. Nina met
Trigorin, a successful writer, who was and still is Arkadina's lover. Trigorin led Nina, a beautiful, fragile young
girl, into believing he loved her. He ended up breaking
her heart and going back to Arkadina. It is two years
since Nina has seen Trigorin or Konstantin. Her health
is not good, physically or mentally. She has come back
to see the old theater where she had found so much
happiness. It is winter now. The house has been opened
up for a weekend for Arkadina and her family. Nina sees
the lights on in the house and comes to visit Konstantin.

Situation: Konstantin is thrilled to see Nina. He confesses
that he still loves her and would like to marry her. Occasionally, Nina lapses into short disconnected phrases

that recall for her her past relationship with Trigorin.
They hear Trigorin and Arkadina enter the dining room
in great spirits. Nina and Konstantin both realize that
Nina still loves Trigorin, whom she can never have.

Comments: It will be necessary to have other actors do the
offstage voices of Trigorin, Arkadina, and a few other
guests enjoying the dinner party. The coach will have to
cue these actors. Konstantin, in the actual play, goes off
and kills himself right after this scene with Nina, realizing
his love will never be consummated. This is important
for the actor to know so that he understands Konstantin's
state of mind. Konstantin's heart is breaking for Nina,
and Nina's for Trigorin. The actress playing Nina must
be aware of her deteriorating physical and mental state.
Her mind keeps reliving snatches of that happy summer
in the theater with Trigorin. This is not to imply that
the character has lost her mind. Chekhov's characters
are often in this predicament of loving the wrong person
and experiencing the heartbreak that accompanies that.
The seasons are important in Chekhov; the actors should
be aware of the difference between summer and winter.
Summer is a time of relaxation, joy, and falling in love.
The winter is cold, bleak, a time of despair.

_____ 14 _____

Source: *Seconds*, a film by John Frankenheimer, screenplay
by Lewis John Carlino, based on the novel by David Ely

Characters: One male and one female: Arthur and Emily
Hamilton, husband and wife

Place: Their living room

Background: An executive of a bank becomes bored with
his life and wants to start over. He learns of a secret

organization that creates new lives and identities for people. He pays the organization to simulate his death in a hotel room fire. They then give him a new face, fingerprints, etc.—a whole new identity. His "death" takes place when he is in his fifties, but in his new identity, he appears to be in his thirties.

Situation: About a year has passed and Arthur decides to visit his wife. He returns to the house as an old college friend of her husband. He, of course, knows a great deal about the husband because he *is* the husband. He tells Emily that the reason he has come is because he's an artist and wants to paint a portrait of her late husband. He asks her to tell him about her husband so that he'll be better able to paint him. All the time she is describing her husband, he is listening to a portrait of himself.

Comments: The actors must be clear about what their relationship was before the husband supposedly died. They must answer the following questions: What is it that made the husband want out of this life so badly? How did his wife feel about losing him, and what is her life like now? How does she feel about meeting an old friend of her husband's? There is much subtext going on for both characters. The organization has the husband in its power and he is sworn to secrecy. It is very important that the actor decide why he chose to see his wife again.

———— 15 ————

Source: *Sessions,* a film for television by Richard Pearce, teleplay by Barbara Turner

Characters: One male and one female: Dr. Walter Hemmings and Leigh Churchill, lovers

Place: His apartment

Background: Leigh is a high-class, high-priced hooker, but Walter, a young doctor, does not know this about her; he thinks she is a fashion designer. They love each other, but she will not make a long-term commitment because of her profession. She knows that if she tells him the truth, it will destroy their relationship. This is the first time she's really been in love, so this is painful for her. She knows he is not the type of man who could accept her kind of life.

Situation: Walter wants her to move in with him and make this relationship more permanent. She tells him the relationship can never go any further than this, but she cannot reveal the reason why.

Comments: The actress must realize that this woman is not a hard-boiled hooker. She has come to the point where she doesn't want to do it anymore, but she cannot give up the power she has over men and the financial advantages. She is torn apart by her inner conflict. This is an exercise in subtext for the actress, but if the actors want to explore what would happen if she revealed herself to him, they can do so. It would then become a discovery for the actor.

16

Source: *Suspicion,* a film by Alfred Hitchcock, screenplay by Samson Raphaelson, Joan Harrison, and Alma Reville, based on the novel *Before the Fact* by Francis Iles.

Characters: One male and one female: John and Lina Aysgarth, husband and wife

Place: Wife's bedroom

Background: Lina is very wealthy; John had no money of his own when they were married. He has gotten himself into some business difficulties from which he feels he cannot recover. He has purchased some books on poison and has been asking people strange questions about ways to die. All this has made his wife very suspicious; she is convinced he is planning to kill her. In actuality, he is planning to kill himself.

Situation: Lina has become ill and believes "Johnnie" has been slowly poisoning her. He insists on bringing her a glass of milk before she goes to sleep; she is positive that it is poisoned. He brings her the milk because he is concerned that she hasn't been eating properly. He really loves her, but he can't deal with his own troubles.

Comments: The subtext is that the wife believes her husband is trying to kill her, but she doesn't say anything because she is frightened of him. The subtext for the husband is that he doesn't want her to know the despair he feels and that he plans to take his own life. The actor playing the role of the husband should find a strong enough reason for his decision to end his life.

———— 17 ————

Source: *Vertigo,* a film by Alfred Hitchcock, screenplay by Alec Coppel and Samuel Taylor, from a novel *D'entre les morts* by Pierre Boileau and Thomas Narcejac

Characters: One male and one female: Scottie (a detective) and Judy (an actress posing as the person he was following)

Place: Judy's hotel room

Background: A year ago a man hired Scottie to follow his wife, Madeleine. Actually, she was not his real wife but an actress, Judy, who was hired to pose as his wife. An accident occurred, and the supposed wife appeared to fall off a high tower. Scottie had been hired for the job because he was known to suffer from vertigo. He did have a vertigo attack at the time of the so-called accident and did not see that a different woman (the real wife) was pushed off the tower by the husband. The actress, Judy, who posed as the wife disappeared. Scottie had fallen in love with her and she with him. He tried to run up and save her when he saw her falling but was prevented from doing so because of his vertigo. It is now a year later, and he sees her walking out of a store with a different hairstyle and hair color, but she still looks like the woman he loved and lost. He follows her to her hotel.

Situation: Scottie knocks at the door of her room, and when Judy opens the door, he tells her that she looks like someone he loved who died a year ago. She tries to get rid of him. This is difficult for her since she loves him also, but because murder is involved, she cannot reveal her identity. She realizes that he would no longer love her if he knew she had been involved in such a scheme. She finally agrees to go out with him, hoping he will love her for herself and not for her resemblance to Madeleine, the woman she was posing as in the past. He asks her to change her hair color and hairstyle to look the way Madeleine did. He is obsessed with her former appearance.

Comments: These two people had a passionate love affair the likes of which neither will have again, and they both know this. They both want to recapture the relationship they had in the past, but she is living a lie and he's attempting to make her over into someone he remembers rather than who she actually is. Although this is an exercise in subtext, the actors might want to experiment with Judy's telling him the truth.

——————— **18** ———————

Source: *Wreath of Roses,* a short story by Elizabeth Taylor
Characters: One male and one female: two strangers
Place: A compartment on a train
Background: Each actor can decide why he or she is on this train, where they are going and why.

Just before getting on the train, these two people witnessed a man jump to his death in front of another train. Needless to say, they are both quite shaken.

Situation: They enter the same compartment and the train starts to move. At first, they do not say anything to each other. Neither one has had a chance to talk to anyone about what they have seen. Both are rather reserved types, who do not tend to talk to strangers. Eventually, one of them initiates a conversation, which finally leads to their revealing their feelings about the accident. A relationship develops from this shared experience.

Comments: Today we live in a society where we see a lot of violence on television and film, but rarely do most of us see it before our own eyes. The actors must allow themselves to be affected by the horror of what they have just seen—that is their subtext and it cannot be something that is easy for them. This could take place in any country.

_____ **19** _____

Source: _Your Place or Mine_, a television pilot by Dee Caruso

Characters: One male and one female: Archie, middle-aged, and Teresa, an interior decorator, late twenties/ early thirties

Place: An apartment belonging to Archie's brother

Background: Archie's wife divorced him after fifteen years of marriage. He has come to live with his younger brother, Allan, who is a swinging bachelor. Archie's confidence has been damaged by the divorce. Not only did his wife leave him, but she left him for a younger man. It has been fifteen years since Archie dated, and he feels lost. Allan calls a friend, who is a hooker, and invites her over to help Archie. Allan also has an interior decorator, Teresa, whom he has on retainer. She comes by once a week to work on the apartment.

Situation: Allan has gone out and Archie is awaiting the hooker. There is a knock at the door, and Teresa arrives with her fabrics, ready to work. Archie mistakes her for the hooker. The entire improvisation consists of his treating her like a hooker while she's redecorating Allan's apartment. Archie, being inexperienced, assumes that whatever she is doing is part of the game and goes along with it. She probably thinks he's a little strange, but she's there to do her job and Allan's paying her good money.

Comments: This is a situation of mistaken identity. The rules are that Archie must never ask her if she is a hooker. He simply makes the assumption that she is and does whatever she wants him to do. A lot of the fun in this is derived from her getting him to assist her in redecorating: rearranging furniture, measuring things, holding up pieces of fabric, etc. If he gets too affectionate with her, she must deal with that. There is no way of telling where this improvisation might end; the actors should leave the door open for any possibility.

_____ **20** _____

Source: *The Bad Seed*, a play by Maxwell Anderson, based on the novel by William March

Characters: Two females: the mother, Christine Penmark, and her daughter, Rhoda, about ten years old

Place: The living room of the Penmark home at night

Background: Christine has been having strange dreams in which she was running in a field beside a house and someone called her by the name of Ingo Denker, even though she knew her name was Christine. When she heard the name Denker, she became frightened because Bessie Denker was the name of a notorious murderess. She later found out from her father that Bessie Denker was her mother. Her father was a journalist covering the murder trial. He adopted her and renamed her Christine. She has just learned all this from her father; all she knew before was that she was adopted. She has a daughter, Rhoda, who is a sociopath, i.e., she commits crimes with no sense of remorse. Sociopaths can be very charming, which Rhoda is, but they lack morality. They do not come off as maniacs. Since this personality trait will often skip a generation, Christine doesn't have the qualities of her mother or her daughter. Christine has just made the discovery that her little girl, Rhoda, is a murderer. She killed a little boy by the name of Claude because she wanted his penmanship medal. She believed the medal was rightfully hers—that she should have been the winner. Claude refused to give it to her, so she hit him with her shoe and pushed him off a dock, drowning him.

Situation: It is Rhoda's bedtime. Christine gives Rhoda some pills, which she says are vitamins. In reality, they are a lethal dose of sleeping pills. Later, she plans to kill herself as well. After she gives Rhoda the pills, she reads her a bedtime story, knowing her daughter will never wake up. Rhoda plays very sweet with her mother and lies to her about everything she has done, but she is unsuspecting of her mother's intentions.

Comments: The many facts given in the background need never be used directly in the improvisation. They are only for the actor's knowledge. The main issue in this situation is not sociological; it is about a mother who is faced with the horrible task of having to kill her own daughter, whom she dearly loves despite her crimes. Rhoda may sense something about her mother and try to win her love back. She is used to wrapping her mother around her little finger. She knows she must convince her that she did not kill Claude because she will get in trouble—not because she thinks she did anything morally wrong.

_____ **21** _____

Source: _From the Life of the Marionettes_, a film by Ingmar Bergman (Situation #1)

Characters: Two males: Peter, the patient, and Mogens, his psychiatrist

Place: Mogen's office on a Saturday

Background: Peter is married to Katarina, whom he loves, but he has been having recurring nightmares about killing her. This desire to kill her always seems to be connected to his sexual feelings. In this dream, they are both naked and she is watching him in the mirror. Her hair is wet because she has just stepped out of the shower. He has a knife in his hand, and as he moves toward her to cut her throat, she turns around, moving toward him as if she knows what's in his mind. Their bodies touch and he kills her. He then plans to kill himself but always wakes up at that point.

Katarina has been seeing Mogens, but as a friend, not a patient. Although nothing has happened in their relationship, Mogens is in love with Katarina, which makes it very difficult for him to listen to Peter's dream.

Situation: Peter is worried that he is really going to kill Katarina, so he seeks psychiatric help from Mogens, who has opened his office on a Saturday especially to see Peter. After listening to Peter's dream (and fearing for Katarina's life), Mogens suggests that Peter go to a hospital. Peter refuses.

Comments: This improvisation contains strong subtext for Mogens because he has his own sexual feelings about Katarina and yet he has to listen to Peter describe their sexual relationship. It is important for the actor playing Peter to have the dream clearly in his mind, detail by detail. He is truly frightened by it.

See *From the Life of the Marionettes*, #2, page 184.

_____ 22 _____

Source: *Quartermaine's Terms,* a play by Simon Gray

Characters: Two males: St. John Quartermaine, a teacher in his forties, and Henry Windscape, the administrator

Place: The faculty room of the Cull Loomis School of English for Foreigners in Cambridge, England

Background: Quartermaine has devoted his life to teaching English to foreign students in this private school. He is a bachelor and has befriended everyone on the faculty, lending a sympathetic ear to their problems. However, people have seldom considered that *he* might have problems. He spends his holidays near the school when everyone else leaves because he lives in town and has no other place to go. The students find him a boring teacher and he has become increasingly incompetent. Henry Windscape, one of the teachers there, has just been appointed the new administrator. The man who preceded him, though he had heard reports of Quartermaine's incompetence, never would have dismissed him.

Situation: Windscape, who is a friend as well as a fellow teacher, is forced to let Quartermaine go. He dismisses him as gently as possible. Quartermaine, who is a deeply kind person, attempts to make it easy for him. He may have suspected this was coming.

Comments: The actor playing Quartermaine must remember that the Cull Loomis School has been this man's whole existence; he has no family and no place to go. But although he is dying inside, he is still concerned about Windscape's feelings. There are moments, however, when some of his true emotions might be exposed.

_____ **23** _____

Source: *The Basement,* a play by Harold Pinter

Characters: Two males and one female: Law, Stott, and Jane, Stott's girl friend

Place: A restaurant

Background: Law and Stott were old friends, but they had not seen each other for many years. One day, out of the blue, Stott showed up at Law's apartment with his girlfriend, Jane. The three of them have now been living together for about a month. Jane has since become Law's lover.

Situation: Law, Stott, and Jane are at a restaurant having drinks. There is much dialogue about the drinks. Law and Stott are reminiscing about old times. There is an undercurrent of tension owing to the triangular situation. However, nobody ever refers directly to this. The underlying anger and competition between the two men surfaces from time to time indirectly.

Comments: The actors must bear in mind that this is based on a Pinter play and is therefore an exercise in subtext. Everything these people talk about reflects the underlying circumstances. The actors must be clear about their relationships with one another, and they must know what they want from one another.

_____ **24** _____

Source: *Fatal Attraction,* a film by Adrian Lyne, screenplay by James Dearden (Situation #2)

Characters: One male and two females: Dan; his wife, Beth; and Alex, Dan's ex-lover

Place: The living room of the couple's apartment in the city

Background: One weekend when his wife was out of town,

Dan had an affair with Alex, a woman from his office. The affair meant nothing to him, but Alex is determined to make this a life-long relationship. She has become pregnant. Dan has been ignoring her phone calls, and he finally changed his number. He has decided to move his family to the country to get away from her. However, Alex has seen the ad in the paper regarding the rental of their apartment.

Situation: Dan enters the living room to find Alex and his wife together. They are in the process of signing contracts for rental of the apartment. Beth, having no idea that these two people know each other, introduces Alex to Dan, telling him that she is pregnant and needs a nice apartment to live in during her pregnancy. Neither Alex nor Dan let on that they know each other. He attempts to talk his wife out of renting the apartment to this woman, but his wife has been charmed by Alex and cannot understand Dan's attitude.

Comments: Dan's subtext is the fear that Alex is going to destroy his marriage. Alex enjoys the game of revenge because he has been trying to disentangle himself from her. Beth is bewildered by her husband's strange behavior.

See *Fatal Attraction,* #1, page 90, and #3, page 91.

25

Source: *The Final Days,* a film for television by Richard Pearce, teleplay by Hugh Whitemore, based on the book by Bob Woodward and Carl Bernstein

Characters: Four males and three females: President Richard Nixon; his wife, Pat; his two daughters, Tricia and

Julie; their husbands; the photographer (male or female)

Place: A room in the White House

Background: Richard Nixon was the first president of the United States to resign from office. He resigned so that he would not be impeached. A group of men were hired to break into the Democratic headquarters in Watergate to steal information. When they were caught, Nixon attempted to cover it up—an obstruction of justice.

Situation: Nixon tells his family of his decision to resign. At that point, a photographer enters, and Nixon tells them the photographer has been given instructions to take pictures of everything. The president directs his family to pose for a picture. They say they don't feel like having it taken, but he persuades them it must be done for the sake of history. They have to smile and hide their sorrow as the photographer snaps some shots.

Comments: This situation demands strong subtext on the part of all the actors, including the photographer. The actor playing Nixon should not attempt to do an "impression" of him—he should not be played as a caricature. These are all real people with real emotions.

_____ 26 _____

Source: *Golden Boy,* a play by Clifford Odets (Situation #1)

Characters: One female and two males: Lorna, Moody's girl friend (in love with Joe but loyal to Moody); Moody (a middle-aged fight manager, married but waiting for a divorce so that he can marry Lorna); Joe Bonaparte (a young boxer managed by Moody and in love with Lorna)

Place: Moody's office

Background: Lorna and Moody have been down and out

most of their lives. Moody finally discovers Joe—a very talented fighter. Moody believes he can become successful as Joe's manager. This would enable him to divorce his wife and marry Lorna. Joe, though he wants financial success as a fighter, is also an accomplished violinist and is afraid of injuring his hands. Moody has sent Lorna to persuade Joe to fight. In the process, Joe and Lorna realize they're in love and they spend the night together. Joe convinces Lorna to leave Moody. She is reluctant because Moody rescued her when she was destitute.

Situation: It is the next morning and Lorna is in Moody's office to break the news. Before she has a chance, Moody announces to her that he is getting a divorce so that they can finally get married. He is so happy about it that Lorna does not have the heart to tell Moody about Joe. Joe arrives, assuming Lorna has kept her promise, but soon realizes Moody knows nothing of their relationship. Moody suspects that something has happened between Lorna and Joe, but he never addresses it. Moody's main interest in Joe is whether or not he is going to fight, since Moody's livelihood depends on it.

Comments: This is a subtext exercise for all three actors. Lorna and Joe must hide their love for each other, and Moody senses something is wrong. It is possible that this situation could develop into a confrontation, but it is basically a subtext exercise. In the actual play, the relationship between Joe and Lorna is never revealed.

——————— 27 ———————

Source: *Golden Boy*, a play by Clifford Odets (Situation #2)

Characters: Three males: Joe Bonaparte, a young fighter; his father; Tokio, Joe's trainer

Place: A locker room before a championship boxing match

Background: Joe could have become a great violinist, but he gave this up because he could make more money as a fighter. The woman he loves, Lorna, has just told him that she is going to marry his manager, Moody. Tokio is preparing to give Joe a massage before the fight.

Situation: Joe's father comes to see him, not to encourage him, but to express his disappointment. He is not going to stay for the fight because he doesn't feel Joe is the same person anymore. He tells him that he feels sorry for him and leaves. Joe lies down on the massage table. He is about to fight the lightweight champion of the world, and the only two people he loves, Lorna and his father, have deserted him. Tokio massages Joe while giving him a pep talk. Throughout the massage, Joe is sobbing, but neither man makes any reference to it.

Comments: It doesn't matter how the actor arrives at his tears, but they must be real. The important element in this is that neither man ever refers to the fact that Joe, a boxing champion, is crying.

See *Golden Boy*, #3, page 71.

28

Source: *Home*, a play by David Storey

Characters: Two males and two females: Harry, middle-aged or older, and Jack, a man of the same age (both upper-middle-class); Kathleen, middle-aged, and Marjorie, a woman of the same age (both lower-middle-class)

Place: The garden of a hospital for the mentally ill, with a table and several chairs

Background: Harry, Jack, Kathleen, and Marjorie—owing to various circumstances in their lives and personal makeup—have been committed, either voluntarily or by someone else, to a hospital for the mentally ill. Their lives have become structured around the various routines of daily hospital life—i.e., lunch, tea, recreational activities, crafts workshops, etc. But none of them really regard themselves as belonging in this place. They cling steadfastly to any vestige of normalcy in order to maintain their self-images as people not really in need of special help. But each of them carries within himself or herself some great personal pain too sharp and deep to openly acknowledge. Only occasionally, in subtle and brief ways, does their pain show itself.

Situation: Harry and Jack, then Kathleen and Marjorie, meet in the garden of the hospital to pass the time in small talk and reminiscence. Never do the two men directly confront the issues that brought them there, though the two women, being of a slightly lower class, are more open about themselves and goad the men for information. Gradually, they all acknowledge precisely *where* they are and talk about it. Until then, it has seemed as if the place were a public park.

Comments: The actors should not portray these people as obviously "crazy." They must create a detailed background for their characters. They must also be acutely aware of the deep pain that flows beneath the surface of everything the characters say, only occasionally breaking through. This is especially true of Harry and Jack, who are much less self-revealing than the women.

The outcome of this situation should not be predetermined. Rather, it should be allowed to evolve naturally at its own pace.

Note: Just because the two men are of a slightly higher class than the women does not mean that these characters should be portrayed as "stuffy." Remember, they are real people, not caricatures. The actual play is set in England, but this situation could take place anywhere.

——— 29 ———

Source: *I, the Accused,* a British television mini-series based on an actual case in the early 1900s.

Characters: Two males and one female: two lovers and a prison guard

Place: A visiting room in prison

Background: The man was unhappily married to a woman who refused to give him a divorce; in fact, he hated her. He met another woman whom he truly loved, but they were unable to be together as long as his wife was alive. His wife was already ill and he slowly poisoned her. He was found guilty of her murder and sentenced to death. In this scene he is in prison, awaiting execution the following day.

Situation: His true love comes to visit him for the last time. Because a guard is standing nearby, they are restricted in their conversation. More is said in the unspoken dialogue or by innuendo.

Comments: The actor must keep in mind that this man is not a cold-blooded murderer who killed his wife so he could be with some young "chick." He was desperate to have happiness with the woman he loved rather than be miserable with a woman he despised. This took place in a time when it was not socially acceptable to live together and the two of them saw no other way out of their situation.

_____ 30 _____

Source: *Macbeth*, a play by William Shakespeare (Situation #2)

Characters: Six males and one female: Macbeth and Banquo, generals in the Scottish army; Macduff and Lennox, noblemen of Scotland; Donalbain and Malcolm, the two sons of Duncan, the murdered king; Lady Macbeth

Place: The courtyard of the castle of Macbeth and Lady Macbeth, two A.M.

Background: Lady Macbeth and Macbeth plotted to kill King Duncan by inviting him to their home for a banquet and then murdering him in his sleep. The motivation for the murder was their ambition to become king and queen. With Duncan and his two sons out of the way, Macbeth would be in line for kingship. Macbeth killed Duncan with a dagger. Lady Macbeth drugged the two bodyguards, smeared them with blood, and put the bloody daggers in their hands to make it appear as if they had committed the murder.

Situation: Macduff and Lennox arrive at the castle to talk to King Duncan. Macbeth, acting the gracious host and pretending all is well, directs Macduff to Duncan's room. A few moments later, Macduff reenters, screaming about the brutal murder of Duncan. This wakes up the whole castle, including Banquo, Donalbain, and Malcolm. Lady Macbeth comes out of her bedroom, pretending that she has no idea what is causing all the commotion. Macbeth and Lady Macbeth must feign ignorance regarding any knowledge of Duncan's murder and show the same horror as their colleagues.

Comments: In the actual play, Lady Macbeth faints at the news. It has been debated whether this is fake or if she actually faints from the realization of what they've done. The major task for the actor and actress playing Macbeth and Lady Macbeth is to use subterfuge to hide their crime and feelings of guilt. Macduff is the only one who suspects them, but he does not reveal it until he gets proof later on. Donalbain and Malcolm realize that their father has been assassinated; though they are grief-stricken, they become aware that they are next in line and make the decision to flee.

The actors should not get caught in the trap of playing kings and queens or make any attempt at Shakespearean style. They must experience the discomfort of this situation, which could happen in any time period.

See *Macbeth*, #1, page 54.

_____ **31** _____

Source: *A Man for All Seasons*, a play by Robert Bolt

Characters: Three males and two females: Sir Thomas More; his wife, Alice; their daughter, Margaret; Roper, Margaret's fiancé; and the jailer.

Place: A prison in the Tower of London during the reign of Henry VIII in 1535

Background: Sir Thomas More was the chancellor of England and a devout Catholic. Henry VIII separated himself from the Catholic Church and made himself supreme head of the Church of England in order to implement his divorce, which the Catholic Church would not recognize. More refused to sign the Act of Supremacy granting Henry VIII a divorce from Katharine of Aragon. The Act of Supremacy is an actual document that acknowledges Henry as the supreme head of the Church of England. All the necessary signatures for the document had been acquired, with the exception of More's. He refused to sign it because it was against his religious beliefs. He did not acknowledge anyone but the Pope as supreme head of the church. Were he to sign this document, it would be like selling his soul. If he did not sign it, he would be beheaded. Thomas Cromwell, who implemented the divorce, has had More imprisoned for a year without books to read, with little food, and no visits from his family. Cromwell has summoned More's family to visit him in prison for the purpose of having them persuade him to sign the document and be freed.

Situation: Alice, Margaret, and Roper arrive with a basket of food, which they lay out for Sir Thomas. There is much talk about his favorite foods and no direct reference to the real reason they are present. Alice is repressing great anger toward her husband for not signing the document and coming back to them. Sir Thomas tells her that he cannot die with her hating him. Margaret is the only family member who understands her father's stance. After a short visit, the jailer comes to the cell and tells them their time is up. More asks Roper to give the jailer some money in exchange for added time. The jailer accepts this but returns again shortly and demands that the family depart. The family knows this will be their last moment together because Sir Thomas will not alter his decision.

Comments: When More requests that Alice not let him die with her hating him, the actress must decide, at that moment, how she will respond. The actors must bear in mind that this family love one another deeply and this is not an easy encounter. The great courage these characters have is in the subtext.

--------- 32 ---------

Source: *A Raisin in the Sun*, a play by Lorraine Hansberry

Characters: Three males and three females: The Younger family, all black—Lena, the mother (in her sixties); her son, Walter Lee (early thirties); his sister, Beneatha (early twenties); Walter's wife, Ruth (late twenties/early thirties); their son, Travis (about nine or ten); a white man (he can be any age, but is not especially young)

Place: The kitchen in the Younger family's present home

Background: The Younger family has recently purchased a new home. They have worked long and hard to make the purchase. This home is located in what has always been an all-white neighborhood. They have not yet moved in.

Situation: A white man from the new neighborhood's "welcoming committee" comes to pay a call at the family's original home, ostensibly to welcome them to their new neighborhood. In reality, however, this person (a veiled racist representing the bigotry of the entire community) tries subtly to persuade them not to move into their new home. This person tries to make it seem as though it would be to their advantage not to make this move.

Comments: The actors must realize that this play was written in the late 1950s, when the climate for the black community was different from what it is at present. At that time, blacks moving into a white community was a major event.

--------- 33 ---------

Source: *Room at the Top*, a film by Jack Clayton, screenplay by Neil Paterson, based on the novel by John Braine

Characters: Two males, three females, and ensemble: Joe Lampton, a man working in an office; Mr. Brown, his boss; Susan Brown, his boss's daughter; two secretaries, and other office workers

Place: A corporate office

Background: The main character in this improvisation is Joe Lampton, who has had a love affair with an older woman, Alice, whom he loves deeply. Mr. Brown has offered him a very important position in the company contingent upon his marriage to his daughter Susan. Joe breaks off his relationship with the woman he truly loves in order to rise to the top.

Situation: Joe has now become engaged to Susan, and the office is throwing a party for him. They are opening the champagne when he overhears the secretaries talking about an accident in which Alice has been killed. They enjoy discussing the gory details about how she crawled around in her blood, all mangled, for hours until a farmer found her. She had been driving drunk. Joe has to listen to this horror story without betraying that he is falling apart inside or indeed that he even knew her.

Comments: This improvisation is an exercise in subtext primarily for the main male character. His fiancée might be bewildered by his behavior because although he attempts to hide his feelings something is bound to show through.

------- 34 -------

Source: *She Stoops to Conquer*, a comedy by Oliver Goldsmith

Characters: Three males and one female: Mr. Hardcastle, the innkeeper/host; Marlow, Miss Hardcastle's suitor; Hastings, Marlow's friend; Miss Kate Hardcastle, the daughter of Mr. Hardcastle

Place: Living room in the Hardcastle manor, a large country house in England in the late 1700s

Background: Marlow and Hastings are upper-class young men used to being waited on. They've just come from a nearby pub, inquiring about a good local inn where they might stay the night. A young man, Tony, actually the son of Mr. and Mrs. Hardcastle, realizes Marlow is the expected suitor of his sister. Knowing Marlow has never laid eyes upon her or any other member of the family, Tony directs the two men to his father's house, as a practical joke telling them it is a local inn.

Situation: The young men arrive at the house, naturally assuming Mr. Hardcastle to be an innkeeper—which he most emphatically is *not*. Mr. Hardcastle, however, unaware of the deception and expecting his guests, is nevertheless bound by the class conventions of the time to treat them with hospitality. He is also bound *not* to broach certain topics, one of which is the courting of his daughter. Kate Hardcastle passes through the room a few times, and Marlow and Hastings, thinking she is the maid, treat her accordingly. Marlow and Hastings, assuming Mr. Hardcastle to be the innkeeper, quickly grow annoyed with his overfamiliarity and are taken aback by his acting as though he were on an equal social level with them—which, of course, he actually *is*. Being a cultured man, who is well schooled in the social graces appropriate to his class and standing, Mr. Hardcastle does his best to contain his shock and eventual outrage at being treated by the young men as though he were a servant.

Comments: In approaching this improvisation, the actors must have some awareness of the class conventions and rules of social behavior in the Neo-Classic Period. This same situation would be handled in a completely different manner if it were set in the twentieth century. Out of its own time period, this situation would not make sense. The actors must also accept the rules of the game in this mistaken-identity type of humor.

The coach may wish to supply the audience with the background for this improvisation beforehand, thus setting the scene.

--------- 35 ---------

Source: *The Winslow Boy*, a play by Terence Rattigan

Characters: One female and two males: Kate Winslow, a young woman; John, her new fiancé; and Desmond Curry, the family solicitor, who is an old friend of the family

Place: The Winslow family's living room

Background: Kate and John have just announced their engagement. Desmond has always been in love with Kate

and hoped to marry her. Kate knows this but has never
had any interest in him. John is also aware of Desmond's
feelings.

Situation: John and Kate are alone when Desmond unexpectedly pays a visit. Kate announces to him that she
and John are engaged to be married.

Comments: Kate and John know how devastating this news
must be to Desmond, but they try to preserve his dignity
by not mentioning their awareness of his pain. Desmond
must congratulate them without letting on how he feels.
It is an exercise in subtext for all three actors.

SUBTEXT

Cross-References

Other improvisations in this book that involve Subtext can be found in the following categories:

RELATIONSHIP

One male and one female

CONFRONTATION/CONFLICT

Two males

CLIMACTIC MOMENT/DISCOVERY

One male and one female

SOLO MOMENT

One male

One female

FANTASY

Two females

5

SOLO MOMENT

Some of the most powerful and important moments in a play can be those in which an actor is onstage alone. Solo moments are not entirely unlike multiple-character scenes and can conform to any of the categories in this book. For example, a situation with a man grieving over the sudden death of his dog, just killed by a hit-and-run driver, would qualify as a climactic moment. Other solo moments may not conform to any category other than SOLO MOMENT— i.e., coming in out of the cold and warming oneself by the fire, or checking oneself in the mirror before an important date. These are moments in a character's life but not climactic ones. The actor, however, must learn to make these moments full.

In Shakespeare, an actor will likely be confronted with many soliloquies. Therefore, he will experience periods of time on stage when he is talking to himself, to an imaginary person, or to the audience. These moments can occur in contemporary pieces as well. At such times the actor must find within and around himself what is real at that moment. In that way, these moments will not appear set or contrived to the audience as they might seem if they were done in an arbitrary manner.

Almost any form of private activity, no matter how ordinary or exotic, can provide useful material on which to base a solo moment. But included in this section are solo moments that would be particularly interesting or challenging for an actor.

SOLO MOMENT

List of Situations

One male

One female

_____ **1** _____

Source: *Adam*, a film for television by Michael Tuchner, teleplay by Allan Leicht, based on a true story (Situation #1)

Characters: One male (two males—see Comments): John Walsh, the father of Adam, a missing child

Place: A small room in a police station

Background: Mr. Walsh has been living in a state of torment and anxiety regarding the whereabouts and well-being of his missing son. At length, he is summoned to a police station by one of the detectives assigned to the case.

Situation: Mr. Walsh has just been asked to listen to a tape recently found in an abandoned warehouse. The tape contains the sounds of children being tortured. The tape was made by the man who killed them. The police thought that one of the voices on the tape might be that of his son. Mr. Walsh has been cautioned about the highly upsetting nature of this tape, but he has agreed to listen to it for purposes of identification. His son's voice is not among those on the tape. Nevertheless, this is a harrowing experience for him. He listens to the tape through earphones.

Comments: This may be done completely as a solo moment, with the father sitting down, putting on the headphones, and listening; or as a two-person scene, with the detective setting up the situation for him and telling him about the tape, etc. This could also be done with Reve Walsh, the mother of the child. The actor must be prepared to deal with the discomfort of this material.

See *Adam*, #2, page 86.

2

Source: *The Adventures of Huckleberry Finn*, a novel by Mark Twain

Characters: One male: Huckleberry Finn, Caucasian, anywhere between fourteen and seventeen years old.

Place: The shore of the Mississippi River. The South during the time of slavery.

Background: Huck has run away from home along with an escaped slave named Jim. They have been traveling down the Mississippi on a raft. It is nighttime. Huck has just saved Jim from capture by some men in a boat who were looking for a number of runaway slaves, Jim among them. Since it was dark, they were not able to see whether Jim was black or white, and Huck covered for him by saying he was white. In Huck's mind, he has just committed a terrible sin, slavery being the norm in the South at that time, and harboring an escaped slave a grave crime.

Situation: At this moment, Huck is alone, talking to God about what he has just done, trying to explain why he did what he did, even though he knows he will probably "go to Hell for it."

Comments: The actor must be willing to place himself in this period and accept the social mores of the time. He must bear in mind that Huck is himself rebelling against the injustice of the time, although not intellectually— he is incapable of that—but, rather, because he loves

Jim. He is willing to lose his soul for the sake of a friend and take the "consequences." From Huck's point of view, this is quite a sacrifice. The actor must also remember that Huck is still a young boy.

_____ 3 _____

Source: *Child's Play*, a play by Robert Marasco (Situation #1)

Characters: One male: Jerome Malley, a middle-aged teacher

Place: The faculty room in a school

Background: Malley has been under much emotional strain recently, caring for his terminally ill mother.

Situation: Malley receives a phone call, informing him that his mother has just died. He is very aware of other people in the room.

Comments: The close proximity of coworkers and the sensitive nature of the news received are both key factors in the possible responses of the actor in this situation. Careful consideration should be given to these elements. The actor can use imaginary people or other actors for the coworkers.

_____ 4 _____

Source: *The Dead Zone*, a film by David Cronenberg, based on the novel by Stephen King

Characters: One male: Dr. Sam Weizack, a man in his sixties

Place: Weizack's office in a hospital

Background: The doctor has a patient who has just regained consciousness after being in a coma for five years. The patient has found that he now has psychic powers he did not formerly possess. When he takes a person's hand, he can see things from their past, present, and future. He takes the doctor's hand and sees him being torn away from his mother during World War II. He then sees the mother in present time and tells him where she lives. The doctor finds this hard to believe because it has been almost fifty years since his separation from her, and he had heard confirmed reports that she had been killed.

Situation: Weizack decides to contact his mother. He acquires the telephone number and places the call. Someone else answers the phone, and when he mentions his mother's name, he is told to hold. At that moment, he realizes she is still alive. She comes to the phone, and he hears the voice of his mother whom he's loved and missed all these years.

Comments: The actor playing the doctor must identify with that little boy who was torn away from his mother and what it would mean to talk to her. In the film, the doctor is unable to speak to his mother, feeling it was somehow not meant to be, and hangs up. But the actor in this improvisation should allow himself the freedom to respond as he chooses.

5

Source: *The Execution of Private Slovik,* a film for television by Lamont Johnson, teleplay by Richard Levinson and William Link, based on the book by William Bradford Huie

Characters: One male: Eddie Slovik, a young soldier in his twenties

Place: Standing in front of a firing squad, waiting to be executed, in 1945

Background: Private Slovik is being executed for cowardice because he was seen running away from battle. He had been in reform school for being a thief before he was drafted. He is an unstable and nervous person who can't handle high-pressure situations and is, therefore, a misfit in the army.

Situation: Slovik is staring death in the face. He is allowed to say anything he wants before the order is given to fire. The actor may choose to say nothing, or he may speak or pray.

Comments: The actor must imagine the firing squad lined up in front of him, with their rifles loaded. The acting coach might say "Fire," or the actor can imagine the moment he is hit.

_____ **6** _____

Source: *A Field of Honor,* a University of Southern California student film by Robert Zemeckis

Characters: One male or one female: a mental patient

Place: Outside a mental institution

Background: The person has been institutionalized for several years. The actor should decide what the nature of the mental illness was, what happened that catapulted him into the institution, and what made the doctors decide to release him today.

Situation: This is the person's first moment out in the world in quite some time. He is alone; nobody has come to meet him or help him back into the world.

Comments: The actor must decide whether or not he is ready to face the world again. It is very important that

he fill in the background information because this will
help determine how he feels now.

──────── 7 ────────

Source: *From the Life of the Marionettes,* a film by Ingmar
Bergman (Situation #2)

Characters: One male: Peter, a married man

Place: A stripper's dressing room backstage. The time is
three A.M. The room is one with little ventilation and
no windows. It smells of makeup and cigarette smoke.
The doors leading outside are locked. The only open
door leads to the stage.

Background: Peter has been seeing a doctor because he
has been having strong desires to kill his wife after sexual
contact with her. He has gone to see a stripper, who
functions as a prostitute after work. The doorman at the
theater has locked them in the dressing room, and he
will return at six A.M. to let them out. Peter, feeling
pent up at one point, attempts to leave but cannot get
out. Strangely, the stripper has the same name as his
wife—Katrina. They play soft music while making love.
He ends up strangling her and then making love to the
dead body.

Situation: This is the moment after the murder/rape. He
realizes that it was his wife whom he imagined he was
killing, and he is also aware that he is mentally ill. He
is locked in the dressing room with the body until the
doorman returns in three hours.

Comments: Peter is a highly intelligent, upper-middle-class
man, successful in business. He has been relatively happily married until this peculiar desire overcame him. He
has gradually lost his grip. The actor should be cautioned

not to play the character as a stereotypical lunatic. If desired, an actress may be used to represent the dead body.

See *From the Life of the Marionettes*, #1, page 157.

—————— **8** ——————

Source: *La Strada*, a film by Federico Fellini, screenplay by Fellini, Ennio Flaiano, and Tullio Pinelli (Situation #2)

Characters: One male: Zampano, a strongman for a traveling carnival. Optional: woman he talks to.

Place: A beach at night

Background: Several years ago Zampano purchased a young woman named Gelsomina from her mother. The mother sold her daughter because Gelsomina was simpleminded and she needed money for her other children. Zampano taught Gelsomina how to play the trumpet to accompany his strongman act. They traveled from town to town in a caravan. Sometimes he brought other women into the caravan, making Gelsomina wait outside. He slept with her when there were no other women available. Finally, they joined a carnival, where they met Il Matto ("The Fool"), a high-wire artist who was very kind to Gelsomina. Although she adored Il Matto, she chose to stay with Zampano because she felt he needed her more. One day, Il Matto, who enjoyed poking fun at Zampano, went too far—and Zampano, in his anger, accidentally killed him. Gelsomina, heartbroken, could no longer play the trumpet with any joy. Zampano deserted her on the roadside, feeling she was of no further use to him.

Situation: Five or so years later, Zampano goes to a town and hears a woman humming a melody he had once

taught Gelsomina, and asks her where she learned it.
The woman tells him about a strange young woman who
used to walk the streets playing this melody endlessly
on the trumpet until one day she was found dead. That
night Zampano goes to a deserted beach. He realizes for
the first time that he really loved Gelsomina and how
terribly he treated her. With this realization, he breaks
down completely.

Comments: The actor playing this role can react in any way
he wants to this discovery, but whatever his choice, this
is a painful acknowledgment for him. This improvisation
can include the woman who tells him about Gelsomina's
death, or it can commence after he has acquired the
information from her and internalizes it.

See *La Strada*, #1, page 196.

————— 9 —————

Source: *The Last Emperor*, a film by Bernardo Bertolucci,
screenplay by Mark Peploe with Bertolucci, based on
the autobiography *From Emperor to Citizen* by Pu Yi

Characters: One male: Pu Yi, a man in his late sixties, the
last emperor of China, now a gardener

Place: The throne room in China's Forbidden City, now a
public museum

Background: Pu Yi, from birth, had been the emperor of
China, his every need cared for by countless servants.
And yet he remained a kind of prisoner inside the For-
bidden City, a vast walled maze of palaces and temples.
Then, when Pu Yi reached full maturity, he was suddenly
thrust out into an unfamiliar world, a new China under
Communist rule. And in this new China, Pu Yi was

forced to take on a new life as a gardener—a citizen no different from any other.

Situation: Pu Yi, having bought a ticket, walks through the Forbidden City—now as a tourist. He explores the throne room and sits on the throne from which he once ruled all China. He remembers having placed a small cricket cage behind the cushion in the throne. He reaches back and finds it still there.

Comments: The enormous irony and subtext inherent in this situation is obvious and provides rich material for the actor. The tremendous contrast between Pu Yi's former and later positions, i.e., from emperor to gardener, would inevitably have staggering psychological and emotional ramifications, and the actor must, of course, be aware of these in approaching this improvisation.

After the actor has been seated on the throne for a while, the acting coach might send in a guard to tell him that sitting on the throne is prohibited.

_____ **10** _____

Source: *Los Santos Inocentes (The Holy Innocents)*, a film by Mario Camus, screenplay by Camus, Antonio Larreta and Manuel Matji

Characters: One male: Paco, a retarded man

Place: A field

Background: A man finds a wounded bird, which he brings to his retarded brother, Paco. Paco nurtures the bird back to health, and it becomes his beloved pet. Each day it flies free but always returns to him when he calls it. He works for a man who hunts birds for recreation. Paco's job is to pick up the dead birds. This day he sees his pet bird flying and screams to his boss not to shoot it. Having not, as yet, shot any birds this day, the boss ignores his pleas and shoots the bird. When Paco becomes distraught, he tells him to pull himself together and pick up the dead bird. Leaving Paco behind, the boss continues on in pursuit of more birds.

Situation: This is the moment when the retarded man comes to terms with seeing his lifeless pet lying on the ground.

Comments: The actor must decide how his grief over the bird will manifest itself. He must also bear in mind that this character does not have a normal facility with language. Therefore, the actor must find another means of expression.

_____ 11 _____

Source: *The Morning After*, a film for television by Richard T. Heffron, teleplay by Richard Matheson, based on the novel by Jack B. Weiner (Situation #2)

Characters: One male: Charlie Lester, a middle-aged, self-destructive alcoholic

Place: A telephone booth in a bar

Background: Charlie is a confirmed alcoholic. He has a wife and two children, a beautiful home, and a successful job as a speechwriter for an oil company executive. However, he is a ghost writer who never gets credit for his speeches. He has been in a special hospital to cure his alcoholism. All the same, he feels his situation is hopeless, and for this reason has left the hospital. His wife has tried to help him, but she was finally told he would have to help himself.

Situation: This is Charlie's final telephone call to his wife, in which he tells her he has given up and left the hospital.

He has made up his mind that he will never recover. He's calling to say good-bye to her and the children. He wants them to know he loves them deeply, but he just can't pull himself together.

Comments: He will now become a derelict who sits on the beach and drinks all day. The self-destructive part of Charlie has taken over. The actor must find this quality within himself. There may be some hope that his wife will say something to rescue him, but in his own mind, he is really beyond being rescued.

See *The Morning After*, #1, page 120.

12

Source: *Othello*, a play by Shakespeare

Characters: One male: Othello. Optional: one female

Place: Othello's bedroom in Venice

Background: Othello, a Moor, who is a soldier of fortune in the pay of the Venetian senate, has risen to the rank of commander of the Venetian armed forces. Recently, he married a young white woman, Desdemona, whom he loves passionately. Iago, Othello's ensign, secretly resents his commander and wishes to destroy him. To accomplish this, Iago began to convince Othello—whom he knows to have jealous tendencies—that Desdemona has been having a secret affair with one of his officers. One night, in a final burst of jealous rage, Othello strangles his innocent bride. Then Iago's wife tells Othello the truth about her husband's evil scheme.

Situation: Othello holds Desdemona's body, realizing what he has done.

Comments: An actress may be used as the lifeless Desdemona. The actor playing Othello must come to terms with the enormity of what he has done. How this realization manifests itself should be unpremeditated, spontaneous.

——— 13 ———

Source: *The Picture of Dorian Gray,* a novel by Oscar Wilde (Situation #2)

Characters: One male: Dorian Gray, a good-looking young man in his twenties.

Place: Dorian's living room

Background: Dorian was engaged to an actress by the name of Sibyl Vane. He loved her as an actress but not as a person. One night, when he brought some friends to see her perform, she disappointed him. He felt humiliated and disillusioned by her abominable performance. He went backstage to her dressing room and broke off his engagement to her. She was so devastated that, later that evening, she committed suicide.

Recently, a portrait was painted of Dorian, which he keeps in his living room. It shows a young, handsome man—an excellent likeness.

Situation: Dorian comes home to his apartment after rejecting Sibyl and notices that a cruel line has appeared in the portrait at the corner of his mouth, but his own face has not changed.

Comments: The portrait must be very clear in the actor's mind. He may not have had any concern for what he did to Sibyl until this moment. This is the first time he's seen his portrait change.

See *The Picture of Dorian Gray,* #1, page 100.

_____ **14** _____

Source: *Sandburg's Lincoln*, a television mini-series, based on the biography by Carl Sandburg

Characters: One male: Abraham Lincoln

Place: The bedroom of William, Lincoln's ten-year-old son

Background: Lincoln's son, Willie, liked to collect railroad timetables. He was fascinated by the names of the stops. Many of them had strange-sounding, poetic names, such as Utica, Schenectady, Syracuse, etc. He liked to have his father read the timetables to him, finding them comforting.

Situation: Lincoln is sitting beside his son's bed. Willie has a high fever and is near death. To comfort him, Lincoln begins to read the timetables. He puts on a smiling face, but, inside, his heart is breaking because he knows he will lose his son.

Comments: The actor can use any reading material for this. He can be reading from a book or reciting something from memory. He should be clear in his mind as to the nature of his son's illness.

_____ **15** _____

Source: *All Summer in a Day*, a short story by Ray Bradbury

Characters: One female (or male): Margo, approximately twelve years old

Place: Another planet, locked inside a closet.

Background: This is a planet where the sun shines only once every seven years for about an hour. The rest of the time it rains. The children have to spend time each day beneath a sunlamp. Originally, Margo was from Earth and kept telling the other children that she had seen the real sun. She was the only one in art class who could paint a picture of it. One little boy became jealous of her, labeling her a know-it-all. It is now the seventh year and the sun is due today. Because of his jealousy, the boy has locked Margo in a closet. Suddenly the sun appears, and all the children go running off to see it, forgetting completely about Margo.

Situation: Margo realizes that she will not see the sun, and it will not return for another seven years. Suddenly, she spots a ray of sun coming under the door. She puts her hand out to touch it.

Comments: The actor must accept the reality of these circumstances. The sense memory of that single ray of sun becomes of enormous importance.

_____ 16 _____

Source: _An Act of Murder,_ a film by Michael Gordon, screenplay by Michael Blankfort and Robert Thoeren, based on the novel _The Mills of God_ by Ernst Lothar

Characters: One female: Catherine Cooke, a married woman

Place: The living room of the Cooke home

Background: Catherine has been dying of a brain tumor for many months. Her husband, Judge Calvin Cooke, knows this, but Catherine does not. She has had severe headaches, for which her husband was giving her what she thought was aspirin. In actuality, he was giving her pain killers prescribed by the doctor. They were very toxic and the husband could give her only two a day. Therefore, he had to keep pretending he had run out of them.

Situation: Catherine finds a letter to her husband that makes reference to her fatal illness. This is the first moment she has known about this. The letter doesn't mention that it is an inoperable brain tumor. The letter states the following: "In the final extremity, we do not feel that your wife should be informed of the fatal nature of her illness."

Comments: It is important that the actor have no anticipation of the contents of the letter. She comes across it quite accidentally, perhaps by cleaning off her husband's desk. She never thought of her headaches as being any more than just headaches. She is totally unprepared for this news.

_____ **17** _____

Source: *The Collector,* a novel by John Fowles

Characters: One female: Miranda Grey, a young art student

Place: A basement room

Background: Miranda has been kidnapped by Freddie, a deeply disturbed young man. He has been holding her prisoner in his basement. He leaves her alone, tied up in a chair, for long periods of time. He has given her some food and water but not a sufficient amount.

Situation: Miranda has been here for a number of days and this is the first time she has been untied. At last she is free to move around. The room is securely locked; there is no way out.

Comments: The actor must be acutely aware of the girl's state of mind after several days of sexual terror and captivity. Her responses while exploring her environment will obviously be colored by her recent experiences and would, therefore, not be the responses of someone exploring a room in a normal situation.

——— 18 ———

Source: *The Entity*, a film by Sidney J. Furie, screenplay by Frank DeFelitta from his book (Situation #1)

Characters: One female: Carla, a woman in her thirties

Place: Carla's bedroom, evening

Background: Carla has three children and a fiancé, who is out of town on business.

Situation: Carla is at her makeup table, getting ready for bed. She may be removing her makeup, brushing her hair, etc. Suddenly, she is assaulted by a powerful invisible force. This force beats her, then throws her onto her bed, where it attacks her sexually, raping her.

Comments: This unseen force must be very real to the young woman and not a figment of her imagination. This film was based on an actual case study conducted by UCLA's parapsychology department. The woman was *not* diagnosed as mentally disturbed.

See *The Entity*, #2, page 213.

——— 19 ———

Source: *Gertrude Stein, Gertrude Stein, Gertrude Stein*, a play by Marty Martin

Characters: One female: a professional writer, Gertrude Stein, who has lived in the same place for thirty-five years

Place: Her Rue de Fleurus apartment in Paris, from which she has just been evicted

Background: Gertrude Stein has written many great works in this apartment. She has entertained many famous people and had intimate relationships here. This is the last time she will see this apartment.

Situation: She is looking at the apartment, with its multitude of memories, for the last time.

Comments: The actress may choose to do this with words or in silence. This is vaguely based on an incident in Gertrude Stein's life in 1938. However, this is a situation that could happen to anybody. It is crucial to keep in mind that this apartment holds many rich associations.

_____ **20** _____

Source: *I Never Promised You a Rose Garden,* a film by Anthony Page, screenplay by Gavin Lambert and Lewis John Carlino, based on an autobiographical novel by Joanne Greenberg

Characters: One female: Deborah, a girl in her midteens

Place: The restroom of a mental institution

Background: Deborah was brought to the institution by her parents because of her severe schizophrenia. Deborah has for some time been living in an imaginary world with its own language and customs. Through much painful work with her psychiatrist, a woman named Dr. Fried, she has managed to break through much of her psychosis and readjust to life in the "real" world. One of the symptoms of her illness has been an inability to feel certain types of physical pain, usually self-inflicted, i.e., cutting her wrist or arm with sharp objects, banging her head on the floor, or burning herself with cigarettes.

Situation: Deborah has gotten permission to use the bathroom, but she has ulterior motives; she has hidden cigarettes in a secret compartment in the bathroom, along with a pack of matches. Lighting a cigarette, she pauses for a moment in anticipation, then touches the lighted tip of the cigarette to her arm. Instantly, she gasps and

withdraws the cigarette, stunned to feel this pain for the
first time in a long while. She burns herself again and
yet again to reinforce the reality of her sensation. She is
profoundly grateful for this pain, since it means she is
on the road to recovery.

Comments: In the film, this moment became one of great
joy and ecstasy. However, each individual actor doing
this improvisation should find out for himself exactly how
he will respond to this moment of self-discovery. The
actor must deal with the sense memory of being burned,
though not necessarily by a cigarette.

———— 21 ————

Source: *La Strada,* a film by Federico Fellini, screenplay
by Fellini, Ennio Flaiano, and Tullio Pinelli (Situation
#1)

Characters: One female: Gelsomina, the helper to a carnival strongman, Zampano

Place: A country road in northern Italy

Background: Zampano hired Gelsomina, a mildly retarded
woman, to work for him. Actually, he purchased her from
her mother. He taught her to play the trumpet to accompany his act. They traveled from town to town in a
caravan. Sometimes he brought other women into the
caravan, making Gelsomina wait outside. When there
were no other women around, he slept with her. Eventually, they joined a carnival company and met a high-
wire artist, Il Matto ("The Fool"), who was extremely
kind to Gelsomina. He was probably the first person in
her life who treated her with respect, even offering to
let her travel with him. She refused because she thought
Zampano needed her more. She loved Il Matto because

he cared so much for her. Zampano got into a fight with
Il Matto and accidentally killed him.

Situation: Gelsomina watches, in horror, as Zampano and
Il Matto struggle. Finally, after one wild blow from Zampano, Il Matto falls to the ground, lifeless. This is the
turning point in Gelsomina's life. Not only has she lost
Il Matto, who gave her dignity, but he has been killed
by Zampano, whom she loves.

Comments: Although Gelsomina is somewhat retarded, she
feels deeply and this moment breaks her heart. In fact,
she never recovers from the grief this causes her. Eventually, she dies from her sorrow.

See *La Strada*, #2, page 185.

––––––––– **22** –––––––––

Source: *Losing Time*, a play by John Hopkins

Characters: A young single woman living alone

Place: The woman's apartment

Background: The woman has just been mugged and raped
while outside.

Situation: The woman returns home alone from her traumatic experience.

Comments: The actress should not decide beforehand what
her actions and responses will be. She should allow things
to happen in a fresh and immediate way. The actress
must, however, have a very definite idea of exactly what
has just happened to her.

——————— **23** ———————

Source: *Manhunter,* a film by Michael Mann, based on the novel *Red Dragon* by Thomas Harris (Situation #2)

Characters: One female: Reba MacLaine, a blind woman in her twenties or thirties

Place: A veterinary clinic in a zoo

Background: Reba MacLaine, a young blind woman, has been working in the darkroom of a photo processing laboratory. A coworker, Francis Dolarhyde, has offered to take her somewhere after work as a surprise. She accepts.

Situation: Francis brings Reba to a veterinary clinic at a nearby zoo, where a Bengal tiger lies anesthetized on a table waiting to have his tooth capped. Reba is allowed to touch the tiger as she pleases. This is the first time she has ever been able to feel an animal of this kind, and she is profoundly affected by the experience.

Comments: For obvious reasons, the actress will have to call upon sensory skills and reserves of imagination. It is unlikely a life-sized stuffed animal tiger will be available, but this sort of substitute object may be used if desired.

——————— **24** ———————

Source: *Request Concert,* a play by Franz Xavier Kroetz

Characters: One female

Place: The woman's dingy one room apartment

Background: This whole play consists of a woman preparing for her suicide. No specific background is given, and there is no dialogue. All character is delineated solely through the woman's actions and the furnishings of her apartment.

Situation: A woman comes home from work and goes about the minute details of her household chores. She seems to be putting her house in order. At the end, she commits suicide.

Comments: The actor may choose the means of suicide and must also be clear about the reason. The important element here is the meticulousness with which the preparations are made. The setting and properties are an important element in this improvisation; therefore, preparation time must be allowed. Obviously, this situation could work just as effectively with a man.

25

Source: *Resurrection*, a film by Daniel Petrie, screenplay by Lewis John Carlino (Situation #2)

Characters: One female: Edna McCauley, a recent widow, in her late thirties

Place: Husband's grave

Background: Edna has just recovered from an automobile accident in which her husband died. She is in a wheelchair because her legs are paralyzed. This is her first outing since her release from the hospital.

Situation: Edna talks to her husband at the gravesite. Up to this point she hasn't really spoken about what has happened to her.

Comments: The actor should not have any preconceived idea of what she is going to say to her husband. This needn't be approached as something overly heavy, and it should not become an exercise in morbid self-indulgence. The actor might make discoveries about the marriage, and she should try to balance the seriousness of the situation with lighter elements so that the improvisation is not dragged down into bathos.

See *Resurrection*, #1, page 102, and #3, page 319.

_____ **26** _____

Source: *Shirley Valentine*, a play by Willy Russell

Characters: One female: Shirley Valentine, a middle-aged housewife

Place: A table by the sea at an outdoor café in Greece

Background: Shirley Valentine, tired of the mundane life of waiting on her husband hand and foot, decides to go to Greece with a girl friend. Knowing her husband would persuade her not to go, she simply leaves him a note of farewell. Her friend, Jane, with whom she is traveling, finds a male companion on the plane and leaves Shirley alone when they arrive in Greece. Shirley is now sitting by herself in a café. Having imagined herself sitting at a romantic café by the sea, Shirley asks the waiter to move her table down to the beach, which he does.

Situation: Shirley sits at the table, realizing that it's not quite as romantic as she had fantasized. She reviews her life and comes to the conclusion that she has thrown it away. She has lost herself somewhere in taking care of her husband, Joe, and in raising her daughter, Millandra. She tries to remember who she really is.

Comments: The entire play is a one-woman monologue, although in the film version other characters were realized. The actress may wish to verbalize some of her thoughts or do it all internally. She may or may not come to some conclusions about the direction her life is now to take.

_____ 27 _____

Source: *Summer*, a play by Edward Bond

Characters: One female: Xenia, middle-aged

Place: A house overlooking the sea in Eastern Europe

Background: Forty years ago, Xenia's family owned and lived in this house. It was taken from them under the German occupation during World War II. At one time Xenia's family threw dinner parties for the German officers in this very house. Marthe, the family servant, was taken prisoner, along with many of the townspeople, and was condemned to be shot. Only Xenia's intervention saved Marthe's life. At this point Xenia lives in England, and Marthe now owns Xenia's old house.

Situation: Xenia has returned to her old home for the first time since the German occupation. It is now safe for her to make this visit, but nothing in this country belongs to her family anymore. Needless to say, the place is fraught with memories both pleasant and painful. When she arrives, she is alone in the house.

Comments: The actor needs to do sufficient preparation for this moment, since it is dependent on what she has experienced in the past. The memories should be specific; each object should be meaningful. The fact that her one-time servant, Marthe, now owns the house should be taken into consideration as well.

28

Source: *This Child Is Mine*, a film for television by David Greene, teleplay by Charles Rosin

Characters: One female: Bonnie (and Craig) Wilkerson, adoptive parents of a two-year-old

Place: Lawyer's office

Background: Bonnie and Craig adopted a baby two years ago. The natural mother has now decided that she wants her baby back. The case has been in court for two years and the natural mother has won. The child will now be returned to its natural mother and the adoptive parents must part with it forever. These parents have doted on the child, whom they love as much as if it were their own.

Situation: The child has just been delivered to the natural mother, who was waiting in the outer office. Bonnie will never see her child again.

Comments: It is important for the actress to establish this child clearly in her mind. She may still be holding an object that belonged to the child. This improvisation could also be done with both the father and the mother present.

29

Source: *What Ever Happened to Baby Jane?*, a film by Robert Aldrich, screenplay by Lukas Heller, based on the novel by Henry Farrell

Characters: One female: Blanche, an invalid

Place: Blanche's bedroom

Background: Many years ago, Blanche, in a jealous rage, attempted to run over her sister, Jane, with a car. Instead, she ended up injuring herself, becoming crippled, and being confined to a wheelchair. Because Jane was drunk at the time, Blanche was able to convince her that she caused the accident. Jane has been burdened with caring for her sister since the accident and has come to resent Blanche. As a result of this resentment, Jane has become abusive to her sister and punishes her in various ways.

Situation: Jane has just served Blanche's dinner on a tray. Blanche, who has been made to wait a long while, is exceedingly hungry. She lifts the cover off the dish and finds a dead rat on her plate.

Comments: The actress must remember that Blanche is totally dependent on Jane for everything and has been kept a prisoner in her own house for a long time.

SOLO MOMENT

Cross-References

Other improvisations in this book that involve Solo Moments can be found in the following categories:

CONFRONTATION/CONFLICT

One male and one female

SPECIAL PROBLEMS

One female

One male

PART II

THROUGH THE LOOKING GLASS

6

UNUSUAL CIRCUMSTANCES

This chapter deals with situations of an unusual nature which could conceivably occur and in some cases actually have occurred. In *Devour the Snow*, based on a real-life occurrence, a member of the Donner party is put on trial for cannibalism. In the play *The Child Buyer*, based on John Hersey's novel, a man in the employ of a large government corporation attempts to buy children from their parents for use in medical experiments. Although the latter situation has not (it is hoped!) actually occurred, it is nevertheless within the realm of possibility.

These improvisations will challenge the actors' limits. Actors will be confronted with highly unusual situations, to which they must respond with the same degree of honesty as they would to more everyday occurrences. There are many circumstances we will never confront in our lives. Films and theater, however, often deal with out-of-the-ordinary situations. Actors must develop the skill required to plunge themselves into these strange waters with total believability. A problem that amateurs often experience is that they find these unusual circumstances ridiculous and do not know how to put themselves in the characters' circumstances. However, an actor must learn how to throw himself into the most bizarre situation and still remain truthful within its off-beat context.

Many of these improvisations, which are situations rife with opportunities for subtext, confrontation, conflict, discovery, and so on, provide an exciting synthesis of elements dealt with in previous chapters.

UNUSUAL CIRCUMSTANCES

List of Situations

_____ **1** _____

Source: *A Kind of Alaska*, a play by Harold Pinter

Characters: One male and one female: Deborah, a woman in her mid-forties, and Dr. Hornby, her physician, a man in his fifties

Place: A hospital room

Background: At the age of sixteen, Deborah fell prey to a type of sleeping sickness that has kept her in a comatose state for twenty-nine years. She has just been injected with a recently discovered cure, a drug called L-dopa. Dr. Hornby has administered the drug and is waiting for her to awaken. He has been her doctor all these years and has gradually fallen in love with her. He is married to the afflicted woman's sister, Pauline. His obsession with Deborah has taken its toll on his marriage.

Situation: After twenty-nine years of "sleep," Deborah awakens. It was her sixteenth birthday when she succumbed to sleeping sickness. Her parents are no longer alive, but she is unaware of this. Dr. Hornby must inform her that she is no longer sixteen but is now a grown woman of forty-five.

Comments: The actress playing Deborah must remember that in her mind she is sixteen—a pretty, young, flirtatious girl still living with her parents. To her this seems like the day after her birthday party. The actress must also deal with the physical aspects of not having used her body or voice for twenty-nine years. It is important to be very specific about the party, who was there, the gifts, the food, and so on. She knew Dr. Hornby before, but as a young man.

This is also a big moment for Dr. Hornby because he has waited twenty-nine years for Deborah to regain consciousness. He has been at her bedside every day. He has probably fantasized a great deal about this woman.

The source material on which Pinter based his play was *Awakenings*, by Dr. Oliver Sacks, which also formed the basis for the film of the same title.

2

Source: *Blue Velvet*, a film by David Lynch

Characters: Two males and one female: Frank Booth, a sexually unbalanced, violently disturbed man in his fifties; Jeffrey Beaumont, a young and very inquisitive man in his early twenties; and Dorothy Vallens, an attractive and mysterious lounge singer in her thirties. (Note: It is possible to do this improvisation excluding the character of Frank Booth.)

Place: Dorothy's apartment

Background: Jeffrey Beaumont, a young man home on vacation from a university, was walking in a field one day and found a severed human ear lying in the grass. Some amateur detective work on his part eventually led him to the apartment of a woman named Dorothy Vallens, who works as a lounge singer in a local nightclub. (The actor playing Jeffrey may choose to ignore the above reasons for his being in Dorothy's apartment and invent his own.) Dorothy allows Frank to be abusive to her because he is holding her husband and daughter captive. The actress may need this information to motivate the role she plays with Frank, or she may choose her own reasons.

Situation: Jeffrey is in Dorothy's apartment, looking around for possible clues. Suddenly he hears approaching footsteps and a key in the lock. Quickly he hides himself in a closet, where he watches secretly through the wooden slats in the door. He sees Dorothy arrive and begin to undress. She puts on a bathrobe. At this point, there is a knock on her door. She opens the door and lets Frank Booth into her apartment. Booth is older than Dorothy and seems to be a tough customer. As it turns out, that is an understatement. He engages Dorothy in a bizarre and frightening ritual of sexual humiliation. During the course of this ritual he hits Dorothy, calls her names, chews on her clothes, makes baby sounds, and eventually rapes her. There are many ways to be abusive and the actor can invent his own; those cited above are suggestions. At the conclusion of the ritual (throughout which he remains clothed) Booth exits from the apartment, leaving behind a shattered, traumatized Dorothy. As she begins to pull herself back together, she hears a noise in her closet. Moving cautiously and grabbing a knife, she goes to the closet and yanks open the door, discovering Jeffrey. He has seen everything that has happened and has now been caught red-handed. Pointing the knife at Jeffrey, she orders him to disrobe. Her decision to do this comes about gradually.

Comments: The actor need not disrobe entirely but at least to the point of discomfort. The scene is about degradation, which cannot be avoided. The actress playing Dorothy should take into account that Dorothy is hardly the average girl-next-door; therefore, she would not be likely to react in the expected manner to finding a young man hiding in her closet. She can be inventive about how she humiliates Jeffrey for his indiscretion. It is essential that the actor playing Jeffrey not get caught up in the story of why he is in Dorothy's apartment. The scene is not about his detective work or Dorothy's reasons for participating in the bizarre behavior with Frank; it is about what happens between these two people at this moment. The actor playing Jeffrey must remember that she has a knife on him, so he is in her power. If a knife is not available, another "weapon" can be used.

The actor playing Frank will have to do intensive preparation concerning his unique relationship with Dorothy. There is danger in this scene, and the actors must tap into the part of themselves that would lead them away from "safe" choices. At the same time, of course, the actors must trust that they will not hurt each other. It is recommended that this improvisation be given to actors of a mature nature, and preferably to those who have not seen the film.

Special properties: a stage knife and a bathrobe or coat.

———— **3** ————

Source: *The Entity,* a film by Sidney J. Furie, screenplay by Frank DeFelitta from his book, based on an actual case study done by UCLA's parapsychology department (Situation #2)

Characters: One male and one female: Carla Moran, the victim of a violent unknown force, and her fiancé, Phil

Place: Carla's kitchen

Background: Carla is living with her three children, two young girls and a boy of about seventeen. Phil, her fiancé, has been out of town on business. She has been experiencing rape and other physical abuse by some powerful unseen force. After these attacks, her body was covered with scratches and bruises. She then went to a psychiatrist. But she was not hallucinating; this was really happening to her. At first, she was alone when the attacks came, but eventually she was attacked when her children were present. This "force" followed her from her house and attacked her while driving, nearly causing a fatal accident. It even attacked her while she was staying at a friend's house, severely damaging the place. Eventually, scientists come to Carla's home and observe the phenomenon.

Situation: Phil, who has just returned, finds her in an anguished state. She tries to explain to him that she is being repeatedly raped by the unseen force. Needless to say, this is neither easy for her to explain nor easy for him to accept.

Comments: The actress must keep in mind the fact that the character is not mentally deranged. This is something that is actually happening to her, and she is terrified. The actor must realize that he loves Carla very much, and although what he hears is nearly impossible to believe, he knows that Carla is a very strong, stable woman, who is not given to wild flights of imagination.

See *The Entity*, #1, page 194.

_____ 4 _____

Source: *Foolish Love*, a film by George Panousopoulos, screenplay by Panousopoulos, Phillpos Drakonpaidis, and Petros Papsopoulos

Characters: One male and one female: a young astronomer and a middle-aged woman who lives across the way from his apartment

Place: The astronomer's apartment

Background: Through his telescope, an astronomer has been watching the window across the way from his apartment. Originally, he was observing a pretty young girl, but in the process he became more intrigued by her mother. He has watched her making love with her husband many times and sees that it is not satisfactory. He has begun calling her on the phone but hangs up whenever she answers. This time he calls her and identifies himself. He tells her that he has been watching her for months, even supplying her with some of the details of her life.

Situation: The woman across the way makes a visit to the voyeur. She finds his telescope, looks through it, and realizes that he truly could have seen every intimate detail of her life.

Comments: The actors should have no preconceived idea of what this meeting will be like. There are any number of possible ways this relationship could develop. The actress must keep in mind that this is a respectable woman and that it took some courage for her to knock on the door of the young man's apartment. The actor must decide why his character became so intrigued by this woman's life. He has spent a lot of time observing her.

5

Source: *Gotcha*, a teleplay by Ray Bradbury, based on his short story

Characters: One male and one female: a romantically linked couple of any age beyond adolescence

Place: A hotel or motel room—or a bedroom in either character's home

Background: These two people have only recently fallen in love, and neither knows much about the other.

Situation: The woman has suggested to her partner that they play a game called Gotcha. The rules require that he agree to lie on the bed and not make a sound or move off the bed for a set period of time—let's say, fifteen minutes. She then lights some candles and turns off the lights. When this is done, she stands at the foot of the bed and begins the game by slowly sinking down out of sight beyond the edge of the bed. Then, for the ensuing period of the game, she begins to unnerve him by moving, unseen by him, about the room and around the bed, displacing objects, running her fingers like a spider over the edge of the bed or across furniture and then drawing them out of sight again, making little sounds and almost inaudible whispers. At a certain point during this, he begins to protest, not enjoying the game at all. At first, he hears her telling him "shhh," but after a couple of minutes she no longer says anything. It is clear that he is becoming very frightened by this "game" and wants her to stop. But he gets no response. Finally, he lapses into uneasy silence. Then, after a long period of silence, she leaps up onto the bed and pounces down upon him, looking almost possessed or deranged, and screams into his face the single word: "Gotcha!" He, to say the least, is not amused. (How he reacts can be left up to the actor.)

Seeing his distress, she is immediately remorseful and tries to apologize. It becomes obvious, however, that during the ensuing dialogue there is a tension between them that was not present before. On a deeper level, the actor playing the victim of this game must convey that this single event has somehow made it impossible for him to continue loving her in the same way. The interaction between them must convey that their relationship is ultimately doomed.

Comments: This improvisation may be done in reverse as well, with the man suggesting the "game" and the woman being the uneasy "victim," but in most cases this would tend to be a more conventional, and therefore less interesting, choice. This improvisation will not work unless the actors take the game very seriously. He may make a joke out of it at first, but he is willing to go along with it because he loves her. Their relationship is relatively new, and he doesn't want to do anything to jeopardize it. The whole relationship was initially founded on game-playing. They met at a costume ball, where he was dressed as Laurel and she as Hardy. This is what brought them together. There has been a trust established between them.

The actor must allow himself to become truly scared. A lot of his fear comes not from what she does but from his imagination. As he lies there in the semidarkness, he conjures up things stimulated by her actions. Much of what happens is triggered by his own childhood fears. It is best for the actor to do this scene with his eyes open but in the semidark. Eventually, the actress must pounce on him with a loud noise, which should come unexpectedly. The important thing is that the actor allow himself to become truly scared. He cannot snap back when she says "Gotcha!" Their relationship has been greatly altered and damaged.

──────── 6 ────────

Source: *The Hairdresser,* an original situation

Characters: One male and one female: an actor and a hairdresser

Place: A hair salon

Background: The actor had at one time mentioned to his hairdresser his need for custom-made quality human-hair wigs and mustaches for an upcoming role in a classical drama. Eager to please, she said that she would be able to help him in this regard, since, as a hairdresser, she had connections with people who did this type of work. Upon his next visit, she informed the actor that the hairpieces had already been ordered and would soon be completed, all at no charge. The actor is astonished and grateful, knowing how costly such work can be. But as he comes to suspect after a while, the hairpieces are, in fact, entirely nonexistent. The hairdresser is clearly a pathological liar who is willing to go to any absurd length to please a customer, regardless of the verbal logistics required to stall her unwitting victims or to extricate herself from the corners she has painted herself into. Each time the actor comes to the hairdresser to pick up the promised hairpieces, the hairdresser has an increasingly elaborate and convoluted excuse as to why the pieces are not yet in her possession.

Situation: The actor and the hairdresser have had several meetings before this one. At this point, the actor has just come from a wig shop she had directed him to, telling him that the hairpieces had been sent there for styling and that he was expected by the shop owner for a fitting. The actor has now confirmed what he suspected—that he was not expected for the said appointment and that the owner of the shop has heard nothing about the hairpieces. The actor has just returned to the hairdresser's salon to confront her with this knowledge.

Comments: Since the actor desperately needs the hairpieces for an upcoming performance, he must actively pursue the matter. The actor playing the hairdresser must find, of course, an inner justification for her monumental and convoluted lies. She must truly believe that what she is doing is motivated by having her victim's best interests at heart. Liars of this kind are masters at it because they do it all the time. They can cover up anything. However, the hairdresser might slip up for a moment, get caught in her lie, and then make a recovery. She will always find an excuse, however, no matter how improbable.

The improvisation might be handled as a series of scenes based on this situation and then lead up to the final confrontation described above. In each scene, the actress playing the hairdresser must find a new explanation for the unavailability of the elusive hairpieces, even though she may have told the actor by telephone just moments before that she indeed had them in her possession.

7

Source: *The Missing Clothes,* an original situation

Characters: Two males and one female: an American girl and her boyfriend, who is Mexican, both in their teens, and an old Mayan hermit

Place: A stream in the jungle just outside a small Mexican village

Background: This stream is in a remote village that sticks to old traditions. A girl and a boy, who are not supposed to go out together unchaperoned, sneak off in the middle of the day and swim naked in the stream.

Situation: They have just emerged from their swim to find that their clothes have been washed away by the current. They are in quite a predicament because not only did they sneak off together, which is forbidden, but they also now have no clothes. Upon making this discovery, they encounter a hermit who speaks no English or Spanish, only Mayan, and they must communicate their dilemma to him.

Comments: The actors must keep in mind the seriousness of these cultural traditions. The American girl is living in this country so she is obligated to play by the rules. Their action is equivalent to committing a crime and they will be in real trouble—not only with their parents, but with the whole village as well. This may be humorous to the audience but it is devastating for these two people. Because they will most likely be clothed during this improvisation, the actors will have to call upon their sense memory of nakedness. The actor playing the hermit must also see these people as nude. The actors cannot communicate using spoken language so they have to find other means. The girl and the boy can understand each other to some extent, but their communication is also limited. The actor playing the hermit can speak in gibberish. The actor playing the Mexican boy can also speak in gibberish if he doesn't know Spanish.

_____ 8 _____

Source: *Salomé*, a play by Oscar Wilde

Characters: One male and one female: Salomé, King Herod's stepdaughter, and King Herod

Place: King Herod's palace

Background: Salomé is King Herod's stepdaughter; her mother, Herodias, is his queen. John the Baptist calls Salomé's mother an adulterous whore because she divorced Herod's brother and married Herod. Herod has John imprisoned for his slanderous tongue. Salomé has fallen passionately in love with John, who rejects her. Herod tells Salomé that if she dances for him, he will give her anything she wants, including half his kingdom. He is a man of his word and never breaks an oath. Salomé's mother, Herodias, begs her not to dance for Herod. She does not want her daughter to be looked at in this lascivious manner by her stepfather. Salomé disobeys her mother and dances the Dance of the Seven Veils for him.

Situation: Salomé has just finished the dance for Herod, and he asks her what her wish is. She requests the head of John the Baptist be brought to her on a silver platter. During John's imprisonment, Herod has become rather fond of him. Herod begs Salomé to ask for anything else. A woman scorned, she is unrelenting.

Comments: The actors should not play this in any particular time period in terms of style. The actor playing Herod must understand that an oath is not to be broken. He does everything he can to talk Salomé out of this horrible request. In Oscar Wilde's play (and in the Bible) Herod grants Salomé her wish. However, in Wilde's version, when Herod sees the head, he orders Salomé killed.

This situation may be difficult for the actors to believe, but a woman scorned is a universal and timeless theme. If this improvisation should take a humorous twist, that's fine.

_____ 9 _____

Source: *The Ultimate Solution of Grace Quigley*, a film by Anthony Harvey, screenplay by A. Martin Zweiback

Characters: One male and one female: Grace Quigley, a woman in her seventies, and Seymour Flint, a young hit man

Place: Seymour's apartment

Background: Grace Quigley has seen this man commit a murder and knows he is a paid killer. She finds out where he lives and pays him a visit. He has been considering retiring from the business because he really hates killing people.

Situation: Grace comes to Seymour's apartment and announces to him that she has seen him commit a murder. She proceeds to make a bargain with him—that she will not go to the police if he kills someone for her. She reveals to him that the person she wants him to kill is herself. She doesn't want to live anymore.

Comments: It is one thing to be a paid killer and another to have a sweet old lady ask you to kill her. The young man really doesn't want to do it, but the dilemma is that she could turn him in. The actress must decide exactly why she doesn't want to go on living. It is best not to pick something like a fatal disease because then there is no way out. It should be a psychologically motivated reason, something she could conceivably change her mind about if her feelings changed.

———— 10 ————

Source: *Year of the Hare*, a film by Risto Jarva, screenplay by Jarva and Kulleryot Kukkasjaryi based on a novel by Paasilinna

Characters: One male and one female: husband and wife

Place: Their apartment in Helsinki

Background: The husband worked for a large advertising corporation in Helsinki. One weekend he went on a business trip with a colleague. While he was driving in the country at night, the car hit something. Getting out to investigate, they found an injured hare. Its leg was broken. The driver, having no concern for the animal, checked his car for damages and prepared to leave. Meanwhile, the husband disappeared into the woods to nurse the wounded hare. His colleague called for him but, getting no response, became impatient and continued on his journey alone.

    The husband lived in the woods, caring for the animal for several weeks. Its leg healed, but then it became ill. This forced him to take the hare to a veterinarian in Helsinki. During his time in the woods he found a way of letting his wife know that he was all right, but he gave her no specific information. On his return trip from the veterinarian, he has now decided to visit her.

Situation: His wife is surprised to see him. He attempts to explain to her his decision to live in the woods and care for the hare. She brings to his attention the fact that since he stopped working, none of their bills have been paid. Naturally, she would like him to return home. His plan is to go back to the woods as soon as the hare is cured by the veterinarian.

Comments: The important factor here for the actor playing the husband is to establish for himself his reasons for this drastic change of life-style. He was heavily entrenched in the advertising business. He must decide why he walked out of his job and out of his marriage. Both actors must examine their relationship as husband and wife. The actress should know what these past few weeks have been like for her. Although the actor's objective is to return to the woods, the improvisation may take another turn.

———— 11 ————

Source: *Berlin Alexanderplatz*, a film by Rainer Werner Fassbinder, based on the novel by Alfred Doblin

Characters: Two females: close friends—a woman in her early twenties and a woman in her thirties

Place: The older woman's apartment

Background: The younger woman is very much in love with her husband, but she is unable to give him a child. She knows it would mean a great deal to him to have one.

Situation: She asks her friend to have intercourse with her husband and bear a child for them. This is her best friend, and she wants the child to be conceived by two people whom she loves.

Comments: The relationship between these two women must be clearly established. They are dear friends, but this is not an easy request. It brings with it a grave responsibility.

12

Source: *Stevie Wants to Play the Blues*, a play by Eduardo Machado

Characters: Two females: Stevie Herman, a young woman posing as a man, and Ruth Scott, a singer with a jazz group

Place: A nightclub after hours

Background: This play is based on the true story of a successful female jazz piano player, who posed as a man throughout her adult life in order to be allowed to perform professionally. The play takes place just after World War II, when women could participate in the jazz world as singers but could not play an instrument publicly. Stevie, who is actually a girl, auditioned for this job posing as a man and was hired. The female singer, Ruth Scott, has fallen in love with Stevie, thinking she is a man. It is probably the gentleness that attracted her because she'd been treated pretty roughly by most of the men in her life. Stevie cannot reveal her identity because she will lose her job. Her job is more important to her than anything. She is totally devoted to being a piano player.

Situation: It is late evening and the other musicians have gone home for the night, leaving Stevie and Ruth alone. Ruth, thinking Stevie is male, propositions her. Stevie is very fond of Ruth and doesn't want to hurt her, but her whole career is at stake if she reveals her identity.

Comments: In the actual play, Stevie does eventually confess her true identity to Ruth. This decision should be left up to the actors but not decided beforehand. This is a challenging role for the actress playing Stevie because she must attempt some masculine mannerisms. But it is important that she not fall into masculine clichés. Remember, it is her gentleness that attracts Ruth. It is advised that the actress playing Stevie be dressed as much like a man as possible. She wouldn't be wearing a dress, obviously.

_____ **13** _____

Source: *A Death in Canaan,* a film for televison by Tony Richardson, teleplay by Thomas Thompson and Spencer Eastman, based on the book by Joan Barthel

Characters: Two males: a middle-aged policeman who is a polygraph specialist, and Peter Reilly, a seventeen-year-old boy

Place: The interrogation room of a police station in the small New England town of Canaan, Connecticut

Background: Peter has been accused of the brutal murder of his mother. Peter has never had a father. His mother told him that she had been raped at one time and that he was the product of that violation. Peter is easily influenced by male authority figures; therefore, he finds himself unconsciously trying to please the officer who is interrogating him.

His relationship with his mother, though he loved her very much, had often been a stormy one. For some years she had been a heavy drinker, and she became known as one of the town characters. She and Peter had become used to living in relative poverty.

Peter's main activity outside of school has been his interest in rock music, principally through playing the guitar in a local band. At the time of his mother's murder, he was at band practice.

Situation: In this interrogation scene, Peter is practically in a state of shock. He has been kept without sleep for some time, and his barriers of defense are down. Peter is rather naïve regarding his right to the presence of an attorney, and he has not requested one. During the course of the interrogation, the officer succeeds in making Peter believe that he actually committed the murder. He convinces Peter that he cannot remember having done it because the horror of the crime caused him to blank it out of his memory. The interrogating officer tries to establish a connection between a straight-razor, which Peter used on model airplanes, and some of the wounds found on the body.

Comments: The actor playing the interrogating officer must understand that there is absolutely no direct physical evidence tying Peter to the murder. The police simply have no other suspect at this time. They are grasping at straws and trying to conclude the case as speedily as possible. Also, being aware of the boy's past, the officer consciously manipulates the boy by playing upon his need for a father figure. The actor playing the interrogator must come across as sincere if he is to build up a trust with Peter. But at the same time, he has to be a master of intimidation. The actor must be warned not to fall into the trap of playing the stereotyped cool professional. He should find his own personal reasons for getting Peter to confess.

The actor playing Peter must be acutely aware of the confusion and emotional trauma the boy has recently undergone; also, he must take into account his lack of sleep.

14

Source: *K-2*, a play by Michael McClure

Characters: Two males: mountain climbers and close friends

Place: The top of a high mountain, designated K-2

Background: The two men have reached a small ledge partway up the towering rock face of K-2. One of them has badly injured his leg, and is unable to make the return trip down the mountain.

Situation: The injured party must convince his friend to return alone, his argument being that there is no way to get help and no point in both of them dying. Also, he has messages that he would like delivered to his family. The able-bodied man does not want it on his conscience that he left a friend to die.

Comments: It is important that the relationship between these two men be well established. They have a history together, which binds them. This is what makes it a particularly difficult decision for the person leaving his friend behind. The actors must accept that the injured climber cannot be saved. It is a long way down the mountain, and by the time the able climber reaches the bottom, his friend will probably be dead.

15

Source: *Manhunter*, a film by Michael Mann, based on the novel *Red Dragon* by Thomas Harris

Characters: Two males: Freddy Lounds, a journalist with *The Tattler*—a supermarket tabloid; Francis Dolarhyde, a psychopathic killer

Place: The living room of Francis Dolarhyde's home, an isolated house in the country

Background: Freddy Lounds has been writing lurid articles on a series of gruesome serial killings in which entire families have been brutally slaughtered. He has called the killer an "animal" in his articles and has questioned his sexuality. Lounds was surprised by the killer in the underground garage of the *Tattler* office building, chloroformed, and transported to the killer's house. The killer, Francis Dolarhyde, is a tormented, deeply disturbed man, who believes that his victims are sacrifices who contribute to his "great becoming"—a process of imagined transformation in which he will change into a powerful godlike being known as the Red Dragon. The killer refers to himself by this name and wants all people to tremble at his feet in a mixture of awe, terror, and adoration.

Situation: Freddy Lounds regains consciousness in the killer's living room. He is blindfolded and has been strapped into a chair so that he is unable to move. The killer speaks to him, revealing to Lounds what has happened and where he is. He then removes his blindfold. Lounds sees that the upper half of Dolarhyde's face is concealed by a nylon stocking, making him unrecognizable. Lounds knows that if he sees the killer's actual face, it means he will not be allowed to live. His extreme terror makes him almost childlike, in marked contrast to his usually abrasive manner. The killer shows slides of his victims to Lounds, forcing him to watch the frightful images of his crimes as they were being committed. He then forces Lounds to read a prepared speech into a pocket tape-recorder—a message to the police warning them of the power and terrible wrath of the Red Dragon. Lounds knows he is almost certain to be the next victim, but he doesn't want to accept the terrible reality of this.

Comments: This improvisation can be left open-ended or carried through to some conclusion. This scene in the film *Manhunter* ends with an act of sadistic violence, which is implied rather than explicitly shown. In the book, a nonvisual medium, the violence is more graphic. It should be left up to the taste of the individual actors in this improvisation how far they wish to take the situation, and the two actors should agree on this. The actor playing Dolarhyde may write the speech beforehand. He must have his face covered in some way and Lounds must be blindfolded at first. The actors will have to use their imagination for the slides. The actor playing the killer should enjoy his ability to create terror in his victim.

_____ **16** _____

Source: *The Meeting Between Charles de Gaulle and Bozo the Clown,* an original real-life situation

Characters: Two males: Charles de Gaulle, the president of France, and Bozo the Clown

Place: Charles de Gaulle's office in Paris

Background: Larry Harmon, the actor famed for creating Bozo the Clown, has recently received an unexpected (to say the least) phone call from Charles de Gaulle, asking him to meet with de Gaulle in France to discuss the children of the world. The only catch is that Harmon must come to the meeting in full costume and character as Bozo the Clown.

Situation: The actors can pretty much take this wherever they want to go with it, but they must stay in character no matter what happens or what is discussed. This situation comprises the meeting between de Gaulle and Bozo. De Gaulle is a big fan of Bozo's and expresses an almost childlike delight in his company, despite the seriousness of some of the issues discussed.

Comments: If the actors are familiar with either of these characters, naturally it would help. De Gaulle, of course, speaks with a heavy French accent, addressing his visitor as Monsieur Bozo, and Bozo uses specific phrases such as "Whoa, Nelly!" If he prefers, the actor playing de Gaulle may pick another political figure, with whom he is more familiar. The actor playing Bozo may play a generic clown. The humor in this real-life situation comes from these two men attempting to discuss serious issues while one is acting like a clown and the other like a child.

Though the pretext of this meeting was ostensibly to discuss the children of the world, de Gaulle's actual motivation may have been to recapture a bit of his childhood, thus relieving some of the enormous strain of his job. Bozo, sensing this, does his best to make de Gaulle laugh and forget his troubles for a while. This is quite a challenge for the actor playing Bozo.

____ 17 ____

Source: *Strongman's Weak Child*, a play by Israel Horovitz
Characters: Two males: Franny and Fast Eddie, both weight lifters
Place: Franny's garage, Gloucester, Massachusetts. The garage contains weight-lifting equipment.
Background: Men come to this garage to do body building every day. Franny is the trainer. Gloucester, which used to be an important fishing port, is suffering from severe

economic change. As a result, these men are out of jobs. Thus, body building has become their main focus. For Fast Eddie, body building is his ticket out of Gloucester, his avenue of escape from a disappointing life. For Franny, it is an arcane discipline that he can master. For all the men, this gym has become hearth and home. Franny has a young daughter, Dede, who has leukemia. Fast Eddie is her real father. He deserted Evvie, Franny's wife, years ago, when he realized she was pregnant. Franny has been going to the hospital to give bone marrow to his daughter. This is a painful process that saps one's strength. However, the transplant has not been working because the bone marrow must be donated by the person's own flesh and blood, in this case Eddie.

Situation: Franny approaches Eddie, Dede's real father, and asks him to donate his bone marrow. For someone like Eddie, this is a rough request. Body building is his whole life, and the process of extracting bone marrow is debilitating.

Comments: The outcome of this situation can be left open-ended for the actors. Franny has known all these years that Eddie was the real father, but it was never discussed openly. The actor playing Eddie can decide what his feelings are, but Dede is his flesh and blood. Whatever he decides, it is not an easy decision. The characters must discover the true test of strength, which has nothing to do with how much iron one can lift. It would be a good activity for the actors to be working out during this confrontation.

——————— **18** ———————

Source: *Twin Peaks*, a TV series created by David Lynch and Mark Frost

Characters: Two males: special agent Cooper, a young FBI man in his late twenties; a room-service waiter in his late seventies or early eighties

Place: Cooper's room in the Great Northern Hotel in the small town of Twin Peaks

Background: Special agent Cooper has been dispatched to Twin Peaks to solve the brutal murder of a beautiful high school cheerleader named Laura Palmer. He has uncovered many bizarre clues but has not yet found the killer. Events and people in the town have become increasingly weird since Cooper's arrival in Twin Peaks.

Situation: Special agent Cooper has just been shot at point-blank range by an unknown assailant. Cooper now lies on his back, his white shirt soaked with blood. Not his *own* blood, however, but that of a bloated wood tick that had fastened itself to Cooper's bulletproof vest. But to any outside party, Cooper would seem to be in dire need of emergency medical care. As the improvisation begins, a decrepit room-service waiter comes into the room bearing a glass of milk on a tray. The man's immediate concern is with where Agent Cooper would like him to put the milk. At the sight of Cooper on the floor seemingly injured, he responds in no expected way. As it happens, Cooper *does* have a few broken ribs owing to the impact of the bullets on the vest, and he is unable to get up. He requests assistance from the room-service man, but the man just doesn't seem to "get it." He smiles amiably and begins to talk about inconsequential things. He tells Cooper: "I've heard about you!" He makes a major production of hanging up the telephone, which is off the hook. However, he makes no effort to call for assistance. Through his dazed discomfort, Cooper tries to reach the man and get him to help.

Comments: In the actual television show, Agent Cooper's requests for help were very understated, and the waiter finally left the room without helping at all. But in order for the improvisation to have some kind of tension, the actor playing Cooper must not give up too easily in his efforts to reach the slow and addled mind of the waiter. Though Cooper is not fatally wounded, he *is* in a great deal of discomfort.

————— **19** —————

Source: *Audrey Rose,* a film by Robert Wise, screenplay by Frank DeFelitta, based on his novel (Situation #1)

Characters: Two males and one female: Bill and Janice Templeton, and Elliot Hoover, a middle-aged man, whom they haven't met before

Place: A restaurant in New York City

Background: Mr. Hoover makes an appointment to meet the parents of Ivy Templeton, a ten-year-old girl, who is deeply troubled by nightmares. Mr. Hoover has been hanging around Ivy's school, watching her. The parents have agreed to meet him because they are afraid for Ivy, and they hope to convince him to leave her alone.

Situation: Mr. Hoover tells the Templetons that their daughter, Ivy, is really his daughter, Audrey Rose. He explains to them that Audrey Rose, along with his wife, was killed in an automobile accident exactly ten years ago. He had talked with a clairvoyant who told him that his daughter was not dead. After her death, she had returned in another body. He didn't believe any of this

until a year later, when he encountered another clairvoyant, who told him the same story. Mr. Hoover called
up every hospital in New York City to find out what
babies were born at the exact moment of his daughter's
death. In this way, he had located Ivy. He is now convinced that Ivy is his reincarnated daughter. All he requests of the parents is that they let him see Ivy
occasionally.

Comments: This improvisation works well if the only information given to the actors playing Bill and Janice Templeton is that their daughter is troubled, and that a man
named Mr. Hoover has been hanging around her school
and insists on meeting with them. In her dreams, Ivy
gets hysterical from memories of an automobile accident.
Her parents, having no knowledge of any such accident,
assume that she has a mental disorder. The actors may
deal with this in any way they like; obviously it is a
difficult story to accept. They may or may not. It is Mr.
Hoover's problem to convince them.

The actor playing Mr. Hoover must not treat him as
a crazy person. He is a normal man, the last person to
believe this kind of "nonsense," and yet he is convinced
that Ivy is really Audrey.

_____ **20** _____

Source: *Audrey Rose*, a film by Robert Wise, screenplay
by Frank DeFelitta, based on his novel (Situation #2)

Characters: Three males and two females: Elliot Hoover,
a middle-aged man; Bill and Janice Templeton; their ten-
year-old daughter, Ivy Templeton; and their lawyer

Place: The living room of Mr. and Mrs. Templeton's New
York apartment; later, Ivy's bedroom

Background: (See preceding Situation #1.) The parents have agreed to let Mr. Hoover come to their home to see their daughter, but under false pretenses. They have hired a lawyer to record Mr. Hoover's visit in order to use it as evidence against him. They want to put an end to his phone calls and his visits to Ivy's school. Mr. Hoover is unaware of their plans.

Situation: Mr. Hoover arrives at the apartment and is surprised to see it decorated just as the clairvoyant had described it. When he mentions the name Audrey Rose, there is a scream from Ivy's bedroom. The parents rush into her room and see Ivy standing at the window, her hands touching the glass frantically and then pulling away as though the glass were very hot. Her hands are blistering. Mr. Hoover then says again and again: "Audrey Rose, it's all right, I'm here. It's Da Da." Recognizing his voice, she slowly calms down and then goes to Mr. Hoover, collapsing in his arms crying. The parents and the lawyer all witness this. Again, how they react is up to the actors at that moment. Mr. Hoover proceeds to tell them exactly how his daughter died—trapped inside a burning car.

Comments: As mentioned in Situation #1, these are all normal people, who do not particularly believe in supernatural events. However, they see before them some strange happenings that they cannot ignore or explain away. The parents are very worried about their daughter's troubled state and have not been able to help her. Although they have doubts about Mr. Hoover, this is the first time they've ever seen anybody calm Ivy down during one of her hysterical fits.

_____ **21** _____

Source: *Las Bicicletas Son para el Verano* (*Bicycles Are for the Summer*), a film by Jaime Chavarri, screenplay by Salvador Maldonado

Characters: A family group: mother, father, daughters, sons; there must be one daughter with a young child

Place: The dinner table in the apartment of a family in Madrid during the Spanish Civil War

Background: During the Spanish Civil War (1936–39) there was a widespread food shortage. Most of the time the average family had only lentils to eat, and very few of those. The daughter's husband is killed in action, and she is left with an infant. She finds that because of her own malnutrition, she has gone dry and has no milk for her baby.

Situation: The mother calls the family together for a meeting because the lentils are disappearing. She believes the mother-in-law is stealing them. Eventually, the truth emerges that each member of the family has been sneaking spoonfuls. This is a difficult confession to make because they're taking food out of loved ones' mouths.

Comments: This improvisation might turn out to be humorous; if it goes in that direction, the actors should flow with it. It does not have to take place during the Spanish Civil War. It can be any situation in which a family does not have enough to eat, and there is no more food available. The actors must use their imaginations to experience what this situation must be like. Certainly everybody can relate to hunger pangs.

———————— 22 ————————

Source: *The Child Buyer,* a novel by John Hersey

Characters: Two males and one female: Wissey Jones, a
middle-aged man, representing the United Lymphomiloid Corporation; a couple (husband and wife) in their
late thirties to early fifties

Place: The home of the couple

Background: The United Lymphomiloid Corporation is de-
veloping a very important secret project involving national defense. For this project, the company needs a
number of children possessing genius-level IQ's. Money
is no object. With the company's nearly limitless financial
resources at his disposal, their representative, Wissey
Jones, is sent to several small Middle American towns
to actually buy brilliant children for the corporation. The
project involves altering the children surgically—removing their organs of sight, hearing, smell, etc., removing their limbs, and then mentally conditioning them
to become human thinking machines. This couple has a
preadolescent child (boy or girl) with a genius IQ. The
child is about ten years old.

Situation: Wissey Jones tries to convince the husband and
wife to sell him their child. When they react unfavorably
to this proposal, he begins to use various approaches to
persuade them. He preys upon their patriotism by stress-
ing the vital national importance of the project. When
this approach begins to gain some ground, the parents
become more inquisitive, wanting to know the exact nature of what will be done with and to their child. At this
point, Jones must detail, in a very careful manner, the
process of reconditioning described above (in Background). When the parents, understandably, react with

some degree of horror, Jones moves into his final area of persuasion—money. It is important to note here that the parents have a low income and are hurting financially, a point that Wissey Jones is acutely aware of. With this in mind, Mephistopheles–like, he begins the process of breaking down the parents' objections through the temptation of larger and larger sums of money, as well as other material inducements, such as a new car, a new home, medical benefits, paid vacations, and so on. What the end result of this process will be, however, can be left up to the actors.

Comments: Before beginning the improvisation, the actors playing the couple must decide on a background for the child, his or her name, their relationship with the child, some family history, etc. All of these factors will influence their response to Mr. Jones's unusual proposal. Also, they must decide whether they have other children or only this child.

The coach or the actors must set up this improvisation so that it is a difficult decision for the parents to make. For example: They are struggling, poor, and have many children, whom they cannot care for. They are at their wits' end. They may even have some reservations about this particular child, who, perhaps, gives them trouble. However, whatever their feelings may be about the child, this is obviously not an easy choice. There may be conflict between the husband and wife in making this decision.

Note to coach: This improvisation works well if the parents are only given information about their child and know nothing about the man from the corporation so that his proposal takes them completely by surprise.

———— **23** ————

Source: *Devour the Snow*, a play by Abe Polsky, based on true-life historical events

Characters: Four males and one female: Lewis Keseberg, mid- to late thirties, a survivor of the Donner party; his wife, herself a survivor; a man, middle-aged, acting as a judge; and two other survivors (male) of the Donner party, who have made inflammatory accusations against Keseberg.

Place: A meeting hall in Sutter's Fort, northern California. The hall is serving as a courtroom. The year is 1847.

Background: The Donner party was a group of settlers in the mid-1840s who traveled west by covered wagon across America. They became snowbound in the Sierra Nevada mountains, and some had to resort to cannibalism in order to survive. At least forty people in the Donner party died of starvation or froze to death. One of the survivors, Lewis Keseberg, was later accused by two other survivors of taking wanton pleasure in eating human flesh. The men have called him "corpse hunter" and "carrion vulture." They also accused him of being a thief and of causing the deaths of their two young children. Incensed by these accusations, Keseberg sues the men for slander.

Situation: A trial is in progress, at which it will be determined whether the accusations of the two men are justified or not. During the course of this situation, Keseberg is questioned by the judge, who in this instance also serves the function of a prosecuting attorney, insofar as he attempts to extract as much information from Keseberg as possible. However, unlike a prosecuting attorney, he does not come off as hostile, merely dogged in his pursuit of the facts. His questions lead Keseberg to relate his actions and explain his motivations during the snow-bound months in the Sierras. Many of these memories are not easy for him to talk about. Throughout the proceedings, the judge, while helping to guide Keseberg in his recollections, also serves largely to handle the verbal accusations of the two survivors.

Comments: The actor playing Keseberg must decide for himself whether his character is guilty or innocent. He must also have a very clear picture in his mind of the events that occurred in the mountains. Keseberg's wife must also have a definite opinion in her mind concerning her husband's actions. The actors may wish to do some historical research on this subject before attempting this improvisation.

In this situation it is vitally important that the actors do not get overly caught up in trying to simulate the detailed specifics of courtroom procedure. Besides, in the period in which this improvisation takes place, and especially in this particular instance, there were marked differences from the rigorously formal legal procedures of the modern-day courtroom. This is an informal trial, and it is first and foremost about people—not legal jargon.

————— **24** —————

Source: *The Green Card*, an original situation
Characters: Two males and two females: foreigners—father, mother, daughter; and a young American man
Place: An outdoor café in New York City or Los Angeles
Background: The family is sitting at a table near a young

American man. The father wants a green card for his daughter immediately, or she will be shipped back to Mexico (or some other country) and they will be separated. Because she was not born in the United States, she is not a citizen and at age sixteen can be deported. The daughter is a little bit on the fat side, but her father believes that his daughter is a prize.

Situation: The father approaches the young man and makes his proposal. He offers him money in return for marrying his daughter so that she can get her green card.

Comments: The actor playing the American should find some reason why he might consider this proposition. For example, he may be very broke and need money right away. However, this girl is in no shape, manner, or form his type. It must be remembered that when you become involved in an arranged marriage like this, you have to live with the person *for a full year* because the immigration department does check up on it very carefully. The father is desperate not to lose his daughter.

—————— 25 ——————

Source: *Hannah and Her Sisters*, a film by Woody Allen

Characters: Two males and two females: two couples

Place: The living room of one couple

Background: A couple cannot bear children because the husband's sperm is not fertile. Rather than go through artificial insemination with a stranger's sperm, they have decided to ask for their friends' assistance.

Situation: What the couple requests of their friends is that the husband donate his sperm. They tell them that they feel this is the only solution to their problem. Since they are their closest friends, the husband is the only man they know whom they would want to father their child.

Comments: This should not be an easy decision, whatever the outcome. The actors playing the friends should not have any preconceived ideas about their reactions. However, the actress playing the wife cannot choose to be an ultraliberal person, who is open to anything, or there will be no conflict.

——— 26 ———

Source: *Man Disappears from Home,* an original real-life situation

Characters: One male and two females: Father, mother, and daughter

Place: The living room of their home

Background: The father was last seen a week ago when he left for a fishing trip. Nobody has heard from him, and the mother and daughter don't know if he is dead or alive.

Situation: The mother and daughter each blame the other for his disappearance. There are conflicting emotions because they both fear that something terrible may have happened to him but they also fear that he walked out on them. At some point in this improvisation, the father returns, and the mystery is solved—but not the problems within the family.

Comments: The actor playing the father must decide what really happened. Whatever he chooses, it must involve emotional problems within the family.

_____ **27** _____

Source: *Paths of Glory,* a film by Stanley Kubrick, screenplay by Kubrick, Calder Willingham, and Jim Thompson, based on the novel by Humphrey Cobb

Characters: Three males: soldiers

Place: A holding cell, where the men await execution

Background: Three soldiers were falsely accused of cowardice under fire and have been court-martialed—sentenced to execution by a firing squad at dawn the next morning. The man responsible for putting them in their present circumstance is a psychotic general, who sent his men on a suicide mission. He ordered the other men to fire on them because they refused to complete the mission. The men refused to fire on their fellow soldiers. Enraged, he chose three representative men to be executed. The men were chosen randomly by drawing lots. The court-martial was a kangaroo court.

Situation: During their time together awaiting execution, the men share something about themselves and their feelings about death. Each of them must deal with the question, "Why me?"

Comments: Each actor must know his own personal history. Each person can decide what he chooses to reveal about himself. The actors may also make discoveries about themselves under these highly unusual circumstances. This is their last chance to feel or expose anything; it is not a time for superficial conversation. This does not mean that the characters have to be humorless.

_____ 28 _____

Source: _The UFO Incident_, a film for television by Richard
A. Colla, based on the book _The Interrupted Journey_ by
John G. Fuller

Characters: Two males and one female: Barney Hill, a
middle-aged black man; Betty, his wife, a middle-aged
Caucasian woman; and Dr. Benjamin Simon, their psychiatrist

Place: Dr. Simon's office

Background: A couple of years prior to the time of this
scene, Barney and Betty Hill, while driving in the New
Hampshire countryside, sighted a UFO, which had
landed nearby. Both Barney and Betty were abducted
by the beings in the ship and subjected to medical ex-
aminations. They were then made to forget what they
had experienced, but memories of their ordeal began to
surface in their dreams. Being very troubled, not only
by the experiences in the dreams themselves but also
by the fact that each of them was having the same dreams,
they at last decided to seek professional help to deal with
this unique problem.

Situation: During a hypnosis session, both Barney and
Betty reexperience their UFO incident with great emotional immediacy. They relive the terror of having been
brought aboard a spaceship and examined.

Comments: This is based on an actual case. These people
are not crazy. The actors must accept that this really
happened to them. The goal of this improvisation is for
the actors to make this experience so real for themselves
that they can visualize in detail what they went through.
It is important to note that if the actors playing Barney
and Betty do not appear to be under authentic hypnosis,
the scene will very likely take a humorous turn. Under

actual hypnosis, a person does not behave in the clichéd robotlike manner that is sometimes depicted. Though their speech is somewhat slurred at times, their eyes are open; they appear awake and alert, although they are seeing and experiencing things that happened at another time. Dr. Simon must guide them through it. He can make his own decision whether or not he believes this incident actually occurred or is, in reality, some kind of shared fantasy. This will depend entirely on what occurs during the improvisation. In the actual case, Dr. Simon arrived at no concrete conclusion.

UNUSUAL CIRCUMSTANCES

Cross-References

Other improvisations in this book that involve Unusual Circumstances can be found in the following categories:

RELATIONSHIP

One male and one female

Two females

Two males

CONFRONTATION/CONFLICT

One male and one female

Two males

Ensemble

CLIMACTIC MOMENT/DISCOVERY

One male and one female

Two females

Ensemble

SUBTEXT

One male and one female

SPECIAL PROBLEMS

One male and one female

One female

Two females

Two males

7

FANTASY

This chapter focuses on situations that take the actor into the realm of the fantastic, calling upon reserves of imagination and invention not frequently required by more naturalistic material.

In *Alice's Adventures in Wonderland* a very real little girl suddenly finds herself in a wildly fantastic place, surrounded by a myriad of strange and often whimsical beings. But whether an actor plays Alice or one of the fabulous characters she meets in Wonderland, the same rules apply: The actor must find within himself an essential "reality" for his character. No matter how fantastical a character might be, the character must still possess an inner life or it will appear as little more than a caricature.

The make-believe we experience as children, which, to varying degrees, stays with most of us throughout our adult lives, is given free rein in situations such as the ones in this chapter. The very concept of fantasy calls directly to the child in each of us. Rediscovering that child, and the child's capacity to play and pretend, is invaluable—in fact, crucial—to any actor who wishes to avoid the danger of over-intellectualization and pedantic stuffiness. In giving the imagination permission to run wild, the actor is shocked out of possible complacency and energized anew—able to

return to more mundane situations with a revitalized out-
look.

Since the genres of science fiction and horror are both
offshoots of fantasy, they are also included within this
chapter.

FANTASY

List of Situations

1

Source: *Dracula*, a novel by Bram Stoker

Characters: One male and one female: Count Dracula, the king of vampires, handsome, late thirties to mid-forties in appearance, and Lucy Westenra, a beautiful young woman in her early to late twenties

Place: Lucy's bedroom in a large English country house, late at night

Background: Count Dracula has recently moved to Whitby, England, from his ancestral home high in the mountains of Transylvania. He is a vampire hundreds of years old, who is beginning to long for the peace of real death. To maintain his immortality, he must sleep in a coffin by day and drink the blood of living mortals by night. He has become taken with Lucy Westenra, a beautiful young woman living in a country house near Carfax Abbey, his new residence. She recently met Count Dracula and found herself irresistibly, hypnotically, drawn to him.

Situation: By supernatural means, Count Dracula gains access to Lucy's bedroom late at night. Then, with the use of his hypnotic powers, he seduces her, promising her eternal life with him. To seal his promise, he "kisses" her neck, drinking her blood in the process. Then, to complete the ceremony, he cuts his own chest with one of his fingernails and pulls Lucy to him, bidding her to drink his blood as well.

Comments: The actors must find some element of conflict, such as Lucy initially resisting Dracula's advances. Time should be allowed to fully explore the eroticism and tension inherent in this situation. Dracula doesn't necessarily have to be played as melodrama; the actors may find humor in it.

2

Source: *The Japanese Gardener,* an original real-life situation

Characters: One male and one female: husband and wife

Place: The living room of their home

Background: They are a happily married couple. The husband is a successful executive. For the past few days, he has stayed home from work with a bad cold.

Situation: The wife comes home from work and finds her husband cowering in a corner, terrified. He says their Japanese gardener, who is seemingly innocuous, is in reality part of the secret vanguard of an invading army from another planet. He has gathered this knowledge during the past few days. He is convinced of this because of something particular that happened today to cement his suspicions.

Comments: The actor playing the husband must be specific regarding the evidence he's been gathering on the gardener's behavior. (For example: One actor who did this improvisation described having seen the gardener arrange his equipment in a circle—i.e. lawn mower, shears, spade—at which point, a beam of light came down from the sky through which descended a box of what appeared to be geraniums.) It is important to note that the husband is not crazy; he is a perfectly normal person, who has been observing bizarre events. The actor must truly believe what he has seen and try to communicate it so that his wife will listen to him. The actress playing the wife must decide how much, if anything, she is willing to believe and how to deal with it. She may, for example, believe her husband's convictions are a result of his being ill. It is the job of the actor playing the husband to convince her that he is telling the truth.

_____ **3** _____

Source: *Peer Gynt,* a verse drama by Henrik Ibsen

Characters: One male and one female: Peer Gynt and the troll/woman

Place: A forest in the mountains of Norway—mid-1800s

Background: Several years ago Peer Gynt, in a drunken stupor, had sexual relations with an ugly old woman. He is now about to be married to a young girl.

Situation: The ugly old woman appears to him, announcing that she is the woman he bedded a number of years ago. She then tells him she is actually a troll. She claims to have his son and insists that Peer Gynt, being the biological father, take him in. She also tells him that she will always be around, watching everything he does with his new bride. They will never be alone even at the most intimate times. His only alternative is to cancel the impending marriage and go to live with her.

Comments: The actors must realize that this play is set in Norway at a time when people still believed in trolls. Peer Gynt has to accept the fact that this woman means what she says and that he is dealing with an evil element. He also loves his bride-to-be dearly.

_____ **4** _____

Source: *The Purple Rose of Cairo,* a film by Woody Allen (Situation #1)

Characters: One male and two female: Cecilia, a young woman; Tom Baxter, a character from a film; a waitress

Place: A restaurant

Background: Cecilia has a very unhappy marriage; she goes
to the movies to escape. She loves one film in particular,
called *The Purple Rose of Cairo*, which she goes to see
every day. She falls in love with the character of Tom
Baxter, the "great white hunter," a very handsome young
man, very much a gentleman, which her husband is not.
One day she goes to the film after a terrible fight with
her husband. The character in the film looks directly at
her from the screen, remarking that she must really love
this film because she keeps coming back. He then proceeds to walk right off the screen toward her, much to
the consternation of the other characters in the film and
to the astonishment of the audience.

Situation: Cecilia and Tom go to a restaurant to have dinner
and get acquainted. They both discover that they are
unhappy with the monotony of their lives and desperately want a change. Cecilia is relieved to get away from
her abusive husband, and Tom is relieved to escape the
narrow confines and repetition of the film.

Comments: Tom is naturally limited by the film from which
he came—i.e., not knowing how to use money or how
to make love. In his experience, the film always faded
to black after the first kiss. All he knows of life and the
world is what is contained within that film. The actor
will have to know clearly the contents of the film from
which he has emerged. He should choose an actual film
with which he is very familiar. It should, however, be a
film from a different era. Whatever film he decides on,
he is the handsome leading man. He knows nothing
about Cecilia's life, but she knows everything about his
from the film. He is her absolute idol.

It is necessary to use a waitress because it creates the

contrast between Tom's film and real life. There are two
improvisations from this film in the book. This one should
be done first.

————— 5 —————

Source: *The Purple Rose of Cairo*, a film by Woody Allen
(Situation #2)

Characters: Two males and one female: Gil, an actor; Tom,
the actor's character in a film; and Cecilia, Tom's girl
friend offscreen.

Place: A restaurant

Background: (See Background in preceding Situation #1.)
The studio and the other actors in the film are furious
that the picture is losing money because Tom, the main
character, walked out. Cecilia and Tom, the great white
hunter, are in a restaurant, and she has just excused
herself to go to the ladies room. Meanwhile, the actor
Gil (not the character) walks into the restaurant. Returning from the ladies room, Cecilia sees him and starts
talking to him as if she knows him (naturally he looks
exactly like her date Tom). At first, the actor brushes
her off, thinking she is just a fan, but he begins to realize
that she thinks he's the character and probably knows
where the character is. He persuades her to lead him to
the table where his character Tom is sitting.

Situation: The actor confronts his character, pleading with
him to return to the film because he is ruining the actor's
career. The character is enjoying his life, he is in love,
and he doesn't want to reenter the limited existence he
had in the film.

Comments: When the "actor" arrives, the "character" immediately knows who he is. The actors must be clear about the difference between the "character" and the "actor playing the character." It must be remembered that the "character" has a much more limited view of the world, an almost childlike innocence, whereas the "actor" is sophisticated and his professional success is everything to him. The conflict comes from this major difference between the two. Tom and Gil should be played by two actors who are as close in type as possible. It would also be interesting to have the actors reverse roles.

6

Source: *Time After Time*, a film by Nicholas Meyer, based on a story by Karl Alexander and Steve Hayes

Characters: One male and one female: a man and a woman in love. The man is, in reality, H. G. Wells, but he is using a pseudonym.

Place: Outdoors in a secluded area

Background: The man (H. G. Wells) invented a time machine back in the 1890s. Jack the Ripper used this time machine to escape to the future—our present day. Wells has followed him in the time machine because he doesn't want him unleashed again on society. He has had to make the rather difficult adjustment to the late twentieth century but has done a good job of it. In the process, he has met and fallen in love with Amy, a young bank teller. They have reached the point where they are talking about possible marriage.

Situation: Wells has asked Amy to take a walk with him because he has something to tell her. He must make her believe that he is from the nineteenth century. He tries

to make her understand that his mission was to capture
Jack the Ripper and return to his own time. The catch
is that he wants her to come back with him. She is a
very contemporary woman and would have difficulty fitting in with the nineteenth-century view of women. She
loves him very much, however, and doesn't want to give
him up.

Comments: The believability factor is crucial here. The
actor playing H. G. Wells must do something to convince
his intended that he is telling the truth. He may decide,
for example, to take her to the location of his time machine and show her that it is real. If this course is chosen,
then the actress must accept the imaginary machine. She
must decide how to deal with her awesome decision.

——— 7 ———

Source: *Vinegar Tom*, a play by Caryl Churchill

Characters: One male and one female: two lovers—Alice
and a man who claims to be the devil

Place: A mountaintop in England during the time of witch
burnings

Background: Alice is an outcast because she had a child
out of wedlock. People call her a whore and a witch, and
if she stays here, she will probably be burned at the
stake. She has no money and feels trapped.

Situation: Alice has just slept with her lover. He announces
to her that he is the devil. To prove it, he shows her his
cloven hooves. He offers to rescue her from this stifling
atmosphere, reminding her of the impending danger of
being burned at the stake. However, if she agrees to go
with him, he will have total power over her. Alice realizes

that, in essence, she would be selling her soul to the devil if she agrees to go with him.

Comments: The actors must be advised not to attempt any special behavior just because this play takes place in a different time. This was a period when people believed that the devil was amongst them in their daily lives. The actors must believe that this man is the devil. Alice must realize what it means to sell her soul—having absolutely no power over her life ever again and living forever with evil. He has great sexual power over her, which he uses as part of his persuasion. The actress should let the decision be made *during* the improvisation, not before. In this play Caryl Churchill is dealing with the historical repression of women.

8

Source: *The Stepford Wives*, a film by Bryan Forbes, screenplay by William Goldman, based on the novel by Ira Levin

Characters: Two females: two young married women, who are very close friends

Place: The kitchen of one of their homes

Background: Stepford is a company town for families of men who work for a Disney-like corporation. These men have gotten together and systematically replaced their wives with highly sophisticated lifelike robots. These robots are like much more advanced versions of the robots seen currently at Disneyland and Disneyworld.

Situation: In this scene, one of the women, Joanna, discovers that her best friend is now, in fact, one of these robots. Her conversation consists entirely of talk about cooking, Tupperware, laundry, cleaning, and making her husband happy. Joanna is naturally very alarmed by this discovery but tries not to show it, not wishing to join the ranks of these robots herself. She feels that if she were to express her horror openly, the robot might act in a violent fashion and subdue her. She tries to cover her fear as best she can until she can get out of the house.

Comments: If desired, the husband of the robot could enter into the scene at some point, returning home from work. Joanna would then have a new problem to confront, since she would be in danger. The actors should keep in mind that these robots have been created to fulfill their husband's sexist fantasies of the perfect wife. The robots have no lives or ideas of their own and are dedicated entirely to their husbands' domestic and sexual needs. The element of danger for Joanna is important. She is now the only woman in the town who has not become a robot.

———— 9 ————

Source: *The Canterville Ghost*, a short story by Oscar Wilde

Characters: Two males: a little boy (or girl) and a ghost, middle-aged or older

Place: Canterville Chase, a castle haunted by a ghost

Background: A family (mother, father, daughter and/or son) moves into this castle, which has a resident ghost. He is not at all happy about their presence and seeks to frighten them away from his home.

Situation: One day the ghost confronts the little boy, attempting to frighten him but to no avail. The child likes the ghost and finds him amusing, much to the ghost's chagrin and vexation. (In Wilde's version, the child is a fifteen-year-old girl, Virginia, but the age and sex of the child are immaterial in our improvisation.)

Comments: There is a possibility in this improvisation for an interesting relationship to develop between the child and the ghost. (For example, the child may desperately need a friend.) The actors should keep this possibility in mind so that the improvisation need not end merely in a stalemate. In addition, if a child is not available, the character may be played by a younger member of the class.

10

Source: *Something Wicked This Way Comes,* a novel by Ray Bradbury

Characters: Two males: Charles Halloway, a librarian, in his late sixties, and Mr. Dark, a carnival owner, about forty-five in appearance.

Place: A small-town public library late at night

Background: Charles Halloway's thirteen-year-old son, Will, and Will's friend, Jim, recently discovered that the carnival that came to town some days earlier is not what it appears to be. They found it to be a façade, beneath which lay pure supernatural evil waiting to capture the souls of the townspeople. Mr. Dark, the sinister and enigmatic ringmaster of this carnival, has discovered that the boys know his secret. He wants to capture them before they can spread the news to those who might believe them. The boys came to the library tonight to tell Will's father of their discovery, knowing that he, more than anyone else, would be likely to believe them. Halloway confirmed their story by producing his father's diary. In this diary, his father, the town's minister at that time, described an identical carnival coming to visit the town in the days of his youth. There was the same mention of supernatural evil at work beneath the carnival's exterior. At this point, the front doors of the library are blown open by the wind, heralding the arrival of Mr. Dark. Knowing why he has come, Halloway immediately sends the two boys off to hide somewhere among the library's labyrinth of book stacks.

Situation: Mr. Dark confronts Halloway with the knowledge that the two boys are hiding. He makes it clear, in no uncertain terms, that he wants them. At first, seeing that Halloway won't cooperate, Dark begins talking to the boys directly, calling out to them with various supernatural inducements and temptations to join his carnival, telling them, for example, that he will make them older and enable them to enjoy all those privileges that only adults have access to. When this approach fails, Dark begins to work on persuading Halloway to reveal the boys' whereabouts. At this point, he presents Halloway with the one temptation he knows will be the most difficult for him to resist—the return of his youth and former vitality. Halloway, being almost obsessed with concern over his age and failing health, finds Dark's proposition enticing indeed. Halloway finds himself in the middle of a battle with his own conscience, with the lives of the boys on the one hand and the return of his youth on the other.

Comments: It is up to the actor playing Mr. Dark to make his temptations as persuasive, seductive, and irresistible as possible. Also, he should be aware that his character is no mere mortal but an ageless embodiment of the dark side of man's nature. The actor playing Halloway must decide how he will respond to this temptation. He must also focus on his obsession with his own age and health.

--------- **11** ---------

Source: *William Wilson*, a short story by Edgar Allan Poe

Characters: Two males: William Wilson, a young man, and his double

Place: An antechamber in a Roman palazzo

Background: William Wilson goes away to an English boarding school and discovers that there is another boy in his class who is a duplicate of himself. He resembles Wilson in his appearance, mannerisms, and speech. He follows him everywhere he goes. Every time Wilson is about to do something immoral, such as cheat at cards or flirt with other men's wives, his double taps him on the shoulder. Wilson enjoys his immorality and finds his double's interference a great bother. He travels all over the world in an attempt to escape from him, but wherever he goes, the other William Wilson shows up. One day his exasperation toward this unwanted conscience reaches a climax.

Situation: While Wilson is attending a ball in Rome given by a Neapolitan duke, he seizes the opportunity to try to seduce the aged man's wife. He is just about to approach her when the familiar tap on the shoulder occurs. In a fury, Wilson rushes into an antechamber adjoining the ballroom, with his double following him. In this room the two Wilsons come face to face with each other. Wilson wants his double out of his life forever.

Comments: In the story, Wilson stabs his double. In this improvisation, however, the actors should let the situation evolve spontaneously. Symbolically, Wilson's double is his conscience. He is determined to obey the evil side of himself and is most perturbed with his other self for interfering. The audience must be told beforehand that the two actors look exactly alike. The actor playing the double should try as much as possible to mimic and sound like his partner.

12

Source: *Alice's Adventures in Wonderland,* a story by Lewis Carroll

Characters: Three males and one female: the Mad Hatter, the March Hare, the Dormouse; and Alice, a girl of about ten

Place: An outdoor tea party in Wonderland

Background: Alice, a young girl, was out playing with her pet kitten one day, when she fell down a rabbit hole. When she reached the bottom, she found herself in Wonderland, a curious place indeed, full of fantastical things, strange people, bizarre creatures, and talking animals.

Situation: Eventually, Alice finds herself at a peculiar tea party, presided over by the Mad Hatter, a no less peculiar gentleman wearing an oversized top hat. The Mad Hatter is, by turns, snobbish, dictatorial, whimsical, and rude. Also, as his name indicates, he is quite, quite mad. The March Hare is no less crazy, although a bit less abrasive. By contrast, the Dormouse is a quiet and gentle creature, who is constantly falling asleep only to be abruptly awakened by the Hatter or the Hare pouring tea on him or giving him a shove. The Hatter and the Hare query Alice relentlessly, giving her riddles and nonsense questions to answer. The Hatter creates extemporaneous poems, equally nonsensical, and insults Alice when she finds herself unable to answer the insane riddles and questions. During all of this, Alice does her best to maintain her dignity and composure.

Comments: The actress playing Alice must accept the reality of what she is experiencing and try her best to find some shred of order amidst the chaos. The actors playing the Wonderland characters must find their own interior logic for why they do and say what they do. To them, the craziness of this tea party is quite commonplace. Each actor should decide on something he wants from Alice, and she should decide what she wants from them. The actors should not try to be zany, since the situation takes care of that. In addition, the actors need not feel compelled to compete with the unique cleverness of Lewis Carroll but should, instead, create their own riddles, poems, etc.

13

Source: *Blithe Spirit,* a play by Noël Coward

Characters: One male and two females: Charles Condomine; Ruth, his present wife; and Elvira, his dead wife, who has just returned as a ghost

Place: The living room of the Condomines's house in Kent, England

Background: Elvira was Charles's first wife, who was killed in an automobile accident a number of years ago. He has recently married Ruth. For the sport of it, Charles invited Madame Arcati, a medium, to his house, with another couple, to conduct a séance. Apparently, during the séance, Madame Arcati accidentally called Elvira back, and Elvira is now present in the house. But Charles is the only one who can see or hear her.

Situation: Charles is naturally rather shocked to see Elvira and doesn't know quite what to do. Elvira, being very feisty, scolds Charles for not giving her a better greeting. Ruth cannot understand whom Charles is speaking to. He has to carry on a conversation with the two women at the same time. Elvira does not plan to leave, nor is she able to leave. Elvira was killed in her prime, and she is still quite delectable. She is a more flamboyant type than Ruth. However, Ruth is alive and she is Charles's present wife. All three characters are in a bit of a dilemma. Charles suddenly has two wives, Ruth has a husband who appears to have become unbalanced, and Elvira finds her husband married to someone else.

Comments: The fun of this material is that every time Charles responds to Elvira, Ruth thinks he is speaking to *her*. This can cause much mischief. For example, Charles might get into an argument with Elvira and tell her to "shut up." Ruth would naturally think he was addressing her. The actress playing Ruth has to really concentrate on *not* seeing or hearing Elvira. The actress playing Elvira can have fun tormenting Ruth in various ways, such as blowing in her face, pulling her hair, and so on. She can even kiss Charles. Charles cannot understand why Ruth doesn't hear or see Elvira. He doesn't try to hide the fact from Ruth that Elvira is present, but Ruth doesn't believe him. The actor playing Charles must know what he wants from both these women.

14

Source: *Harvey*, a play by Mary C. Chase

Characters: One male and ensemble: Elwood P. Dowd, a middle-aged man, and various other characters (to be determined as required)

Place: Any place where there is a group of people gathered.

Background: Elwood P. Dowd, a tippler, believes he has a close friendship with a six-foot-tall rabbit named Harvey, who is invisible to all but himself. He has had this unusual "companion" for some time and is quite at ease with him.

Situation: Whatever situation is selected, Elwood must make it apparent that he fully believes in Harvey's existence and must behave as though he really can see and touch him. It will be up to the other actors in the improvisation to respond to the situation individually.

Comments: It is essential to the actor playing Elwood that he believe in the definite existence of this singular rabbit. If the actor doesn't appear to believe in Harvey, then the audience *surely* won't. The actors should choose a situation in which the existence of Harvey causes conflict, i.e., any locale or situation in which Elwood's interaction with Harvey would cause embarrassment or be disruptive.

15

Source: *I, Spud*, a novel by Reginald Wilton

Characters Two males and one female: A man, his son, and his daughter. They can be any age, providing the ratios are believable.

Place: The man's bedroom

Background: The man has been happily married for some years and has a close relationship with his family. His wife, however, has always been something of a "couch potato," which he may have told her once too often.

Situation: It is early morning. The alarm clock goes off. The man wakes up in bed to discover that next to him, inside his wife's nightgown (arranged as though his wife were still inside it), lies a potato, which he gradually comes to realize is, in fact, his wife. Somehow, during the night, she was transformed into a potato. Once he is convinced of this, he must decide how to handle this admittedly offbeat situation. Eventually, he calls his children into the room one at a time and informs them of their mother's altered condition.

Comments: The actor playing the husband must find his own interior logic for believing the potato to be his wife. The children may or may not believe it, but they must deal with their father, who is totally convinced. It is suggested, for the sake of believability, that an actual potato be used.

_____ **16** _____

Source: _Kaleidoscope,_ a short story by Ray Bradbury

Characters: Ensemble: any number of astronauts of either sex

Place: Outer space

Background: These astronauts were on a spaceship, which was caught in a meteor shower. At that point they were instructed to put on their spacesuits and oxygen helmets. Suddenly their ship was struck by a meteor and the craft exploded, hurling the astronauts out into space, each going in a different direction and traveling away from one another.

Situation: The astronauts are able to communicate through the radios in their helmets. They realize, however, that at the speed they are traveling, the time left to them for radio communication is not long. Therefore, they take this opportunity to say final words to one another. Since it is the last time they will be speaking to a living being, they may say things that they wouldn't under ordinary circumstances. In the process, they reveal much about themselves.

Comments: Before the actors do this exercise, they must create a past for themselves. These people have been traveling together in a spaceship and they know one another well. They should decide on these relationships, with regard to physical staging, since they are, in essence, disembodied voices and cannot see one another. This might be staged effectively by using the entire class or theater with the lights turned off. There is an element of panic here also, since the astronauts have been hurled into space. Each person will respond differently to this.

It is essential that the coach create the atmosphere for this. To denote the explosion, all the lights should go out, signaling the beginning of the improvisation. The whole class should participate. Make sure the actors establish their relationships with one another before beginning the improvisation.

17

Source: *Killer Klowns from Outer Space*, a film by Stephen Chiodo, screenplay by Chiodo and Charles Chiodo

Characters: Two males and one female: Mike and Debbie, a teenage boy and girl; and Officer Mooney, the chief of police

Place: A police station in a small town

Background: Debbie and Mike have just experienced something that, to say the least, could be called unusual. In a clearing in a nearby forest at night they came upon a brightly lit circus tent. It turned out to encase a gigantic spaceship inhabited by grotesque humanoid aliens resembling clowns. The couple also discovered a number of pink cotton candy cocoons, inside of which were the bodies of human beings whom the aliens had captured. One of the persons was a friend of theirs. Debbie and Mike barely escaped with their lives, the clowns having chased them and set loose a dog made of balloons to capture them. The "dog" was hit by a car. They shot at the teenagers with guns that fired popcorn or something resembling popcorn.

Situation: Believing that the aliens are intending to take over the town, if not the world, these kids must do their utmost to convince Officer Mooney that their story is true—not an easy task by any means.

Comments: The actors should feel free to expand on what they saw and give more detailed circus imagery. Before approaching the police chief, the actors playing the teenagers must have a clear picture of what they actually experienced.

—————— **18** ——————

Source: *No Exit*, a play by Jean-Paul Sartre

Characters: Two females and two males: Estelle, Inez, Garcin, and the bellboy

Place: A room with one door, no windows, and three sofas

Background: Each one of the three characters—Estelle, Inez, and Garcin—have done something in their lives that has caused them to be sent to hell after their death.

Estelle had a child by her lover; she didn't want the baby, and so she tied a rock around it and threw it off the balcony into the ocean. When her lover heard about the baby, he shot himself. Estelle was then hit by a truck, and this is how she came to be here.

Inez is a lesbian who broke up a marriage in order to get the woman she wanted. The woman went with her and became despondent over the dissolution of her marriage. One night she turned on the gas, and they both died.

Garcin ran a newspaper with a reputation for telling the truth. He was married and brought a mulatto girl to live with his wife and himself. He made his wife wait on them hand and foot. He made her bring them breakfast in bed. He was shot for being a deserter during wartime.

Situation: The bellboy brings these three characters into a room—a room containing only three sofas and a fireplace, with no windows, no mirrors, and a light switch that doesn't work. Their hell is to be together for eternity. They've never met, and they slowly unfold their lives to one another. Each one eventually becomes the torturer of the other two. Inez will not let Estelle and Garcin get together because she wants Estelle for herself. Garcin basically wants peace and quiet, but they won't allow him that. Estelle is very vain and likes men to be interested in her. She wants to adjust her makeup so Inez becomes her "mirror" and tells her how to put on her lipstick, etc. This hell was designed specifically for these three people, who cannot get along. Since they are already dead, they cannot commit suicide and they can't sleep because they no longer have any eyelids to close. In addition, the light in the room can't be turned off. In short, there is no possible escape of any kind for these three unfortunates. But in their separate ways, they try somehow to make the best of it, none too successfully. Finally, they come to the conclusion that hell is simply "other people." They also come to accept that their situation will go on, unrelieved, throughout eternity.

Comments: It is important that the actors be clear about their backgrounds and know why they were sent to hell. They also must remember that each one wants something from the others that he or she can't get. A good portion of time will be needed for this improvisation to allow the situation and the relationships to evolve organically and not in an arbitrary or forced manner.

———— 19 ————

Source: *Peter Pan*, a play by Sir James M. Barrie

Characters: Two females and one male: Wendy (in her forties), her twelve-year-old daughter, and Peter Pan

Place: The nursery of Wendy's home

Background: It will be remembered by those familiar with this famous story that Wendy, when she was a child, had accompanied her two younger brothers on a marvelous adventure to Never-Never-Land with their guide, Peter Pan, the eternal youth. There they encountered the lost boys, mermaids, Indians, and, of course, the pirates led by the infamous Captain Hook.

Situation: Many years have gone by, and Wendy is now a mother herself with a daughter the same age she was when Peter first came and whisked her away. As the improvisation begins, Peter returns to the nursery, mistaking the daughter for Wendy. At this point, Wendy enters and clears up Peter's confusion by telling him that, unlike him, she has had to grow up and is now a woman.

At this point, the daughter, who is well acquainted with the story of her mother's adventures, pleads to be allowed to accompany Peter to Never-Never-Land. Wendy reluctantly gives her permission, but as Peter prepares to take the daughter with him, Wendy suddenly pleads desperately to be taken along as well; but Peter, with the callousness of youth, informs her that she is too old. Then, taking Wendy's daughter, he leaves.

Comments: The actor (or actress) playing Peter Pan must not fall into the trap of playing Peter as a fantasy character. He is a normal boy, who doesn't realize he's different from others. The actress playing Wendy must decide what Never-Never-Land means to her. If desired, the resolution of this improvisation may be left open-ended, with the actors coming to their own conclusion.

20

Source: *Silent Running*, a film by Douglas Trumbull, screenplay by Deric Washburn, Steve Bochco, and Michael Cimino

Characters: Four males: Freeman Lowell and three other astronauts (Wolf, Barker, and Keenan)

Place: On board the U.S. spaceship *Valley Forge*

Background: These men have been in space for some time, on board a sort of space arc that carries the last of Earth's forests enclosed within protective domes. These contain both flora and fauna. Earth is now too polluted and overcrowded to sustain much natural plant or animal life.

Situation: The men have just received official orders to jettison and destroy all the domes and return to Earth. Freeman, who is fervently dedicated to conservation and has a deep and abiding love of nature, is understandably horrified at these orders. The other men, however, are much more blasé and can only think eagerly about returning to Earth. Freeman tries to make them understand the real and overwhelmingly important value of nature as well as the dire consequences that would ensue as a result of carrying out their orders.

Comments: In the film, Freeman is unable to persuade the other astronauts, but in the improvisation it can be left open-ended. The actors need to orient themselves to being in a spaceship, but need not be preoccupied with the technical aspects. The important thing is whether or not they destroy the last forests in existence. The men must, however, remain in space to keep these forests.

———— 21 ————

Source: *The Twilight of the Vilp*, a novel by Paul Ableman

Characters: Four males and one female, plus ensemble: Clive Witt, a somewhat successful science-fiction writer currently at work on a novel entitled *The Twilight of the Vilp;* his publisher; the mayor; a movie star; Clive's wife; Clive's children (of an indeterminate number); bystanders and several government officials

Place: A construction site: formerly the home of Clive Witt, now the site of a new luxury apartment block

Background: A couple of weeks earlier, Clive Witt's publisher had gone suddenly mad and destroyed Clive's home with dynamite and a bulldozer. In an attempt to make amends, the publisher had commissioned the construction of a twenty-five-story luxury apartment block, topped by a revolving swimming pool, on the former sight of Clive's demolished home. Under veiled construction lasting a mere ten days, the building is now ready to be revealed.

Situation: The people present are here to participate in the ceremony, which includes the traditional cutting of the ribbon by a film star. Several government officials are also present. However, it seems that there has been a disastrous miscalculation on the part of the architect as well as the builders and *inches* have been used as a building reference instead of *feet*. The result is that the entire twenty-five-story apartment block now stands only twelve feet high, and on the roof a doll-size swimming pool slowly revolves. However, unwilling to admit either his mistake or his embarrassment, the publisher makes a pathetic and ridiculous attempt to save face by insisting that everything has gone according to plan and that the building has been constructed to conserve maximum space for reasons of economy. Then, on his knees, he proceeds to point out the delightful features of the Witts' new apartment on the building's ground floor, which, in its entirety, takes up six inches. Clive seems dubious, but not wanting to appear publicly ungrateful, he tries to muster up enthusiasm as his publisher gives him the grand tour.

Comments: The actors must create the imaginary twelve-foot model of the apartment complex. It will be necessary for the people present to bend down on their knees in order to peer into the lower floors. The audience/class should be informed of the architectural mistake in advance in order to understand the situation.

FANTASY

Cross-References

*Other improvisations in this book that involve Fantasy
can be found in the following categories:*

SOLO MOMENT

One male

SPECIAL PROBLEMS

One male

8

THEATER OF
THE ABSURD

Playwrights such as Luigi Pirandello, followed by Eugène
Ionesco, Samuel Beckett, Edward Albee, and Harold Pinter, were at the forefront of a bold new theatrical movement
popularly known as Theater of the Absurd. Works in this
realm of drama incorporate aspects of UNUSUAL CIRCUM-
STANCES and FANTASY. But unlike the characters in most
nonabsurdist plays, the characters here behave as though
the odd goings on were the most normal occurrences in
the world. Something wildly strange may happen and at-
tract no notice, whereas a seemingly ordinary event may
be greeted with astonishment or outrage.

Two plays by Ionesco, *Rhinoceros* and *The Bald Soprano*, are good contrasting examples of this type of play.
In the former, a man is slowly transformed into a rhinoceros. Although a friend, who is present when this occurs,
reacts with fear over what is happening, he expresses no
astonishment at the incredibility of the transformation.
Many other people have also become rhinos, and their
transformation is considered merely an unpleasant fact of
life. In the other play, *The Bald Soprano,* a man and woman
sitting next to each other on a train discover various coincidences in their lives: They live in the same town, on
the same street; each has two children, a boy and a girl; in
fact, as they eventually discover, they live in the same
house, are husband and wife, and have been married for
many years. Their mutual astonishment, though, is at find-

ing so many concidences, not at the patent absurdity of failing to recognize each other.

Beneath the absurd surface of these plays frequently lurk some very serious meanings and implications. *Rhinoceros,* for example, can be interpreted as a commentary on fascism. *The Bald Soprano* may be seen as social criticism aimed at the dehumanization of modern society or the nature of marriage, which would allow two people to share each other's lives and yet, in essence, remain complete strangers to each other.

Theater of the Absurd, frequently nonsensical yet often deceptively serious, can become a treasure trove of possibilities for the daring actor. As with FANTASY, the characters in these improvisations should be treated as living, breathing individuals, not as silly cardboard cutouts.

THEATER OF THE ABSURD

List of Situations

———— 1 ————

Source: *The Bald Soprano*, a play by Eugène Ionesco
Characters: One male and one female: husband and wife
Place: A passenger car on a train
Background: The couple have been married to each other for many years. They have two children and live in a house in suburbia.
Situation: This couple is traveling on a train and believe themselves to be total strangers to each other. They start talking and find out that there are many similarities between their lives, i.e., they live in the same city, in the

same neighborhood, and on the same street. Each of them has a son and a daughter, with the same names. As if these coincidences were not enough, they eventually discover that they live in the same house and have been married to each other for years. This comes as a genuine surprise to both of them.

Comments: Underlying the obvious absurdity of this situation is the serious point that we may know and even live with someone all our lives and never really "know" the person. The actors should either set up mutually agreed upon facts about their lives together prior to doing the improvisation or simply go along with whatever the other actor says during the course of the scene.

———— **2** ————

Source: *Rhinoceros*, a play by Eugène Ionesco
Characters: Two males: John and Stanley
Place: John's apartment
Background: People have spontaneously been transformed into rhinos, seemingly for no reason. This has particularly unnerved Stanley, who is very fearful of becoming one of the herd and losing his individuality. (By the end of the play, as it happens, Stanley is one of the few left who have not been transformed; he finds himself alone in a hostile world.)
Situation: Stanley has just spoken with John on the telephone and, hearing a strangeness in his voice, decides to pay him a visit to see if he is all right. During the scene that follows, John, while maintaining that he feels perfectly fine (in fact, better than usual), begins the process of slowly changing into a rhinoceros. Stanley is horrified by what he sees happening to his friend, but he is

unable to do anything about it. He is losing his friend forever; eventually, there will be no one left with whom he can communicate.

Comments: For the actor playing John, this improvisation presents a treasure trove of imaginative possibilities because he must make the audience believe in both his physical and vocal metamorphosis into a rhinoceros without benefit of makeup or special effects of any kind. The actor playing this role may choose to do special preparation for this scene at home before presenting it to an audience. He may choose to do research about the actual animal either on film or at the local zoo. His main goal here is to capture what he feels to be the essence of the animal through changes in voice and gesture. Also, keep in mind that this is a gradual transformation rather than an instantaneous one. The process should begin in subtle ways and become more pronounced and extreme as the scene progresses.

—————— **3** ——————

Source: *The Chairs*, a play by Eugène Ionesco

Characters: Two males and one female: husband and wife, and an orator, who is a deaf mute (the orator can be played by either sex), plus various invisible guests

Place: A lighthouse

Background: The husband and wife are caretakers of a lighthouse in which they have lived for most of their married life. They have invited various dignitaries and city officials to hear the reading of a document on which the husband has been working for many years. This document distills into one page the meaning of the couple's lives. A professional orator has been engaged to read the document to the group.

Situation: The guests arrive, one by one, and chairs are brought out for them by the old couple. Once the group has assembled and the orator has arrived, the couple feel they no longer have any reason to live and cheerfully jump to their deaths from the windows of the lighthouse (one on either side of the stage). The nasty joke is that the orator, unbeknownst to them, is a deaf mute and can only make gibbering noises and odd sounds, thus making a mockery not only of the document but of the couple's lives as well.

Comments: The main challenge of this improvisation is to make the various unseen dignitaries and city officials real to the audience. A large number of chairs will be needed for this improvisation. They should be brought onto the set for each new "arrival." By the end of the improvisation, the stage should be filled with chairs, each supporting an unseen "person," whom the actors have made real for the audience.

4

Source: A Delicate Balance, a play by Edward Albee

Characters: Two males and two females: two couples—Agnes and Tobias and Harry and Edna

Place: The home of Agnes and Tobias

Background: These two couples are old friends, who have known one another for many years.

Situation: Harry and Edna drop in on Agnes and Tobias one night unannounced. Harry and Edna try to appear casual, but they are obviously distraught about something. After some moments of inconsequential small talk,

Tobias bluntly asks them why they are there. At this point, Harry and Edna haltingly begin to explain the real reason for their visit: They were sitting at home, and although nothing "happened" in a concrete sense, they became absolutely terrified and felt that they had to leave their home. Agnes and Tobias, being their best friends, seemed the right people to go to for comfort and sanctuary. They ultimately ask Agnes and Tobias to take them in for an indefinite period of time.

Comments: Much of this play functions on the level of subtext. Albee seems to be dealing with the terror of emptiness, or "nothingness," be it spiritual or physical. The "terror" that Harry and Edna experience is open to various interpretations, but to the actors playing these roles it must be real and palpable. The actors playing Agnes and Tobias must weigh their years of friendship with Harry and Edna against having their space invaded. Although this play is not typical of Theater of the Absurd, for the purposes of this chapter it meets the necessary requirements.

_____ 5 _____

Source: *Endgame,* a play by Samuel Beckett

Characters: Three males and one female: Hamm, Clov, Nagg, Nell

Place: A basement in an unspecified locale in some future time

Background: It appears as if the earth has been decimated by some unspecified holocaust (nuclear war is never mentioned). This is a world with its own peculiar logic, which should not be rooted in any popular contemporary details, i.e., books, movies, magazines. Hamm's parents,

Nagg and Nell, have become invalids owing to the loss of their legs (which Hamm himself may or may not have had amputated). He keeps his parents in two trash cans from which they pop up from time to time, asking for food or engaging in nostalgic reminiscence. Hamm is blind and crippled and spends his time in a thronelike chair on casters. He wears dark glasses and a whistle around his neck, which he uses to summon his servant, Clov (who may or may not be his own son). Because of a spinal injury, Clov cannot sit down and must always remain standing to do his master's bidding. In this dark and decaying cellar, the only view of the outside world is through two small windows, high up in the wall on either side of the room. These windows are accessible only by means of a tall ladder.

Situation: These four lost souls are living out what time is left to them, performing a series of almost mechanical rituals. The relationship between Hamm and Clov is basically that of master and slave. A good clue to the nature of their dealings with each other may be found in their names—Hamm being short for Hammer, and Clov being similar to *clou,* the French word for nail (and pronounced almost exactly the same way in that language). But no matter how abusive Hamm may be to Clov, he is still dependent on him in many ways—almost to an infantile degree. Clov must wheel Hamm around the room on his casters, fetch things for him, and perform other tasks. Hamm's major concerns are the condition of the world outside—the weather and possible sightings of other human beings. Hamm actually dreads the latter, for it is his fervent hope that mankind has been obliterated. Though Clov is constantly being ordered around, he does have power over Hamm in refusing at any given moment to do what he has been instructed to do. Hamm's other major concerns are knowing that he is being placed in the exact dead-center of the room, when he is done with being wheeled about, and constantly needing to know if it is time to be given his painkiller. Whenever Hamm asks Clov if it is time for his painkiller, Clov seems to take a cruel delight in telling him it is not yet time. Ultimately, when it finally *is* time, Clov takes particular delight in telling Hamm that there is no more painkiller left. Nagg and Nell's major concern is being fed. Hamm resents his parents and is annoyed by their requests for food.

Comments: One cannot hope, within the context of an improvisation, to fully reproduce the unique world that Samuel Beckett has created through language and specific action. Unlike certain plays by other writers in the Theater of the Absurd, Beckett's plays are rather less about situation and plot than they are about language and relationships. Beckett has a uniquely despairing view of life. Once, while he was walking with a friend in Paris, the friend remarked on the beautiful weather, saying, "It makes you glad to be alive." Not missing a beat, Beckett replied, "Well, I wouldn't go so far as *that*." This is typical of Beckett's viewpoint—cynical, sorrowful, yet darkly funny. Almost all of Beckett's plays are shot through with this despairing humor. Beckett's world exists within its own peculiar boundaries, and conventional rules of behavior do not always apply. Frequently, Beckett's humor can become surprisingly raunchy as well—both sexually and/or scatologically. It would do well in approaching an improvisation based on Beckett's work for the actor to familiarize himself to some extent with his plays.

This improvisation requires some special properties. It would be beneficial to have the actors set up something to represent two trash cans—e.g., cardboard boxes large enough for two adults. Also needed are a stepladder and some kind of chair with casters, which can easily be wheeled around.

_____ **6** _____

Source: *The Homecoming*, a play by Harold Pinter

Characters: Five males and one female: Max, the father; Sam, his brother; Max's sons, Lenny, Joey, and Teddy; and Teddy's wife, Ruth

Place: Max's home

Background: Max is a butcher and Sam is a chauffeur. Max has a vicious temper and is, by turns, crude and biting in his speech. By contrast, Sam is much more refined, almost prissy—a bit of a milquetoast. Lenny is sly, cunning, and spends much time at the racetrack betting on horses. His manner is subtly threatening, but unlike his father, he is not physically violent. Joey is a big hulking fellow, who fancies himself a boxer, though he is too slow and lumbering in his movements to be much good at it. Teddy is a college professor, very refined in his manner. His wife, Ruth, is a rather quiet, enigmatic woman, with a strong underlying sensuality. The family, with the exception of Teddy and his wife, all live together under one roof. Teddy has been away from home for some years.

Situation: Teddy returns home for the first time with his new bride. The father immediately assumes she is a prostitute and demands that she be thrown out of the house.

After several patient explanations from Teddy, Max finally gets it through his head that this "tart" is actually his daughter-in-law. Eventually, the father and his sons (except Teddy) come up with the idea of putting Ruth in business, part time, as a professional prostitute and the rest of the time as a private prostitute servicing the family. Oddly enough, Ruth does not object to this, and neither does her husband. He, in fact, makes plans to return home without her, and she, like a hard-nosed business woman, begins to set forth demands regarding her salary and accommodations. Underlying her toughness, however, is pain at being abandoned by her husband. At one point, Sam collapses, as if dead. Max, outraged at having a corpse on his floor, demands that the body be thrown out. It is then discovered that Sam is not really dead after all but has merely fainted. Max seems disappointed at this. No one responds normally to this body in the middle of the living room. Finally, Teddy leaves, and Ruth is now alone with the four remaining family members.

Comments: The actors may resolve this situation any way they like. The play itself ends ambiguously and is open to interpretation. Just because this is Theater of the Absurd doesn't mean the characters don't feel deeply. This is not an easy decision for the husband and wife, although they never discuss their pain. As in most of Harold Pinter's work, much of the tension is dealt with through subtext. When Teddy first brings Ruth home, the father and sons have no idea what the outcome will be. The idea to take her in as a prostitute evolves gradually and ominously.

Like most of Pinter's work, this play defies easy classification. But, for the purposes of this chapter, it meets the necessary requirements. In fact, Pinter's work might well be given its *own* category—the Theater of Menace.

———————— 7 ————————

Source: *The Lesson*, a play by Eugène Ionesco

Characters: One male and two females: a professor in his seventies; a young female student in her early to mid-teens; the professor's housekeeper, a woman in her forties

Place: The home of the professor, in which he does his tutoring

Background: The professor is a man who, though mild and a bit doddering at first, becomes more and more intense as his lessons progress. Every week, for some time, he has been tutoring and then murdering his students. His housekeeper, a strong, formidable woman, has tried to dissuade him from doing this, but to no avail. She has had no recourse but to help him dispose of the bodies.

Situation: The professor's newest student, a young girl, arrives for her lesson. Her manner is shy and mild at first, then progressively whiny and agitated as the lesson goes on. She complains periodically of a toothache that is getting worse and worse. As her pain increases, so does the professor's intensity and the tempo of his speech. Finally, he works himself up into a state of sexual frenzy bordering on hysteria. At the peak of his frenzy, he pulls out a knife and stabs the girl repeatedly while experiencing a sexual climax. Following the murder, he becomes immediately frightened and contrite, shyly confessing his latest crime to the housekeeper, who is not at all happy with him and treats him like a bad child.

But, after helping him dispose of the body, she manages to make the professor presentable again. And just in time too—for there is a knock on the door, signaling the arrival of yet another student!

Comments: In Ionesco's play, the professor teaches a weird, nonsensical combination of grammar and mathematics. The actor can have free rein, since the professor's "teaching" is basically gibberish. But the actor must also keep in mind that the professor takes this gibberish very seriously indeed. He is intent on his student mastering the lesson, whatever that may mean. His underlying sexual motivations must be worked out by the actor and given an organic inner reality. The student's growing uneasiness and discomfort trigger the professor's excitement, urging it on. The more cringing and submissive she becomes, the less feeble and more dominant he grows.

It is Ionesco's belief that the educational system frequently "murders" its students, killing them both creatively and spiritually. He likened bad teaching to a kind of fascism and made this idea explicit by having the housekeeper put a Nazi-type armband on the professor at the play's conclusion, telling him, "Wear this and you won't have to be afraid anymore."

8

Source: *Miss Margarida's Way,* a play by Roberto Athayde
Characters: One female, plus ensemble: a substitute teacher, Miss Margarida, and the students in her class
Place: A classroom of eighth-graders
Background: Miss Margarida is a substitute teacher. She has a huge chip on her shoulder and delusions of grandeur as well. She is also enormously preoccupied with

sex. She is the absolute center of her own universe and truly believes that everyone secretly envies her and would like to *be* her. In her best-of-all-possible-worlds scenario, she would be a dictator and everyone else her unquestioningly loyal subject. But since her daily reality is not this "ideal" world, she becomes a dictator in the classroom, trying obsessively to bend the students to her will.

Situation: It is the beginning of a new school day with a new eighth-grade class. The students are unfamiliar with Miss Margarida's distinctive qualities and at first would assume her to be like many other teachers—rather proper and pedantic. This façade soon begins to crumble, however, as her mania begins to spew forth a bit at a time. She clearly knows absolutely nothing about any of the subjects she teaches—English, mathematics, history, geography, biology (the latter being her favorite subject because it lends itself so well to her sexual preoccupations). She constantly refers to herself in the third person as Miss Margarida, and never uses the word *I*. Thus, instead of saying, "I want you to leave the classroom," she says, "Miss Margarida wants you to leave the classroom." Also, no matter what she "teaches," she always manages to bring the subject back to herself. *Her* life and *her* opinions are all that really matter to her. Her raging egomania enables her to honestly believe that her opinions on every conceivable subject are definitive. As the class progresses, her behavior becomes more and more extreme, her language coarse and vulgar, her manner lewd. In plain fact, she swears like a sailor and loses her temper at the slightest provocation, screaming at her students, hurling epithets, and taunting them sexually.

Her drawings on the blackboard become increasingly bizarre and occasionally pornographic.

Comments: In order for this improvisation to be completely successful, the students in the actual class should ideally interact with the actress playing Miss Margarida, taunting and provoking her in a variety of ways at every possible opportunity—much like a typical eighth-grade class in real life would do. Paper airplanes and spitballs may fly in abundance, anarchy becoming the rule of the day in response to Miss Margarida's rampaging megalomania. The actors in the classroom must remember, however, that she is the focal point of the improvisation and therefore must be heard (if not necessarily obeyed).

Miss Margarida's Way can be viewed as a political allegory, in which Miss Margarida represents any repressive government or military dictatorship. Like Ionesco in *The Lesson*, Athayde uses the educational system as a metaphor for fascism. In fact, in the playwright's native Brazil, the play was considered subversive and immediately banned.

_____ **9** _____

Source: *The Ruffian on the Stair*, a play by Joe Orton

Characters: Two males and one female: Wilson, a young man in his twenties; Mike, a hit man; and Joyce, a prostitute with whom Mike has been living for the past two years

Place: The apartment of Mike and Joyce

Background: Wilson had a very close relationship with his brother—they were, in fact, lovers. The brother was killed a few days ago by Mike, a professional hit man.

Wilson's heart is broken, and he doesn't want to go on living, but he is unable to take his own life. He decides to get Mike to kill him and end his misery.

Situation: Wilson comes to Mike's apartment and finds Joyce there. She has seen him hanging around recently and is frightened of him. She has no idea who he is or what he wants. Wilson knows two things: (1) Mike is insanely jealous, and (2) being a hit man, he undoubtedly has a gun in the house. He plans to make it appear as though he is involved with Joyce so that Mike will shoot him. Wilson proceeds to tell Joyce about the death of his brother. Having no idea what his plan is and feeling sorry for him, Joyce comforts him with a motherly hug. At that moment Mike arrives to find them in what he assumes to be a passionate embrace. Mike behaves exactly the way Wilson had predicted—he goes into a jealous rage and shoots Wilson. As a result of his death throes, a bowl of goldfish gets knocked over. Joyce is far more upset about this than the shooting of Wilson, whose body now lies on the floor.

Comments: The actor may use a knife as the weapon if a gun is not available. The actress will have to justify her concern for the fish rather than Wilson.

Although Joe Orton is not technically part of the Theater of the Absurd movement, he has been placed in this category because this piece has a similar quality.

_____ **10** _____

Source: *The Ruling Class*, a play by Peter Barnes

Characters: Three males: Jack, the fourteenth earl of Gurney; Dr. Herder, his psychiatrist (could be a woman); and a mental patient

Place: The living room of Jack's ancestral home—a mansion

Background: Jack has long been confined to an institution, laboring under the delusion that he is, in fact, Jesus Christ. Jack's father, the thirteenth earl of Gurney, died recently, making Jack the new earl. As such, he was released from the institution and installed as the fourteenth earl of Gurney in his ancestral home. Jack's family, less than thrilled about a madman with a Christ complex assuming control of the Gurney fortune, determine to find a way of shocking Jack out of his delusion. A garden-variety "lunatic" would be tolerable—and would doubtless be labeled eccentric. But a man dressed in sackcloth robes, preaching love and brotherhood and sleeping on a giant crucifix—this is unacceptable and acutely embarrassing. In desperation, Jack's family has summoned a noted psychiatrist to the house to try to snap Jack out of his benign fancy.

Situation: Dr. Herder arrives and brings with him another patient. This patient is a wild-eyed man who declares himself a rival god. A showdown then ensues between the two men to determine which is the One True God, with the doctor acting as the mediator or "referee."

Comments: The actors may resolve this situation any way they like, but whatever the resolution, it must not come about easily. Without conflict, there can be no real tension or excitement in this situation. Each character must prove that he is the One True God. His whole existence is at stake.

_____ 11 _____

Source: *Sticks and Bones,* a play by David Rabe

Characters: Three males, one female: Ozzie, Harriet, Ricky, and David; Ricky is the youngest son and David is just home from the war.

Place: The living room of their home

Background: The characters of Ozzie, Harriet, and Ricky (as their names would suggest) have been living the shallow two-dimensional lives typical of fifties' television sitcom characters. Most likely, the biggest problems these people have had to deal with are what kind of car to buy, what to have for dinner, or what TV program to watch. Their idea of a major tragedy would be their son getting a bad report card. Their speech is also typical of the television sit-com world circa 1955—e.g., *Leave It to Beaver, Father Knows Best,* and, of course, *Ozzie and Harriet.* Statements such as "Gee," "My my," "Oh dear," or perhaps "Darn!" are probably the strongest epithets to escape from the mouths of these characters.

Situation: Into this TV sit-com world of making fudge, mowing the lawn, and watching football games comes the older son, David, home from the Vietnam War, now blind. He is no longer a part of his family's world. Because of all he has experienced in Vietnam, he now finds it impossible to relate to his family in the way he used to. David now represents to the family a strange and dark aspect of life—one they would like to pretend doesn't exist. Ultimately, the family persuades David to take his own life for the benefit of all concerned, even going so far as to help him slash his wrists.

Comments: This treads a fine line between Theater of the Absurd and *very* black comedy. It might best be labeled a savage sociopolitical satire. The actors playing Ozzie,

Harriet, and Ricky must take care not to be so broad in their depiction of these people as to make them caricatures. If this is played too broadly, it will be robbed of dramatic impact or the potential for real conflict. After all, in the 1950s these people were the status quo.

THEATER OF THE ABSURD

Cross-References

Other improvisations in this book that involve Theater of the Absurd can be found in the following categories:

FANTASY

Ensemble

SPECIAL PROBLEMS

One male

PART III

FURTHER
REFLECTIONS

9

SPECIAL PROBLEMS

The actor will, from time to time, encounter special acting problems, which pose a variety of challenges, whether physical, psychological, or both. This chapter focuses specifically on situations in which these problems are central.

Many of these improvisations also require that the actor do a certain amount of research in order to make real or believable the special circumstances of the scene. For example, an improvisation based on Arthur Kopit's *Wings* would require that an actor investigate aphasia and the physical aspects of a stroke. The role of John Merrick in *The Elephant Man* would similarly require a degree of research into the stance, posture, vocal intonations, and so on, of a man with severe neurofibromatosis.

Some of the following improvisations could not be performed adequately without research prior to performance. Without research, some of these improvisations are likely to be superficial, stilted, undisciplined, and possibly ridiculous.

In the course of his career, it is likely that an actor will encounter instances requiring unusual preparation for a given role. Therefore, this chapter is geared toward allowing the actor an opportunity for research and preparation not generally found within the confines of improvisation.

SPECIAL PROBLEMS

List of Situations

Ensemble

_____ 1 _____

Source: *David and Lisa*, a film by Frank Perry, screenplay by Eleanor Perry, based on the book by Theodore Isaac Rubin

Characters: One male and one female: David and Lisa, both in their teens

Place: A recreation room in a school for disturbed children

Background: David and Lisa are mentally disturbed in different ways. David fears that if he is touched, he may die; therefore, he is extremely wary of physical contact. Lisa speaks only in simple rhymes and insists that anyone carrying on a conversation with her speak in like fashion. Lisa has an alternate personality named Muriel, who communicates only by drawing pictures or writing.

Situation: David and Lisa are in the recreation room alone. They have never spoken before but feel attracted to each other. They have a strong need to communicate, but each insists that this communication be on his and her own terms—Lisa must not touch David and David must speak in rhymes such as: "You're a girl, a pearl of a girl."

Comments: Of course, it is not easy to speak in rhyme, and David becomes frustrated by it, as will the actor. The need to make contact must be strong enough to impel the actors to struggle with this difficult relationship. At some point during the improvisation, the actor playing

David may attempt to speak to Lisa without rhyming. How Lisa responds to this should be left up to the actress. She may try to grapple with it or, instead, retreat into her silent alter ego, Muriel. In addition, the actress playing Lisa may wish to touch David. How he responds to this will be up to the actor.

_____ 2 _____

Source: *Gaby—A True Story,* a film by Luis Mandoki, screenplay by Martin Salinas based on the real-life story of Gabriela Brimmer

Characters: One female and one male: Gaby, a young woman, nineteen or twenty, afflicted with cerebral palsy; and Fernando, a young man of the same age or slightly older

Place: The apartment of Fernando

Background: Gaby, though severely handicapped from birth, has a fine mind and a strong will to succeed. These qualities have enabled her to leave her previous school for exclusively handicapped students and enter a standard university. Academically, she has done well, partially owing to the help of Fernando, a young man who befriended her. She has grown very attached to him and he to her. However, she has misinterpreted his friendship and has become romantically enamored of him.

Situation: There is a knock on Fernando's door. He opens it to find that Gaby, in her wheelchair, has been deposited on his doorstep. She was brought by her housekeeper and left there with the understanding that she would be spending the evening—if not the night—with him. Believing that he is in love with her, she expects him to be delighted to see her. Though he is very fond of her, he cannot possibly respond the way she would want him to. He invites her into his apartment, and after some awkward moments, he tells her in his own way that he is not in love with her and has no intention of sleeping with her.

Comments: If she is given this improvisation beforehand, the actress playing Gaby can do research on cerebral palsy. Or she may substitute some other form of extreme and/or crippling handicap with which she is familiar. Neither of the actors should have any preconceived ideas as to how they might react to Gaby's misinterpretation of the relationship. In these situations, people are not necessarily sensitive to the feelings of others, especially when caught off-guard. They may react in unpredictable ways.

_____ **3** _____

Source: *The Heart Is a Lonely Hunter,* a film by Robert Ellis Miller, screenplay by Thomas C. Ryan, based on the novel by Carson McCullers

Characters: One male and one female: John Singer, a deaf mute, in his late thirties/early forties; and Mick Kelly, a girl of about sixteen

Place: A rented room in the Kelly house

Background: Mick's parents have rented a room to Mr. Singer because they are in need of money. Although he is a deaf mute, Mr. Singer can read lips and sign. Mick lives in the house with her parents and her younger brother. She is a tomboy and doesn't fit in with most kids her age. Music is her main source of comfort. Aware of her passion for music, Mr. Singer has bought her an

album of Mozart. Like Mick, Mr. Singer is very lonely.
He has no family, and his only friend is a retarded man,
also a deaf mute, who lives in a nearby institution. Many
people tell Mr. Singer their problems because he is very
compassionate and a good "listener." But not many people think to ask Mr. Singer about *his* problems. Mick is
the first person who has ever really shown concern for
Mr. Singer's emotional needs.

Situation: Mr. Singer has just returned from visiting his
friend at the institution. He finds Mick in his room,
listening to the album of Mozart he bought her. Re-
specting his privacy, she excuses herself and says good
night, assuming he wants to be alone. But he encourages
her to stay. Hesitant at first, she decides to take him up
on his offer and visit with him. During this visit, they
struggle to communicate with each other. He can read
her lips, but because he cannot speak, she has difficulty
understanding him. She tries to find out more about him.
At some point, guessing he is lonely and wanting to
comfort him, she plays the Mozart recording and tries
to make him "hear" the music. As the music is playing,
she attempts to describe it to him through images he can
understand—e.g., comparing a slow and solemn passage
to an old woman walking to church, and so on. She tries
to make the music "visible" through hand gestures, moving to the music in the manner of a conductor. Mr. Singer
responds to this in his own way. Eventually, the music
ends, and these two people are left changed by the experience in some way.

Comments: The actors may conclude this improvisation in
any way they wish. But they should acknowledge that a
special relationship has developed between them. It is
important for the actor playing Mr. Singer to realize that

in reading the girl's lips he must concentrate intently. He must remember that if he looks away while she is speaking, he will no longer be able to "hear" her. He does not sign to her because she would not understand. Therefore, he must communicate through gestures and facial expressions.

Actual music should be used in this improvisation. The actress must address herself to the task at hand, which is to interpret the music for a person who cannot hear. At the same time, the actress must not lose sight of her character's needs.

Special properties: cassette player and music.

——— 4 ———

Source: *Interrupted Melody,* a film by Curtis Bernhardt, screenplay by William Ludwig and Sonya Levien, based on the autobiography by Marjorie Lawrence

Characters: One male and one female: Dr. Thomas King, a general practitioner, and Marjorie Lawrence, his wife, an internationally famous operatic soprano.

Place: The living room and kitchen in the Florida home of Dr. and Mrs. King, 1940s

Background: Marjorie Lawrence, while at the height of a spectacular operatic career, contracted polio and, as a result, became paralyzed from the waist down. Confined to a wheelchair, her vocal power greatly diminished, Marjorie sank into deep despair. Believing her career was over, she ceased to care about life. Her husband, Dr. King, believed she could make a partial recovery, regain her vocal prowess, and learn to use leg braces.

Situation: While she is lying on a couch, Dr. King gives his wife physical therapy, bending her legs and straightening them. She finds this excruciatingly painful. Finally, she gives up and orders her husband to leave her alone. He is about to leave the living room when he gets a sudden idea. Moving to the phonograph, he puts on a recording of Marjorie singing an operatic aria. She begs him to turn it off. "If you want it off so badly," he says, "then turn it off yourself." He then leaves the room and enters the kitchen, where he waits anxiously to see what his wife will do.

Trying to block out the music at first, she eventually rolls herself off the couch and falls to the floor. Then, using only her hands and arms, she drags the dead weight of her lower body all the way across the room to the phonograph, which she then knocks to the floor, breaking it.

Dr. King has been waiting in the kitchen during all this. When Marjorie knocks down the record player, Dr. King rushes into the room to be with her.

Comments: Since the role of Marjorie is as great a physical challenge as it is an emotional one, a word of advice: Make sure the actress has some kind of protection for her knees; otherwise, real damage could be done in dragging herself across the floor should it have a rough surface. The actress must truly believe that the lower half of her body is "dead." The actor playing Dr. King must keep in mind his conflicting feelings—that of a stern taskmaster, on the one hand, and a concerned, loving husband, on the other. In this instance, the two aspects of himself are not mutually exclusive.

Naturally, a cassette player can be used in place of a phonograph. It is essential to have an actual recording of an aria by some great operatic soprano. Care should be taken to not really damage the equipment.

Special properties: cassette player and music.

5

Source: *Lie of the Mind, #2,* a play by Sam Shepard

Characters: One male and one female: Frankie, Beth's brother-in-law, and Beth

Place: The living room of Beth's parents' house in the midwestern United States

Background: Beth's husband, Jake, beat her up. This caused some brain damage. She has just come home from several weeks in the hospital. She is able to move now, but she has lapses of memory and gets words mixed up. Frankie (Jake's brother) has come to see Beth. On his way to the house, Frankie is shot in the leg by Beth's father, a hunter, who accidentally mistakes him for a moose. Frankie has been dragged into the house and is now lying on the couch. Nobody has made any attempt to call for help. There is a fierce storm outside, and as a result, they are snowed in for a few days. Beth and Frankie have been left alone. Beth, who has not fully recovered, believes that Frankie is her husband, Jake. Beth's family hates Frankie, and if there were any suspicion of Frankie's seducing Beth, he would be killed by Beth's brother.

Situation: Beth tries to help Frankie by wrapping his wound with her shirt. This leaves her wearing only a bra. She becomes amorous with him because she believes him to be her husband. Frankie is attracted to her but he is also honorable and fearful for his life. This is a struggle for him.

Comments: The actress playing Beth must deal with the problem of brain damage and its manifestations, some of which have been mentioned in Background above. The actor playing Frankie must deal with the fact that he has had a bullet in his leg for several hours.

See *Lie of the Mind*, #1, page 110.

——— **6** ———

Source: *Like Normal People*, a film for television by Harvey Hart, teleplay by Joanna Lee

Characters: One male and one female: Roger and Virginia, a teenage boy and girl, both retarded

Place: The recreation room of an institution for retarded youths

Background: Roger and Virginia both felt ostracized by society before they came to this institution. They have never felt accepted by anyone outside their families.

Situation: This is the first meeting between them. They feel an immediate attraction to each other. Tentative and halting at first, they begin to open up more as they get to know each other.

Comments: The actors should have some knowledge of retardation. They must keep in mind that no two retarded people are alike. They are as individual as normal persons. In general, however, they are childlike, open, uninhibited, and vulnerable. Like adults, they have romantic and sexual needs. There are certain peculiarities of speech and mannerisms unique to people who are retarded. These should be taken into account so that the actors do not come across as adults playing children.

_____ 7 _____

Source: *Lizzie*, a film by Hugo Haas, screenplay by Mel Dinelli based on the novel *The Bird's Nest* by Shirley Jackson

Characters: One male and one female: Dr. Neal Wright, a psychiatrist in his late thirties/early forties; and Elizabeth Richmond, a young woman in her late twenties, his patient

Place: Dr. Wright's office

Background: Elizabeth is a mousy, joyless girl, who, although quite pretty, strikes people as drab because of her low self-image. This self-image is a result of a severe trauma she experienced on her birthday when she was in her mid-teens. Her mother had come home late, quite drunk and with her boyfriend in tow (a sleazy type named Robin). Enraged at her mother for having forgotten her birthday, Elizabeth struck out at her repeatedly. This triggered a heart attack, from which her mother died. At that point, Robin turned on Elizabeth and raped her. As a result of that devastating experience, Elizabeth's psyche was shattered, her personality splitting into multiple identities. One of these, "Elizabeth," became the person her family and coworkers saw most of the time. Another, "Lizzie," embodied the wild, wantonly sexual, dark aspects of her persona. And the third personality, "Beth," existed only as a sleeping, deeply buried identity—the normal, healthy, lovely girl Elizabeth *would* have been had tragedy not destroyed her life. But thanks to the advice of a concerned and compassionate neighbor, Elizabeth sought help from Dr. Wright, a psychiatrist.

Situation: Elizabeth has had a number of sessions with Dr. Wright, each one uncovering more and more psychological layers. He is now going to put her into a deep hypnotic trance. After making sure Elizabeth is comfortable, he begins the necessary procedures, counting backwards slowly from ten, telling her that with each new number she will fall deeper and deeper asleep. When he is down to one, he tells Elizabeth to open her eyes. When she does, it is not Elizabeth looking out but Beth, who is now seeing and speaking for the first time in many years. Then, with further probing, Lizzie surfaces and tells of her plan to kill Elizabeth by forcing her to commit suicide. Dr. Wright then engages the three personalities in a discussion, one at a time.

Comments: This may be resolved by the actors in any way they choose. The challenge for the actress is in making each of the fragmented selves a real and distinctly separate entity. Each persona must have its own objective, which conflicts with the needs of the other personalities. At some point during the improvisation, Dr. Wright may wish to encourage his patient to relive the trauma that shattered her psyche. While doing this, Dr. Wright can have his patient hold his hand, squeezing it tighter as the pain of her memories becomes increasingly severe. The doctor may wish to role-play the mother on Lizzie's fifteenth birthday or the actor playing Lizzie could do an improvisation, prior to this one, in which she relives this confrontation with her mother.

It is not necessary for the patient to remain glued to her chair. Since she is changing locales in her mind, she can move around the office freely.

8

Source: *Wait Until Dark,* a play by Frederick Knott

Characters: One male and one female: Susy Hendrix, a young blind woman in her late twenties/early thirties; and Harry Roat, Jr., a psychopathic drug dealer in his mid- to late thirties

Place: Susy's apartment in Greenwich Village, New York

Background: Susy Hendrix is a strong-willed, independent young woman, who was recently blinded in an automobile accident. Though this event would shatter many people's lives permanently, Susy has dealt with her situation with remarkable courage and fortitude. In a short time she has mastered a great number of household activities, such as washing the dishes, dialing the telephone, doing the laundry, typing. She is married to a photographer. Recently her husband, Sam Hendrix, landed at Kennedy Airport, where a doll filled with heroin was given to him by an attractive female dope smuggler. She said it was a present for her daughter, who was in a New York hospital, and asked if he could hold it for her until she could pick it up. When she arrived to pick up the doll, Sam could not find it. Earlier, unbeknownst to Sam, a young girl named Amy, who lives in a neighboring apartment, borrowed the doll to play with. The woman believes Sam to be lying about the doll. Eventually, a man arrives to retrieve the doll, when Susy is home alone. This man is a dangerous and clever psychopath named Harry Roat, Jr.

Situation: Harry Roat, Jr., confronts Susy, demanding that he be given the doll. Susy is alone in the apartment and has absolutely no idea what he is talking about. Roat does not believe her, and he is willing to go to any means to extract the information from her and retrieve the heroin-

filled doll. However, Susy is much more resourceful than
Roat anticipated.

Comments: A kind of cat and mouse interplay takes place
between these two people. It is a contest of minds. Roat
might attempt to use brute force, but he would not want
Susy dead unless he had the doll first. Roat's primary
motivation is the sizable cut of money he would get from
the sale of the heroin. The actress playing Susy must, of
course, take into account her character's blindness. Some
research may have to be done. It is important that the
actress avoid any stereotypical mimicry of blindness. In
fact, with only a few exceptions, a sightless person, especially in her own home, would seem remarkably self-
sufficient, although in Susy's case, she still makes little
mistakes—misjudging distances, occasionally fumbling
for objects—but this should not be overdone lest the
scene become comic. In this situation, Susy must find a
way of turning her blindness to her own advantage. A
blind person would not wear dark glasses or use a cane
in her own apartment. Susy must also take into account
her tremendous fear at being in the presence of a men-
acing stranger.

Remember that the main purpose of this situation is
for the actress to explore the special problem of being
blind, with the added element of danger. The actor playing Roat must be cautioned not to fall into a criminal
stereotype.

———— 9 ————

Source: *Wings*, a play by Arthur Kopit

Characters: One male and one female: Emily Stilson, a stroke victim, and her doctor

Place: Doctor's office

Background: Emily Stilson has had a stroke, which has left her memory disordered and severely impaired her speech. This speech dysfunction, known as aphasia, is manifested in jumbled speech patterns, inappropriately placed words, and nonsense language.

Situation: The doctor is asking Emily questions in an attempt to determine the severity of her condition. She answers in partial gibberish. He asks simple questions, like "Where were you born?" He puts objects in front of her and asks her to identify them. She struggles for words, often substituting one for the object that sounds vaguely similar (for example, "two-bridge" instead of *toothbrush*).

Comments: The actress playing Emily and the actor playing the doctor really need to be cognizant of the problems of a stroke victim. They will have to do some research on this. It is crucial for the actress playing Emily to realize that in her own mind she is making perfect sense in what she says, not realizing how she sounds to others. Emily is thus understandably bewildered by the lack of comprehension she encounters in those around her. From her perspective, *they* are the ones impaired. Only gradually does she come to realize the nature of her condition and begin to grapple to overcome it.

——— **10** ———

Source: *Brainstorm*, a film by Douglas Trumbull, screenplay by Robert Stitzel and Philip Frank Messina from a story by Bruce Joel Rubin

Characters: One female (or male): Lillian Reynolds, a scientist

Place: A laboratory

Background: An extraordinary machine has been developed that can record human experiences, retaining full sensory detail. These recordings can later be played back by another person, who can then reexperience all the events as though actually living them himself.

Situation: Lillian, one of the scientists who developed the machine, is working late, alone in her laboratory. She has a heart condition. After some moments of making notes, she begins to experience mild chest pains. She puts down her pen and reaches for a bottle of nitroglycerin tablets on the table in front of her. Just as she is about to grab them, her arm brushes against the searingly hot tip of a nearby soldering iron. This sudden pain triggers a massive heart attack. At this point, Lillian, realizing the danger she is in, struggles first to open the bottle of pills, but failing this, attempts to make a telephone call for help. She is in so much pain that she cannot make herself intelligible. Knowing she is about to die, she struggles to wheel her chair (which is on casters) across the room to the experimental machine. She eventually succeeds in doing this and, activating the machine, puts on the head-set, which will now record her experiences. She realizes that, in a few moments, with her death, she will provide the world with an answer to an age-old question: What happens after death? The tape that will be left behind should provide that answer.

Comments: Again, it is suggested that this improvisation be given to the actor beforehand so that he or she will have the opportunity to gather information on the effects and symptoms of a heart attack. This will help sidestep the easy cliché of clutching at one's chest. In an actual heart seizure, much of the pain is centered in the upper left arm, breathing becomes very difficult, and a great pressure is felt on the chest.

Naturally, the actor won't have all the needed props at hand—substitutions should be made or imaginary objects can be used. This improvisation should be read aloud to the class beforehand to help them understand what is taking place.

———— 11 ————

Source: *The Miracle Worker*, a play by William Gibson

Characters: Two females: Helen Keller, a young girl, and Annie Sullivan, her teacher, in her twenties

Place: The dining room of the Keller home in the Tennessee countryside

Background: As an infant, Helen was stricken with measles and rendered blind, deaf, and mute. The family raised her as well as they could, but despite their best efforts, Helen behaved as little more than a wild animal. When Helen was about ten or eleven, the family hired a teacher for her, a young Irish woman named Annie Sullivan. Annie had problems with her vision and was raised for part of her life in a home for the blind. As a result, Annie wears dark spectacles to shield her sensitive eyes from light. She is highly adept at sign language.

Situation: It is just after breakfast. Annie has been left alone in the dining room with Helen. The doors have been locked to prevent Helen from escaping. Helen has been used to eating off everyone else's plate as she pleases, using her fingers rather than utensils. She is now about to be "tamed" by her teacher. It is Annie's task to teach this "wild animal" the common decencies of table manners. Ultimately, her object is for Helen to learn to use a knife and a fork and to fold her napkin when she has finished eating. In order to accomplish this goal, Annie is prepared to be as physically forceful with Helen as necessary.

Comments: The actors must not be afraid to be a bit rough with each other in this scene. To avoid breakage or injury, plastic utensils, plates, cups, etc., should be used. The actress playing Helen must be aware of her character's frustration at having her daily routine forcibly altered. She should also be aware that Helen is locked within the prison of her own mind, unable to make the connection between names and objects, words and ideas. Helen's world consists exclusively of smells, textures, and physical sensations. It is important to keep in mind that Helen is not retarded—she is impaired by her lack of senses. In addition, the actress playing Helen should do the improvisation with her eyes open in simulation of actual blindness. This is one of the many acting challenges inherent in the situation. The actors should feel free to take as much time as necessary to achieve the ultimate goal of the scene.

Special properties: plastic utensils, cups, paper plates, paper napkins, etc.

_____ **12** _____

Source: *Resurrection*, a film by Daniel Petrie, screenplay by Lewis John Carlino (Situation #3)

Characters: Two females (or two males): Edna McCauley, a healer, and an afflicted person

Place: A medical research clinic

Background: After an automobile accident, Edna discovers that she has healing powers. She has been asked to appear at a research clinic to demonstrate these powers under scientific conditions to a group of doctors and researchers.

Situation: Edna is going to attempt to cure a woman who has a crippling muscular disease. This disease has caused the body of the victim to become twisted and distorted so that the victim is unable to sit upright. She is therefore lying down on a movable bed. In attempting to cure the woman, Edna climbs up onto the bed with her. She then begins slowly to take on not only the woman's pain but the physical characteristics of her disease as well. As this happens, the body of the victim is released from the effects of the illness. The effect on the body of the healer is only temporary and soon begins to wear off.

Comments: The actress playing the afflicted woman must take into account her emotional state upon being released from a lifetime of imprisonment by her painful condition. The actress playing the healer must be aware that her powers are indeed genuine. She is not doing this for any financial reward. Therefore, she is very different from the "healers" we often see on religious television programs. The actors will have to decide on the nature of the afflicted woman's disorder—exactly what parts of her body are affected and in what way. The actress playing the healer will have to be particularly observant in order to manifest the affliction herself.

See *Resurrection*, #1, page 102, and #2, page 199.

——— 13 ———

Source: *The Metamorphosis*, a novella by Franz Kafka

Characters: One male: Gregor Samsa, a young man in his twenties

Place: Gregor's bedroom, early morning

Background: Gregor is a normal man, who goes to work every day in an office. He comes down to have breakfast with his family every morning at the same time. This morning he has not appeared for breakfast.

Situation: Gregor wakes up this morning to find he has been transformed into some kind of gigantic beetle. His parents and his sister keep knocking at the door telling him it's time to get ready for work. He can't answer them because he has a strange, very quiet voice. He finds it very difficult to move because he is lying on his back and has never moved as a beetle before.

Comments: It will take the actor a bit of time to make the discovery regarding his metamorphosis. He must experience his whole body as a gigantic insect. It will demand a great deal of concentration. Whether parents and sister are included in this improvisation is optional. The improvisation begins at the moment Gregor awakens.

_____ 14 _____

Source: *The Strange Case of Dr. Jekyll and Mr. Hyde,* a
novella by Robert Louis Stevenson

Characters: One male: Dr. Henry Jekyll (and his evil alter
ego, Edward Hyde)

Place: Dr. Jekyll's laboratory

Background: Dr. Henry Jekyll is a physician and scientist
who has developed a chemical formula capable of splitting the dual sides of a person's nature—good and evil—
right down the middle.

Situation: Dr. Jekyll is about to test his formula on himself
for the first time. No human being has ever tested this
formula before. It is in the form of a liquid. After making
careful notes as to the details of the experiment, Jekyll
pours the liquid into a glass and drinks it. He then under-
goes a gradual transformation into the evil side of his
own nature—Mr. Edward Hyde.

Comments: The actor doing this improvisation is faced with
a wide range of possibilities in realizing this transformation. It should be up to each individual actor how he
(or she) would wish to portray this evil persona, but they
should find these qualities within themselves. No tricks
of makeup, wig, or costume should be employed; the
actor should express the transformation entirely through
his or her own face, voice, and body.

_____ 15 _____

Source: *Greystoke: the Legend of Tarzan, Lord of the Apes,*
a film by Hugh Hudson, screenplay by P. H. Vazak
(pseudonym of Robert Towne) and Michael Austin, based

on the novel *Tarzan of the Apes* by Edgar Rice Bur-
roughs

Characters: Two males: Lord Greystoke, and John Clayton,
his grandson

Place: The Greystoke family estate in England

Background: John's parents, Lord Jack and Lady Alice
Clayton, were put ashore during a ship mutiny off the
coast of British West Africa, and John was born in the
jungle. His parents died shortly after his birth, and he
was raised by apes. (Hence, his jungle name of "Tarzan,"
which means "little white ape" in their animal language.)
Later, he was discovered by an explorer, who taught him
English and eventually brought him back to England to
the Greystoke family estate.

Situation: This is the first meeting between John and his
grandfather. Lord Greystoke has only recently learned
of his grandson's existence and is overjoyed to see him.
It must be remembered that this is John's first exposure
to civilization. Other than the explorer who brought him
back to England, John has known only apes. He knows
nothing about silverware, sitting in chairs, brushing his
teeth, and so on.

Comments: The actor playing John must keep in mind his
unusual background and behave accordingly. This may
be expressed through vocalizations as well as gestures
and general body movements. The grandfather doesn't
really know what to expect and must adjust to this bizarre
behavior.

_____ 16 _____

Source: *The Mind of Mr. Soames*, a film by Alan Cooke, screenplay by John Hale and Edward Simpson, based on the novel by Charles Eric Maine

Characters: Two males: John Soames, thirty years old, and Dr. Bergen. Optional: other doctors

Place: A special medical clinic

Background: John Soames has been in a state of coma since birth. He has been cared for in a special clinic until doctors could find a means of awakening him. Eventually, a surgical procedure is discovered that will bring him to consciousness. He is given this operation.

Situation: John Soames awakens from his coma. Physically, he is a man of thirty, but he has the mentality and reactions of an infant. Everything he now experiences is completely new to him. Dr. Bergen is there to help him through the tremendous adjustment of learning to fit into an adult world while essentially still a child.

Comments: The actor playing Soames obviously has a great deal of room for invention in this situation. Possibilities of environment and objects in that environment should be fully explored. The primary challenge for the actor playing Soames is to convey the impression of an infant locked within an adult body, without spilling over into the realm of caricature—"Goo goo, gaa gaa, ma ma, da da." The actor must keep in mind that Soames has fully mature vocal cords and should not attempt an imitation of the way an actual infant sounds. In addition, since he has not used his vocal cords until now, the actor must also take this into account.

Soames has been constantly cared for all these years and is in good health. Physical therapy has prevented his muscles from atrophying.

Dr. Bergen has watched over the comatose Mr. Soames for many years, and this is a momentous, triumphant occasion for him. In some respects, it is almost as though Soames were his son. The actor should take this into account so that his manner with Soames does not seem exclusively clinical. He should create some kind of background for his character and consider what the doctor's needs might be. This will ensure that the doctor does not emerge merely as a cold-blooded professional.

———— 17 ————

Source: *Promise*, a film for television by Glenn Jordan, teleplay by Richard Friedenberg (Situation #1)

Characters: Two males: D.J., a schizophrenic man in his thirties, and Bobby, his older brother, a small-town real estate salesman

Place: The kitchen of Bobby's home

Background: Bobby promised his mother that when she died, he'd take D.J. into his home rather than place him in an institution. She recently died, and D.J., who had been living with his mother, has come to live with Bobby. Bobby had little contact with D.J. in the past. He saw him only occasionally, when he visited his mother. This is a very new situation for them both. Bobby lives in the houses he's going to sell, and he is concerned about their appearance. He is unprepared for some of D.J.'s stranger habits, such as digging holes in the backyard and putting cigarettes out on the furniture.

Situation: D.J. has just arrived at Bobby's home. They are sitting down to their first meal together. D.J.'s behavior is quite strange. For example: He gets up and washes his hands several times before beginning the meal. He lights a cigarette and puts it out in his glass of water, then drinks from his brother's glass. Bobby asks D.J. if he's taken his pills, which he is supposed to do every morning. He's been taking these pills for thirty years now and still forgets. He refers to himself as a Hindu and is afraid his mother will be reincarnated as an insect.

Comments: It would help if the actor playing D.J. had some knowledge of schizophrenia so that he doesn't display bizarre behavior for no reason. There is some strange inner logic to all his seemingly illogical behavior. The things D.J. does make perfect sense to him. The subtext on the part of Bobby is strong because he's not sure how he is going to cope with all this. He loves his brother and feels responsible for him, but this may be more than he can handle. D.J. is sensitive to any disapproval from Bobby because he doesn't want to be sent away. He's schizophrenic—but not stupid or unfeeling. He has just lost his mother, with whom he was very close. This makes him very much in need of Bobby's care.

See *Promise*, #2, page 333.

18

Source: *Rain Man*, a film by Barry Levinson, screenplay by Ronald Bass and Barry Morrow

Characters: Two males: Raymond Babbit, an autistic savant in his forties, and his brother, Charlie

Place: An airport terminal

Background: Charlie has only recently found out that he has a brother. This brother, Raymond, has been in Wallbrook, an institution, where he was used to an undeviating routine. or example: watching specific TV shows on a daily basis and eating particular foods on specific days. Raymond's entire life is based on routine and ritual—doing things at a certain time and in a specific way. Any disruption of this pattern upsets him terribly. Charlie and Raymond's father recently died and left all of his considerable wealth to Raymond. Charlie believes he rightfully deserves some share of the inheritance. For this reason, he kidnaps Raymond from Wallbrook in a desperate attempt to gain control over the money. He intends to hold his brother for "ransom," refusing to return him to the institution unless he receives a share of the inheritance. His request is, of course, refused. But by this time Charlie has become attached to his unusual brother and wants to continue being with him.

Raymond is able to speak—replying to questions—but he is not capable of carrying on a conversation in the usual sense. His talk is very repetitive, fixating on certain ideas or subjects within his own range of experience or what he has seen or heard on his favorite TV shows. He echoes certain phrases in a parrotlike fashion and recites innumerable statistics on an endless variety of topics. Since he is what is known as a savant, Raymond, though impaired in many ways in terms of social interaction, has a computerlike mind when it comes to mathematical equations. He can calculate complex problems almost instantaneously with no errors. In addition, he is incapable of making real eye contact for more than fleeting moments and does not like to be touched. He carries a notebook with him at all times, in which he writes down all the "injuries" he has received (which, to his mind, can consist of something as harmless as a friendly pat on the back). When he is made to do something that frightens him, he panics, screaming violently in a wild, uncontrolled manner. But when the source of his fear is removed, he instantly returns to "normal"—there being no gradual change between these two extremes. The effect is like turning a switch on and off. Other than at these occasional moments of crisis, his voice is a flat monotone, reflecting no emotion. He is, however, able to accurately imitate things he hears on TV or the radio. In many ways, Raymond seems almost like a robot.

Until recently, his brother, Charlie, has been a callous, completely selfish young man, uninterested in anyone's welfare but his own. But his newfound relationship with his brother has begun to change him, making him more compassionate.

Situation: Having just abducted Raymond from Wallbrook, Charlie must get him out of Chicago before Raymond's absence is noticed. They are walking through an airport together enroute to a particular flight Charlie has booked to Los Angeles. He does not yet know that Raymond is terrified by the idea of flying in an airplane. Raymond is a storehouse of knowledge concerning airplane crash fatalities. In his mind, the only safe airline is Qantas because it has never crashed. Charlie is determined to get Raymond on the plane, despite Raymond's numerous reasons to the contrary. In desperation, Charlie tries to physically pull his brother toward the gate. This causes Raymond to go into a complete state of panic. He comes out of this only when Charlie tells him he will not have to go on the flight. Upon hearing this news, Raymond immediately becomes calm again. Finally, Charlie sees no alternative but to drive from Chicago to their Los Angeles destination.

Comments: The actor playing Charlie must also be aware

of his surroundings. He has not had much experience with Raymond in a public place before and would probably feel embarrassed by much of Raymond's outrageous behavior. The actor playing Raymond must read the Background for this improvisation thoroughly and incorporate it into his role. If he has seen the film, he should avoid imitating Dustin Hoffman's performance. It may be preferable to give this improvisation to an actor who is not familiar with the film.

_____ 19 _____

Source: _Black Comedy_, a play by Peter Shaffer
Characters: Any number of people, male and female
Place: A cocktail party in a living room
Background: The actors must decide on the relationships they have with one another. They should be encouraged to choose volatile or unconventional relationships as well as more ordinary ones.
Situation: A cocktail party is in progress. All at once the lights go out. This improvisation will begin in darkness, with people chatting amiably and music playing. Then the theater lights will be turned on, at which point the characters react as though they have just been plunged into total darkness. This is a theatrical device, in which, through a reversal of actual light and dark, the audience can see things happening which the characters themselves cannot. The challenge for the actors is to realistically behave as though they cannot see a thing and react accordingly to whatever happens. In addition, because the actions of each character are not visible to any of the other characters, they may do things which they would not normally do in a room filled with people.

Comments: The actors must collaborate beforehand on the nature of their relationships with one another. It is essential that these relationships be well established. For example: There may be a clandestine love affair, two enemies, a thief. In some groups, the coach may want to assign these character traits and relationships. If these relationships are not thoroughly established, the improvisation ends up with actors milling around in the "dark" aimlessly. Also, the coach may wish to have the actors experience real darkness on stage for some minutes before the improvisation begins. This will aid the actors in accessing a more immediate sense-memory experience of moving in darkness.

_____ 20 _____

Source: *The Elephant Man,* a play by Bernard Pomerance

Characters: Two males and one female: John Merrick, the Elephant Man; Dr. Frederick Treves; and Dame Madge Kendal, a well-known actress

Place: John Merrick's room in London Hospital, Whitechapel, circa 1880

Background: John Merrick suffers from a rare medical condition, neurofibromatosis, which has resulted in the severe deformity of his face and body. As a carnival freak, he was known as The Elephant Man. He has an enormous head, a twisted spine, and all but shapeless limbs—with the exception of his left arm and hand, which are as graceful and delicate as a woman's. His voice is also impaired owing to the severity of his facial deformity. Up to this point, his life has not been a pleasant one but rather a catalogue of abuse, rejection, and ostracism.

Situation: Dr. Treves, who has been caring for Merrick,

has brought a visitor to meet him. Dr. Treves has chosen Mrs. Kendal, a noted actress of the day, to meet Merrick. He believes that because of her profession, she will be more successful than most at concealing her true feelings regarding Merrick's physical appearance. Until now, Merrick has been subjected to reactions only of shock and disgust from every woman he has come in contact with—the sole exceptions being the hardened nurses on the hospital staff. Dr. Treves feels that this meeting will be a healthy and beneficial experience for Merrick. During the scene, Mrs. Kendal moves beyond her initial uneasiness at Merrick's appearance (which, true to her profession, she conceals like a pro) and comes to appreciate his humanity, beauty of spirit, and the pure, almost childlike quality of his mind.

Comments: The actor playing Merrick must do some homework in preparation for this scene in order to convey Merrick's distorted body and speech without its getting in the way of his inner being. Though his life experience is limited, Merrick knows a great deal through reading. Despite the brutality of his childhood, he has retained his faith in goodness. The actress playing Mrs. Kendal must use her imagination vis-à-vis Merrick's physical appearance.

21

Source: *Flowers for Algernon*, a play by David Rogers, based on the novel by Daniel Keyes

Characters: One male and one female: Charly Gordon, a good-looking man of thirty-two, retarded; Alice Kinian, late twenties/early thirties, a teacher of retarded adults

Place: Two locales: Charly's apartment and Alice's class-room

Background: Charly is one of Alice's students in her class for retarded adults. Alice hears of a scientific experiment in which, through an operation, a retarded person could become a genius. So far this operation has been done successfully only on mice. The doctors are now ready to perform this surgery on a human being. Alice presents Charly to the doctors because he seems so eager to learn. The problem is that having never done this experiment before on human specimens, the scientists are not sure how long the person will remain intelligent. There is the possibility that, after a time, the person will regress even further into retardation than before.

Algernon is a mouse, who is undergoing the experiment simultaneously with Charly. Charly has now become highly intelligent. In the process of working with Alice, he has fallen in love with her. They have had a normal relationship for several months. Charly, however, has begun to notice that Algernon is slowly losing his intelligence and regressing.

Situation: *Scene 1:* Charly has remained by himself for the last few days. Alice finds him in his apartment. She asks him why he hasn't wanted to see her. He tells Alice of his discovery of Algernon's changed behavior. He knows this means that the same thing will happen to him, and he doesn't want her to be around to see it. She wants them to stay together as long as possible.

Scene 2: Alice is in her classroom, and Charly, who is now completely retarded, comes in with his books and sits down at a desk.

Comments: This is an interesting challenge for an actor because he goes from being a normal man to being retarded. However, the feelings do not go away. When Charly becomes retarded, he still loves Alice, but he doesn't know how to handle it. Charly's two "characters" both love Alice, but each expresses his love in entirely different ways. The actor should have some knowledge of the behavioral aspects of retardation.

The actress playing Alice also has quite a challenge because she has the same feelings for Charly, but she can no longer express them in the same manner.

_____ 22 _____

Source: *My Left Foot*, a film by Jim Sheridan, screenplay by Sheridan and Shane Connaughton, based on the autobiography of the same title of Christy Brown.

Characters: Two males and two females, and ensemble: Christy Brown, an Irish writer in his early thirties, afflicted with severe cerebral palsy; Dr. Eileen Cole, his speech therapist, an attractive woman in her early thirties; Peter, her fiancé, a young man of about the same age; Mrs. Brown, Christy's mother, in her sixties; various friends, male and female

Place: A restaurant/pub in Dublin, Ireland

Background: Afflicted with severe cerebral palsy since birth, Christy Brown was unable to walk, to feed himself, or to speak intelligibly. Eventually, he discovered he could control his left foot well enough to write and draw with it. He then discovered he could use a typewriter, and eventually he began to write his autobiography. An electric wheelchair made it possible for him to get around; he operated the control mechanism with his mouth. A speech therapist, an attractive young woman named Eileen, helped him to speak more clearly so that people other than his family and Eileen could understand him. In the process of working with Eileen, Christy fell in love with her. She was not in love with him and had no clear idea about the nature of his feelings for her.

Situation: Christy has just received news that his book is going to be published, and he has taken his mother, Eileen, a male friend of Eileen's, and a few other people (possibly family members) to a local restaurant/pub to celebrate. In the midst of the celebration, Eileen decides to announce her recent engagement to her male companion. Christy had assumed that Peter was just a friend, and this announcement comes as a complete shock to him. He is quite drunk by the time he receives this news.

Comments: Obviously, the actor playing Christy in this situation has quite a few acting problems on his hands— the distorted speech and spastic movements resulting from the cerebral palsy, the task of playing drunk in a believable manner, and the Irish accent on top of it all. The accent can be eliminated, since this situation could conceivably occur in *any* country, but it *is* an added challenge. Naturally, the actor will have to do some research into the specifics of cerebral palsy, and, therefore, this improvisation should not be attempted without warning. The other actors must determine the exact nature of their relationships with Christy.

23

Source: *Promise*, a film for television by Glenn Jordan, teleplay by Richard Friedenberg (Situation #2)

Characters: Two males and one female, and ensemble: D.J., a schizophrenic man in his thirties; Bobby, his older brother, a real estate salesman; and a waitress (Optional: other customers in the coffee shop)

Place: A coffee shop

Background: See *Promise*, Situation #1, page 324

Situation: This is the first time Bobby has taken D.J. out in public. This is a small town, and Bobby knows many of the people in the restaurant. D.J. wants Bobby to take him to the bathroom so that he can wash his hands. Bobby tells D.J. that it would be embarrassing to escort a grown man to the bathroom. Hearing this, D.J. panics and becomes hysterical. While trying to calm his brother, Bobby is also acutely aware of being watched by customers and the restaurant staff. The waitress must contend with this display of hysteria as best she can. Any pressure from her might send D.J. even further over the edge.

Comments: At these moments of emotional crisis, D.J.'s behavior becomes like that of a small child—petulant, self-pitying, and subject to tantrums. The actor may think of himself as a child who is upset at not getting his way. He must also be aware of the sheer terror D.J. experiences when his usual routine is disrupted. People who work with mentally disturbed individuals know how to deal with them, but Bobby is an ordinary person, who is unprepared to cope with this behavior. Also, it must be remembered that he depends on a lot of the people in this restaurant for his business.

See *Promise*, #1, page 324.

SPECIAL PROBLEMS

Cross-References

Other improvisations in this book that involve Special Problems can be found in the following categories:

UNUSUAL CIRCUMSTANCES

One male and one female

THEATER OF THE ABSURD

Two males

INDEX

FOR THE BEST IN PAPERBACKS, LOOK FOR THE

In every corner of the world, on every subject under the sun, Penguin represents quality and variety—the very best in publishing today.

For complete information about books available from Penguin—including Pelicans, Puffins, Peregrines, and Penguin Classics—and how to order them, write to us at the appropriate address below. Please note that for copyright reasons the selection of books varies from country to country.

In the United Kingdom: For a complete list of books available from Penguin in the U.K., please write to *Dept E.P., Penguin Books Ltd, Harmondsworth, Middlesex, UB7 0DA.*

In the United States: For a complete list of books available from Penguin in the U.S., please write to *Consumer Sales, Penguin USA, P.O. Box 999—Dept. 17109, Bergenfield, New Jersey 07621-0120.* VISA and MasterCard holders call 1-800-253-6476 to order all Penguin titles.

In Canada: For a complete list of books available from Penguin in Canada, please write to *Penguin Books Canada Ltd, 10 Alcorn Avenue, Suite 300, Toronto, Ontario, Canada M4V 3B2.*

In Australia: For a complete list of books available from Penguin in Australia, please write to the *Marketing Department, Penguin Books Ltd, P.O. Box 257, Ringwood, Victoria 3134.*

In New Zealand: For a complete list of books available from Penguin in New Zealand, please write to the *Marketing Department, Penguin Books (NZ) Ltd, Private Bag, Takapuna, Auckland 9.*

In India: For a complete list of books available from Penguin, please write to *Penguin Overseas Ltd, 706 Eros Apartments, 56 Nehru Place, New Delhi, 110019.*

In Holland: For a complete list of books available from Penguin in Holland, please write to *Penguin Books Nederland B.V., Postbus 195, NL-1380AD Weesp, Netherlands.*

In Germany: For a complete list of books available from Penguin, please write to *Penguin Books Ltd, Friedrichstrasse 10-12, D-6000 Frankfurt Main 1, Federal Republic of Germany.*

In Spain: For a complete list of books available from Penguin in Spain, please write to *Longman, Penguin España, Calle San Nicolas 15, E-28013 Madrid, Spain.*

In Japan: For a complete list of books available from Penguin in Japan, please write to *Longman Penguin Japan Co Ltd, Yamaguchi Building, 2-12-9 Kanda Jimbocho, Chiyoda-Ku, Tokyo 101, Japan.*